UP SOUTH IN THE OZARKS

UP SOUTH
— in the —
OZARKS

DISPATCHES FROM
THE MARGINS

Brooks Blevins

The University of Arkansas Press | Fayetteville | 2022

ISBN: 978-1-68226-220-7
eISBN: 978-1-61075-787-4

27 26 25 24 23 5 4 3 2

Manufactured in the United States of America

Designed by April Leidig

⊗ The paper used in this publication meets the minimum
requirements of the American National Standard for Permanence
of Paper for Printed Library Materials z39.48-1984.

Library of Congress Cataloging-in-Publication Data
Names: Blevins, Brooks, 1969– author.
Title: Up South in the Ozarks: dispatches from the margins /
Brooks Blevins.
Description: Fayetteville: The University of Arkansas Press, 2022. |
Includes bibliographical references. | Summary: "Up South in the Ozarks:
Dispatches from the Margins is a collection of essays from Brooks Blevins that
explore southern history and culture using [the] author's native Ozarks region
as a focus. From migrant cotton pickers and fireworks peddlers to country store
proprietors and shape-note gospel singers, Blevins leaves few stones unturned in
his insightful journeys through a landscape 'wedged betwixt and between
the South and the Midwest—and grasping for the West to boot.'"
—Provided by publisher.
Identifiers: LCCN 2022026314 (print) | LCCN 2022026315 (ebook) |
ISBN 9781682262207 (cloth; alkaline paper) | ISBN 9781610757874 (ebook)
Subjects: LCSH: Ozarkers. | Marginality, Social—Ozark Mountains. |
Ozark Mountains—Social life and customs. | Ozark Mountains—History. |
Southern States—Social life and customs.
Classification: LCC F417.O9 B65 2022 (print) | LCC F417.O9 (ebook) |
DCC 976.7/1—dc23/eng/20220623
LC record available at https://lccn.loc.gov/2022026314
LC ebook record available at https://lccn.loc.gov/2022026315

For Gordon McCann
and in memory of W. K. McNeil

CONTENTS

Introduction
3

ONE
The Ozarks and Dixie:
Considering a Region's Southernness
7

TWO
Fireworking Down South
25

THREE
The South According to *Andy*
47

FOUR
Where Everything New Is Old Again:
Southern Gospel Singing Schools
59

FIVE
Against the Current:
Landowners and the Fight for Ozarks Streams
75

SIX
The Country Store:
In Search of Mercantiles and Memories in the Ozarks
101

SEVEN
Rethinking the Scots-Irish Ozarks:
Diversity and Demographics in Regional History
121

EIGHT

Revisiting Race Relations in the Upland South:
LaCrosse, Arkansas
135

NINE

The Spruills: Who and Why?
155

TEN

Collectors of the Ozarks: Folklore and Regional Image
171

ELEVEN

The Ordinary Days of Extraordinary Minnie:
Diaries of a Life on the Margins
187

TWELVE

A Time Zone Away and a Generation Behind:
Appalachia and the Ozarks
211

THIRTEEN

Back to the Land:
Academe, the Agrarian Ideal, and a Sense of Place
223

Notes 235

UP SOUTH IN THE OZARKS

INTRODUCTION

I T WOULD BE DIFFICULT to imagine a more unlikely inspiration for a career exploring southern and Ozarks history. But inspiration rarely follows the dictates of logic. It was the winter of 1992, and I found myself in one of the cramped, windowless faculty offices in the attic of the Alphin Building on the campus of Arkansas (now Lyon) College. Senior thesis time was upon me, and I had dropped by this afternoon to run some thoughts by one of the professors tasked with shepherding me and about half a dozen other expectant graduates through the writing of research papers beyond the scope of anything we had yet accomplished. Sitting behind the tidy desk was Charles Kimball, a young historian who had just finished his first semester at this tiny liberal arts school perched on the southeastern tip of the Ozarks. Raised in suburban New York City and educated at Harvard and Stanford, Professor Kimball must have wondered more than once just what strange collision of events landed him in this town of ten thousand people in flyover country, this place where you could toss a rock in any direction and hit a Protestant church house but where bars and liquor stores were banned by law. Such a fish out of water was he—or at least that was the assumption—that we students endearingly called him "Bubba Chuck." We were pulling for him.

I had just recently made the "discovery"—with assistance from Milton D. Rafferty's *The Ozarks, Land and Life*—that the rocky little farm on which I'd been raised, and the community surrounding it, was a part of this region called the Ozarks. It seemed like the kind of thing someone would have told me. I knew we were hill people. I just didn't know we had a brand. The Ozarks was a place that was obviously important enough to warrant an entire book by an esteemed cultural geographer, but the stacks in the college library revealed that the region had yet to inspire much in the way of published history. At this point I only knew that I wanted to focus my senior thesis on the Ozarks. I had no idea how to frame such a study.

I don't how much time Professor Kimball had spent exploring the hills and hollers that folded out beyond the horizon to the north and west of Batesville, Arkansas, but I do know that he had made the forty-five-minute drive to Mountain View, home of the Ozark Folk Center State Park and self-proclaimed "Folk Music Capital of the World." And I'm certain he was familiar with Michel Foucault's theories on social constructionism and with the "invented traditions" analyzed by British historians Eric Hobsbawm and Terence Ranger. "Have you ever thought about what it means that businesses in Mountain View purposely misspell things on their signs and cultivate a rustic image?" he asked. I don't recall the details of the conversation that followed, but I remember leaving his office that day with a budding realization that the true picture of a region didn't always match regional image, that there could be a wide gap between reality and perception. Professor Kimball knew no more than did I about the history of the Ozarks, and unlike me he couldn't even draw on a lifetime of residence in the region to supplement a lack of formal knowledge. But he understood the broad contours of cultural history and the marginal position that a place like the Ozarks must occupy in the American consciousness.

The mission may not have been fully formed in my mind at that moment, but it wasn't long before I devoted myself not just to the exploration of the history and culture of the South but to telling the story of my particular corner of the South, a place that had been misunderstood and marginalized (when noticed at all) by scholars. That forty-page senior paper grew into a master's thesis two years later and eventually expanded to become my dissertation, which was revised and published in 2002 as *Hill Folks: A History of Arkansas Ozarkers and Their Image*, my first book-length study of the Ozarks. My guide on *Hill Folks*—and in the field of southern history in which it was anchored—was historian Wayne Flynt, whose appreciation for the complexities of the South's stories and whose insistence that good scholarship is not synonymous with blandness continue to inspire me to this day. Wayne's understanding of southerners living on the margins helped inform my framing of a peripheral place filled with socially and economically marginalized people. Along the way, I found valuable mentors within the Ozarks. Folklorist W. K. McNeil, my supervisor during a summer job as oral historian at the Ozark Folk Center State Park, illustrated the historical and cultural ties between Appalachia and the Ozarks, without dismissing the latter as simply a smaller version of the former. By the time I met historian Lynn Morrow, he had been immersed in researching, writing, and revising the history of the Ozarks for two decades, and he has generously shared information and insights ever since.

The essays that follow are a sampling of my attempts to explore various facets of the South and the Ozarks, often focusing on the juxtaposition of the history and experiences of the mainstream South and the marginal South—places like the Ozarks or Appalachia. Many also focus on marginal groups or institutions within these places—migrant workers, southern gospel singing schools, fireworks peddlers, the poor. Seven of the essays were previously published in academic journals or books, though four of them have been significantly revised or updated for this collection. The other six essays are published here for the first time. Whether old or new, all of them emanate from the margins. Most of them are rooted right where I am, Up South in the Ozarks.

THIS HAS BEEN A collaborative effort. In addition to the scholars mentioned above, this book would not have been possible without the various journal and book editors who worked to make these essays better and without the library and archives staffs that provided assistance over the years. Three of the essays in this book first appeared in the terrific journal *Southern Cultures*, and I appreciate the improvements made by the journal's editorial staff. I am also indebted to the keen editorial oversight provided on the other previously published essays, expertise offered by Ted Olson, Zachary Michael Jack, Patrick Williams, Gordon Harvey, Richard Starnes, and the late Glenn Feldman. I appreciate the helpful comments and suggestions of anonymous readers, as well as others who have read and commented on one or more of these pieces, including Dan Pierce, David E. Whisnant, Tom Lee, Steven Nash, Blake Perkins, the late Ellen Compton, Mike Luster, George Lankford, Kathleen Kennedy, Brooke Whisenhunt, James J. Johnston, and Elizabeth Jacoway. I also thank several people who helped in various other ways: Terri Crawford, Laura Reed, and Twyla Wright at the Old Independence Regional Museum in Batesville, Brian Grubbs at the Library Center in Springfield, the staffs at the University of Arkansas Special Collections in Fayetteville and the Missouri State University Special Collections, Mark Arslan, Christopher Cooper, Gibbs Knotts, Rachel Reynolds, Beverly Meinzer, and the late Kevin Johnson.

This book would not be possible but for the many writers and scholars who came before me to tell the world about this upland region wedged betwixt and between the South and the Midwest—and grasping for the West to boot. They include early twentieth-century geographers Curtis F. Marbut and Carl O. Sauer and such Depression-era crafters of an enduring regional image as Vance Randolph, Charles Morrow Wilson, May Kennedy McCord, and Otto Ernest Rayburn. More than a few of my predecessors at Missouri State University legitimized Ozarks studies as a worthy field of scholarship, including Robert K. Gilmore, Bob Flanders, Russel Gerlach, Milton Rafferty, and Donald Holliday.

Finally, this book is dedicated to two men in the intimate world of Ozarks studies. The late W. K. "Bill" McNeil spent most of his career on the margins of academe, but in almost three decades as the folklorist at the Ozark Folk Center State Park in little Mountain View, Arkansas, he bequeathed the region an eclectic treasure trove of scholarship. A native Appalachian possessed of a photographic memory, Bill was Google for friends and colleagues before any of us had ever heard of a search engine. I'm proud to have known him as a friend and mentor. Despite his deep roots in the Ozarks, Gordon McCann was a forty-year-old small-business owner when friends first introduced him to the thrill of live traditional mountain music more than half a century ago. He went on to become a self-taught authority on Ozarks history and culture and the foremost expert on the region's rich heritage of fiddle music. In the process, Gordon became a confidante to an elderly Vance Randolph, whose seminal book, *The Ozarks: An American Survival of Primitive Society*, debuted the very year Gordon was born. Even age and physical infirmities have not dampened his spirit for his beloved region.

CHAPTER ONE

The Ozarks and Dixie

CONSIDERING A REGION'S
SOUTHERNNESS

I AM A SOUTHERNER. My father is a southerner. His father was. We all knew it, just knew it. I'm also an Arkansawyer, and just about everybody knows Arkansawyers are southerners. But I'm an Ozarker, and, like our kinfolk back in Appalachia, we have always been a little different.[1]

At the age of twenty-two I left home to have my southernness challenged. I had never spent more than two weeks at a time outside the Ozarks—except for a summer of National Guard training in Texas and Illinois, and all drill instructors, whose keen sense of American regional stereotypes lends flavor and occasional irony to their blustery condescension, certainly know that Arkansas is a key component of the benighted South. But at twenty-two I left for graduate school at Auburn University in Alabama, the "true" South, as I was about to discover.

Much to my surprise, my southernness wilted in the face of such a test. Utterly unimpressed with my peripheral claim on the South, my apathy toward football, my disdain for grits and greens, and my predilection for *you'ns* over *y'all*, the Alabamians chewed me up and spit me out. In the Deep South—the "Heart of Dixie" emblazoned on license plates—there was a different perspective. Back home, I could be in Missouri with a drive of less than forty-five minutes. In Alabama there was nothing but the old Confederacy for a full day's journey in every direction, and it didn't take those of us who made the trip *down* there long to appreciate the power of cultural geography. My wife later encountered this on her first day in an Auburn classroom. When the professor asked if anyone in the class was

---

This is a revised version of an essay originally published in Ted Olson, ed., *Crossroads: A Southern Culture Annual* (Macon, GA: Mercer University Press, 2004).

"from up north," only one young woman near the back of the room raised her hand. My wife was shocked—as was the professor, I expect—when it turned out that the young woman was from Tennessee. The Tennessee Yankee may have simply been very literal minded, but I prefer to think she had also begun questioning her own southernness. The Deep South could do that to you. Stripping me of my southernness, these southerners rendered me a regional misfit, a native of the South whose southernness was suspect at best.

Southerners have for generations participated in the exercise of self-definition. What is the South? Who are southerners? How do we define *southern*? Inherently confident in their southernness, southerners often describe themselves in the process of definition. Consequently, there are almost as many different definitions or descriptions of the South as there are southerners. A Cajun's definition of the South would differ significantly from that of the Tennessee mountaineer. At some point in my youth, I may have been myopic enough to define the South by my own experiences in the Arkansas Ozarks, but my four years in Alabama divested me of any notion that my little corner was representative of an entire region. Thus, in the late 1990s, as a trained southern historian preparing to write a dissertation on the Arkansas Ozarks, I began contemplating just how southern the place was.

Scholars have stepped in to weigh statistics, history, cultures, mindsets, and their own experiences in a general attempt to decide which definition, if any, comes closest to capturing the essence of the American South—the Cajun's or the mountaineer's, or perhaps the Carolina millworker's, the Alabama coal miner's, or the Delta bluesman's. These scholars and pundits have defined the South in numerous ways, using gauges as diverse as race, lethargy, workstock, kudzu, and even fireworks on New Year's. Some deal with the southern mind, others with a physical South of indeterminate borders.

The southern part of the United States is full of subregions that, depending on one's definition, may or may not fit neatly into the scholar's South. The Ozarks region is among these. Stretching from northern Arkansas to central Missouri—with a sideways lop over into northeastern Oklahoma—this geographic entity straddles political boundaries imposed by a federal government unmindful of the area's physical integrity. The line that separates Missouri from Arkansas has proved exceedingly important to American history (remember the Missouri Compromise?) and to the Ozarker's regional affiliation. It threatens to derail our endeavor right off the bat. For historians Missouri remains a regional no-man's-land. The state's legalization of human bondage in the antebellum era rendered it at least somewhat southern, but no state was more divided by Civil War–era loyalties. The Show-Me State—with its strong two-party political system harkening back to wartime divisions—gradually became more associated with the amorphous Midwest than with the South as the postwar years rolled on. Most twenty-first-century Missourians answer the "Are you a southerner?" question in the negative, but there are those who proudly hang their hats on southern identification. If it's possible, the Oklahoma Ozarks provides an even more confusing case study for regional identity and image. Not only does the West tend to pull Oklahoma into its orbit, but the portion of the Ozark Uplift in the Sooner State largely overlaps with the grounds of the Cherokee Nation and the lands of a few of their Indian neighbors. Adding Native American heritage to the jumble of identities in the state's northeastern corner certainly muddles the task at hand.

So, in true Ozarks fashion, we'll make do with what we've got and con- sider the question of the southernness of the Ozarks—not just the portion in Arkansas that would seem our best candidate for inclusion in the South, but the whole region. We'll use as guides or gauges various definitions offered by scholars. Perhaps we will discover the Ozarks's rightful place in the panoply of American regions; perhaps the discussion will simply confuse the matter for those Ozarkers who know in their gut exactly who it is that they are. I'm a historian, so the following observations will for the most part be couched in terms of historical descriptions of the South and the Ozarks. Group identity is, after all, rooted in shared history. But it also relies on the survival of a certain degree of cultural distinctiveness, which requires us to occasionally consider the present, or at least the very recent past.[2] And one other bit of housecleaning before we begin. In an attempt to avoid skewing the statistical computations, for the purposes of this little exercise I have trimmed away the "border" counties of the Ozark plateau, the ones that encompass the valleys of the Missouri, Mississippi, Arkansas, and Grand Rivers and those that straddle the escarpment sep- arating the plateau from the lowlands of the Mississippi Alluvial Plain (Delta). That leaves us with a nice, round "Interior Ozarks" of sixty coun- ties that lie completely (or almost so) within upland terrain.

One of the first scholars to define the South using its history was U. B. Phillips. In his 1928 *American Historical Review* article "The Central Theme in Southern History," based largely on his observations of the plan- tation South, the historian described the "cardinal test of a Southerner and

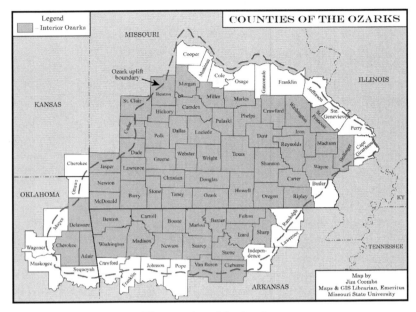

The counties of the Ozarks.
Courtesy of Jim Coombs.

the central theme of Southern history" as the "common resolve indomitably maintained that it shall be and remain a white man's country."[3] Thus, the central theme of the South and its history is the subjugation of African Americans. Here, we are immediately challenged by the fact that throughout history in the greatest part of Ozarks territory there have been few Black people to subjugate. The hilly terrain and generally poor soil prevented the development of plantation-style agriculture, which in turn limited the number of enslaved people brought to the region before the Civil War.[4]

In the twentieth century the Black population of the core Ozarks counties, those lying wholly within the upland plateau, never exceeded 1.4 percent of the total population. In 1930, two years after Phillips's article was published, African Americans constituted less than 1 percent of the region's core population, and in only three interior counties—Greene and Morgan in Missouri and Cherokee in Oklahoma—did they account for at least one in fifty residents. Fourteen counties—almost 20 percent of all core counties—numbered not a single African American among their

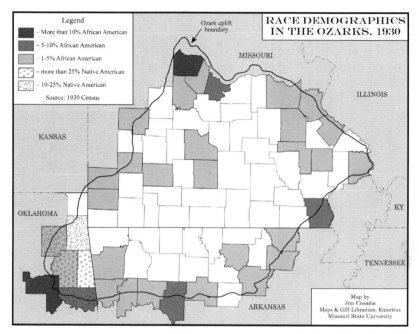

Racial demographics in the Ozarks, 1930.
Courtesy of Jim Coombs.

populations, and the census found fewer than ten Black residents in sixteen additional Ozarks counties.

Demographic shifts in the late twentieth and early twenty-first centuries have witnessed a significant rise in the Black population of the interior Ozarks, now roughly three times the size it was in 1900, but African
Americans remain a distant fourth on the region's racial/ethnic demographic chart, behind whites, Hispanics, and Native Americans. And this
modest racial diversification has had a limited geographical scope, as
two-thirds of African American Ozarkers reside in one of three locations:
Springfield, Missouri; the metropolitan "Northwest Arkansas City" corridor stretching from Fayetteville to Bentonville; and the area around the
US Army's Fort Leonard Wood.[5]

According to Phillips's interpretation, and the interpretations of other
scholars who place race relations at the center of southern history and
culture, the Ozarks should have no direct claim on southernness. That
is not to say that the Ozarks has been free from bigotry, that its residents

were not equally determined that their place on the planet would remain a white man's country. The works of scholars such as Kimberly Harper and Guy Lancaster have exposed a dark and long-hidden past of racial injustice and violence in the region, and in some cases Ozarks communities were all white by design. A series of brutal demonstrations of white power and control in the 1890s and the first decade of the 1900s, culminating in a grisly triple lynching of African American men on the court square in Springfield, Missouri, reflect the racial animosities and tensions that lurked beneath the surface of one of the whitest places within the former slave states.[6] It is most probable that in Phillips's world of 1928 the great majority of white Ozarkers shared the racist sentiments of the greater South, and for that matter of most Americans, and consequently at least acquiesced to the white man's hegemony in the former Confederacy. It should also be remembered that no less an Ozarks mountaineer than Orval Faubus occupied Arkansas's governor's mansion during the state's darkest hours of race relations and subsequently became a symbol of southern resistance to racial integration and the civil rights movement. Nevertheless, in most Ozarks communities from Siloam Springs to Marble Hill the paucity or complete absence of African Americans obviated the need to turn racist sentiments into acts of violence or methods of oppression.

Entwined with the notion of race is the identification of staple-crop agriculture, particularly cotton raising, as a component of southernness. The Ozarks may qualify as more southern by this gauge, but its place in the South remains a marginal one. Before the 1960s, many Ozarkers raised the white fiber, though not as intensively as thousands of farmers farther south and east. In the 1870s and 1880s, a wave of cotton cultivation washed up from the Deep South into the hidden valleys and onto the rocky hillsides of the Ozarks. By 1889 only three Ozark counties in Arkansas—Washington, Benton, and Madison in the extreme northwestern corner—produced fewer than one thousand bales of cotton, and farmers in the Missouri border counties stretching from Taney to Ripley devoted time and effort to cultivation of the cash crop.[7] Nevertheless, falling prices, rugged terrain, and infertility forced many Ozarkers out of the cotton business around the turn of the century. By World War I the cotton wave had receded, leaving the South's staple only in the narrow valleys of the interior and the gently sloping plateaus of the eastern and southern Ozarks. On the eve of the Great Depression, and at the peak of the South's dependence on cotton, farmers in the Ozarks devoted almost 160,000 acres to cotton cultivation.

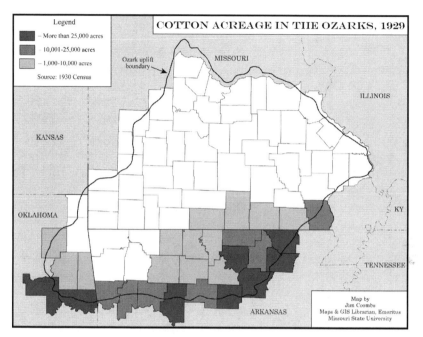

Cotton acreage in the Ozarks, 1929.
Courtesy of Jim Coombs.

More than 75 percent of the agriculturists in four Arkansas counties—Cleburne, Izard, Sharp, and Van Buren—raised some cotton. The interior Ozark region's most intensive cotton county, Cleburne, surpassed the non-Ozark state average in percentage of farmers growing the crop and equaled the average of just under sixteen acres of cotton per farm.[8]

But cotton production was far from monolithic in the Ozarks. Farmers in most Missouri counties and three northwestern Arkansas counties grew no cotton at all, and over half the region's crop was produced in four counties representing the eastern and southern limits of the core Ozarks. By using this test of southernness, we face the prospect of classifying certain areas of the Ozarks as more southern than others.[9] In counties such as Cleburne, Izard, Sharp, Fulton, and Van Buren, cotton growing approached a level of importance and intensity found elsewhere in the cotton state of Arkansas. If a culture of cotton cultivation connotes southernness, then most communities, and by extension most Ozarkers, in these counties at one time qualified as southerners. Conversely, the farther west one traveled in the region, the fewer cotton patches one found and the smaller those patches became. Using the gauge of staple-crop cotton agriculture, most of the Ozarks would not have measured up.

Of course, the cotton argument, at least as applied to the Ozarks, is a purely historical one, for the region has produced no cotton in more than half a century. But the decline of cotton cultivation does not render this particular gauge of southernness useless. With only a few exceptions, nowhere in the modern South is cotton growing as widespread as it was fifty or seventy-five years ago, and now that California is the nation's leading cotton-producing state, one has to question the usefulness of considering cotton-planting a modern sign of southernness. In much of the South, kudzu replaced cotton. In the 1930s and 1940s, New Deal agricultural allotment programs, cooperative extension service agents, and the Soil Conservation Service convinced southern farmers to plant the viney, Asian plant in worn-out cotton fields, a development that most would come to abhor and that would lend another mark of dubious distinction to the post–World War II South. Again, this is a mark that by and large the Ozark region does not share. If one uses sociologist John Shelton Reed's "where kudzu grows" test of southernness, all but the northernmost counties of the Missouri Ozarks fall within the South.[10] But Reed's map is more an indication of where kudzu *can* grow than where it actually *does* grow. Kudzu can be found in the Ozarks, but it is rare enough that it sparks interest when sighted. By contrast, it is so common in areas of Georgia, Alabama, and other Deep South states that the passer-through may only become conscious of the everpresent kudzu when confronted by a succession of pastures and groves not smothered by the vine.

The chief factor in delineating the cotton Ozarks from the non-cotton Ozarks was the same one separating the cotton/kudzu South from the rest of the country—latitude-influenced temperature. Cotton farmers required a minimum of two hundred frost-free days per year, and the two-hundred-day line through the Ozarks hews pretty closely to the old 36°30' line of latitude that divides Missouri from Arkansas. In fact, a study of American agricultural regions in the 1920s found this line to be the northern boundary of the "cotton belt." Almost all the Missouri Ozarks, along with much of northwestern Arkansas and northeastern Oklahoma, fell into a transition zone labeled the "corn and winter wheat belt." Typical of the Ozark region's liminal status, this was a belt where "the crops and systems of farming [were] much the same as in the North, but the people and the social traditions . . . similar to those in the South."[11] Using the cotton belt as a measure of the South's boundaries in the pre-Depression era, then, at least a part (albeit a small part) of the Ozarks had a claim on southernness.

It turns out that weather provided a variety of regional barometers. Clarence Cason defined the South as that part of the country that reached ninety degrees in the shade at least one hundred days a year.[12] That certainly limits our range and offers a first look at the "small South," as opposed to a "larger South" effected by a more inclusive definition. Cason's definition would at best limit the South to a sometimes-narrow swath of plantation land and piney woods stretching from eastern Georgia, just below the Piedmont, down into Florida's swampy hinterland, and across the Gulf Coastal Plain of Alabama, Mississippi, and Louisiana into eastern Texas. Only a southern shard of Arkansas could measure up to such a stiff standard. The Ozarks certainly would not. The highland elevation and the Great Plains weather system claim the Missouri Ozarks and an Arkansas corridor from Eureka Springs to Harrison for the Midwest. There the temperature reaches ninety degrees fewer than sixty days a year.[13]

A similar agricultural gauge of southernness is the mule test.[14] This theory posits that the higher the mule-to-horse ratio in favor of mules as the workstock of choice in a given area, the more southern that area probably is. Using this test we find results comparable to those generated by our cotton survey. Missouri reigned for years as the nation's leading mule-producing state. The Missouri mule became such a common part of American popular culture that Arkansas comedian Bob Burns even made a film about a mule dealer, 1939's *I'm from Missouri*. But farmers in most of the Missouri Ozarks favored the horse over its hybrid offspring. Only in the southeastern Missouri Ozarks did mules slightly outnumber horses in a few counties, a circumstance that may have been due to the mule's favored status in mining and timber operations. Arkansas was certainly a mule state. Mules outnumbered horses almost three to one statewide in 1930.

In the hills of Arkansas, only four counties reported more horses: Benton, Boone, Carroll, and Washington—all located in the non-cotton-growing northwestern corner of the state. But elsewhere in the hills, mules outnumbered horses, and in some areas the difference was southernly striking. Izard County contained two thousand more mules than horses; Van Buren County farmers favored mules three to one. Even in mountainous Searcy and Stone Counties, mules held a two-to-one advantage over horses.[15] The mule gauge absorbs a larger puddle of the Ozarks into the southern pool. Simultaneously, it continues our trend of dividing the region into more and less southern components.

Weather and agricultural definitions introduce us to another complexity in the quest for the essence of southernness—that is, the possibility or

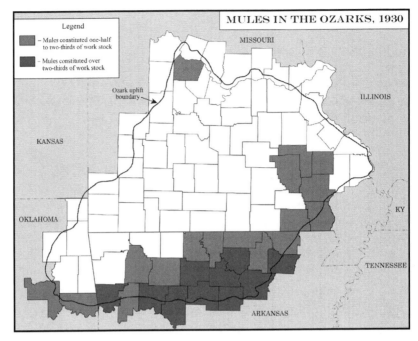

Mules in the Ozarks, 1930.

probability of the existence of several Souths. Some scholars have used the terms *small South* and *large South* to denote the decreasing similarities among southern people as one migrates away from an epicenter of southernness, say, in Clarksdale, Mississippi, or Lower Peach Tree, Alabama, or on some tidewater South Carolina plantation. Again, our epicenters share the distinction of satisfying our stereotypes and definitions—they are, or were, staple-crop producing, African American–majority, ninety degrees in the sultry shade, plantation examples of the South. They so easily pass the tests of southernness because they were the models around which the gauges were constructed. They are all part of the Deep South, where "some Southern characteristics and phenomena were found in their purest, most concentrated forms."[16] The Ozarks never could have been included in this pure, small South. But the large South has room for the Ozarker and for others on Dixie's periphery.

Two additional gauges of southernness reflect the notion of small South versus large South—fireworks and politics. After the Civil War, bitter ex-Confederates urged fellow southerners to halt the practice of celebrating

that Yankee holiday, the Fourth of July. But southerners like their fireworks. Thus was born the tradition of fireworks on New Year's and a
quieter Independence Day.[17] If the South is that part of the nation whose
New Year's fireworks sales surpass those of the Fourth of July, then we
find once again a sorely restricted Dixie. Though New Year's fireworks
were not uncommon in the Ozarks as recently as the 1950s, today they are
found almost exclusively in the Deep South and Southwest. In the early
twenty-first century, Arkansas's largest retail fireworks dealer profited
from New Year's sales in Cleveland, Mississippi; Shreveport, Louisiana;
and Houston, Texas, but never experienced success north of Tupelo.[18]

In terms of politics, most of the South was for generations defined
by a rigid, one-party system. For the better part of a century following
Reconstruction, southern Democrats exercised hegemonic control unpar-
alleled in American history. One-party Democratic rule enveloped more
of the Ozarks into "the South" than any of our previous gauges of southernness. In general terms the areas that emerged from the Civil War and
Reconstruction in the firm control of former Union troops and their allies
became dependable territory for the Republican Party, while counties
in which old Confederates outnumbered their loyal neighbors joined the
solid South of the Democrats. In the Missouri Ozarks this situation created a west-east divide whose map resembles our horse-mule map. With
its greater antebellum prosperity and valuable road system, southwestern
Missouri became a much greater object of the US Army's attention during
the war. Its prairies and ridges, largely swept free of secessionists, became
one of Missouri's most loyal districts for the Grand Old Party. The rugged
hills and hollers of southeastern Missouri, on the other hand, stymied
Union efforts to subdue the territory during the war and attracted former
rebels afterward—a perfect recipe for Democratic domination.[19]

Judging by the party affiliation of Arkansas's elected state and federal
officials during the one-party era, most people in the former Confederate
Ozarks participated in or acquiesced to Democratic dominance. In much
of the Arkansas Ozarks, the party of Jefferson and Jackson held just as
firm a grip on elections as it did in the Deep South. So entrenched were
Democrats on the local level in many Arkansas, Oklahoma, and southeastern Missouri Ozarks counties that Democratic primaries continued to
serve as de facto county elections well into the twenty-first century, long
after Republicans had triumphed in most of the Deep South. But when a
Republican voice made it to the state capitol in Little Rock, it was invariably
sent by a contingent of dissenting Ozarkers. The Ozarks, after all, had been

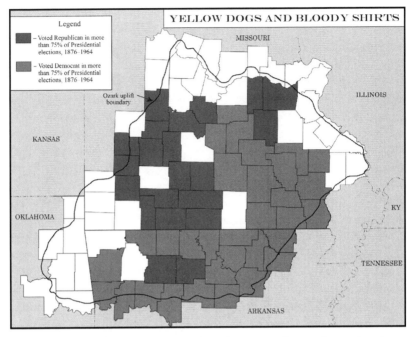

Yellow dogs and bloody shirts: presidential voting in the Ozarks, 1876–1964.

home to the greatest number of Arkansas's anti-secessionists and Union sympathizers. Between 1919 and 1959, five different Ozarks counties— Newton, Searcy, Van Buren, Carroll, and Madison—elected at least one Republican to the Arkansas House of Representatives. In twenty-one general assembly elections during that span, Searcy County sent a Republican to Little Rock eight times, including five consecutive sessions between 1945 and 1953, while her neighbor Newton County elected a Republican representative seven times. Both were consistent supporters of Republican presidential candidates long before the entire white South turned red.[20] It was not uncommon for Republican candidates to garner more than 40 percent of the votes cast in the third, or northwestern, district, and it was no accident when the third district's John Paul Hammerschmidt became Arkansas's first Republican in Congress in almost a century. Similarly, the state's first post-Reconstruction Republican senator (Tim Hutchinson, elected in 1996) hailed from the Benton County town of Gravette.

In more recent years even the bluest of the former Democrat-controlled Ozarks counties have joined most of the South and other parts of rural flyover country as solid red segments of the political map, rendering the once-valuable political test of southernness practically useless. But the historical use of that test continues to hold value. It seems that the Ozarks was, until the present generation, typically divided on the issue of political affiliation—and its impact on southernness. While southwestern Missouri has been a Republican stronghold for more than a century and a half, a large chunk of the region exhibited the one-party Democracy of the century following Reconstruction and, therefore, reflected a very southern political atmosphere.

No discussion of southernness would be complete without at least a mention of religion. Outside of Louisiana and other such religiously marginal locales, the South has long been synonymous with evangelical Protestant Christianity. The 1926 federal census of churches found that such denominations made up 80 percent or more of religious adherents in all but eight of the sixty interior Ozarks counties. In only one—the old mining county of Washington in Missouri—did evangelical Protestants represent a minority of the population. But evangelical Protestants also dominated significant stretches of the Midwest and Plains states, so the presence of large numbers of Methodists, Baptists, and Presbyterians did not in and of itself signal a southern culturescape. Until recent times, and in many places today, the South was dominated by Baptists and Methodists, particularly Southern Baptists and, until the Wesleyans reunited, Southern Methodists. Baptists overtook Methodists as the South's most populous religious group after the Civil War.

If we accept as gospel John Shelton Reed's hunch that you'll find southerners wherever you find large numbers of Baptists, the core Ozarks is fully immersed. Only the counties sprinkled along the northern fringes of the region find another religious group more plentiful. For that matter, however, Baptists account for a plurality in most of the counties of northern Missouri and southern Illinois—and no one expends energy debating the southernness of those places. Yet, Baptist territorial politics in the United States of the late nineteenth and early twentieth centuries thwart any hope of using the presence of Southern Baptists as a gauge of southernness. Comity agreements between Northern and Southern Baptists divvied up territories, ensuring that Missouri would be Southern Baptist country, as were Arkansas and Oklahoma. Thus, with only a few exceptions, Baptists in counties that were rigidly pro-Union during the war and staunchly pro-Republican afterwards remained in the Southern Baptist fold.[21] The old rebels and their allies in the Democratic Party, who achieved only a partial

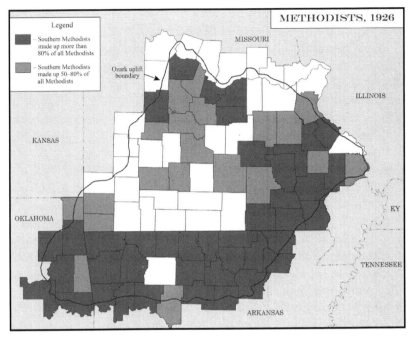

Southern Methodists in the core Ozarks, 1926.

takeover of Missouri's politics after Reconstruction, could have learned a thing or two from the Southern Baptist Convention's complete domination of the state—and the impact that domination must have exercised on whatever *southerning* the Show-Me State experienced in the post–Civil War years.

Methodist divisions provide us with a better gauge, however. Both the Methodist Episcopal Church (Northern Methodists) and the Methodist Episcopal Church, South (Southern Methodists) maintained a presence in all three states. The 1926 census is far from a perfect survey—it ignored tens of thousands of Pentecostals, a thriving body of believers in the Ozarks and elsewhere—but comparing the relative strength of Northern and Southern Methodists is a useful exercise.

Not surprisingly, the Methodist test paints a very southern Ozarks in Arkansas and Oklahoma. Southern Methodist domination extended into the counties of southeastern Missouri—the same areas where mules and Democrats tended to outnumber horses and Republicans—but Northern Methodists held ground in most southwestern Missouri counties.[22]

Thus far, the results from our various barometers of southernness paint a complex and somewhat confusing portrait of the Ozarks set against the backdrop of the South. Using our chosen tests of southernness, it would appear that much of the Arkansas and Oklahoma Ozarks, as well as a block of the region in southeastern Missouri, hold a relatively solid, or middling, claim to southernness—at least in a historical sense. Northwestern Arkansas's inclusion in the South is somewhat less certain, and most of southwestern Missouri appears about as southern as a Zamboni. If you're from Benton County (Arkansas or Missouri) and your momma named you Dixie, don't fret just yet. I'm not calling her a liar or you a Yankee. We'll summon the erudite late Arkansawyer C. Vann Woodward to your rescue. In his classic essay "The Search for Southern Identity," Woodward, no Ozarker, argues that it is history itself that defines the South as a unique region. The South has experienced poverty in a land of plenty, failure in a land of perpetual success, and guilt in a land of innocence.[23] This common heritage of un-American experiences connects mountaineers and sharecroppers, millworkers and landlords, Black people and white people.

Using this now-common definition of southernness—the Civil War as fulcrum—the Arkansas Ozarks would appear to qualify as ably as most regions of the old Confederacy. Though a peripheral and largely forgotten area of the Confederacy, the Arkansas Ozarks was nonetheless a part of Arkansas and, therefore, a part of the losing team. Arkansas Ozarkers, even those who refused to support the Confederacy, suffered through the political unrest and poverty that followed defeat, a plight exacerbated by generations of inept, racist politics. The same state line that coaxed the majority of Arkansas's male Ozarkers into Confederate service prompted most of their Missouri kinsmen to eschew rebellion, ultimately launching loyalists north of the line on a separate trajectory of historical development and consciousness. Culturally and agriculturally, economically and ethnically, the differences in life between Ozark County, Missouri, and Fulton County, Arkansas, may have been almost indistinguishable. In terms of American regional identity, however, the former embraced bloody-shirt Republicanism and Yankee triumph, the latter intransigent Democracy and Lost Cause defeat. But 36°30' was straighter and clearer than the real line of demarcation. The Ozarks of southeastern Missouri and other pockets of the Show-Me State sheltered thousands of former rebels and their kinfolk who experienced the same feelings of failure, guilt, and poverty faced by their fellow Confederates to the south. Here in the land of Democrats, Southern Methodists, mules, and even a little cotton, the orientation toward the South was no less pronounced. Modern America's most seminal event thus played a central role in shaping regional identity and the social construct that is the South.

When pushed to identify the best definition of the South, after all, sociologist and noted chronicler of the South John Shelton Reed turned to a map showing the popularity of the entry "Southern," as opposed to "American," in telephone books of 1976. By this reasoning, if a person, business, or group thinks they are southern and calls themselves southern, then who's to argue? According to this gauge—what might be referred to as the test of southern consciousness—the Ozarks did not fit into the most self-consciously southern part of the South, a sort of Deep South that roughly corresponded with the old Confederacy. The Arkansas Ozarks and almost all of the core Oklahoma Ozarks did, however, squeeze into a broader South that also encompassed areas like Kentucky and East Texas. On the Missouri side of the line, only a thin sliver of the south-central border counties joined this broader South, with the amount of southern territory expanding as the line moved eastward.[24]

The South of Reed's "Southern" test is not starkly different from the South revealed by several of our gauges. Years ago, even before taking a position at Missouri State University, I began asking my Missouri Ozarks acquaintances if they considered themselves southern. The only ones who ever answered in the affirmative hailed from southeastern Missouri, an outcome that makes a lot more sense now. But Reed's bicentennial-year southern test has grown long in the tooth. The Ozarks's peripheral claim to self-conscious southernness from an age when Burt Reynolds ruled the box office and Jimmy Carter prepared to occupy the White House has apparently been in rapid decline. While the use of the term *southern* has persisted much more strongly across the greater South than has use of the "meaner" word *Dixie*—the latter "has more to do with attitude than latitude," Reed observed—neither finds much usage in the modern-day Ozarks. More than thirty years after Reed's study, political scientists Christopher A. Cooper and H. Gibbs Knotts revisited the survey and discovered that the Ozarks (even in Arkansas and Oklahoma) had seceded from the broader South of 1976 and joined the true margins of the South. Cooper and Knotts found self-conscious southernness in the Ozarks to be on par with that in Denver, Indianapolis, and Springfield, Illinois. Not exactly a ringing endorsement for Ozarkers convinced they're also southerners.[25]

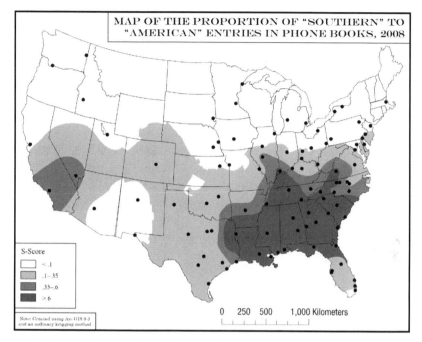

Map of the proportion of "Southern" to "American" entries in phone
books, 2008. From Christopher Cooper and H. Gibbs Knotts, "Declining Dixie:
Regional Identification in the Modern American South," *Social Forces* 88
(March 2010): 1092. *Used by permission of the authors.*

Ultimately, the maps of Reed, Cooper, and Knotts, like Woodward's
thesis, depend on conscious affiliation with some historical and cultural
notion of the South. As historian David L. Smiley observed, "Those of
whatever persuasion or tradition who believe themselves to be southern
are indeed southern, and the South exists wherever southerners form the
predominant portion of the population."[26] While being a native of the
southeastern part of the Ozarks grants me as good a historical claim as
any Ozarker has on the South, it is this consciousness, more than physical
or cultural attributes, that makes me a southerner.

Admittedly, the Ozarks, and for that matter the entire South, is less dis-
tinctively southern today than at any time before. Cultural and corporate
homogenization have taken their toll. The growth of the retirement and
tourism industries have funneled tens of thousands of non-southerners

into northern Arkansas in the last half century. More recently, the population explosion of Northwest Arkansas City—fueled especially by Walmart, Tyson Foods, and other corporate heavyweights—has fundamentally altered demographics in Arkansas's far northwestern corner, and not in a way that makes the area more southern. In some areas of the Ozarks, outlanders outnumber natives; physically and culturally, these areas possess few characteristics that qualify them as southern. Many Ozarkers possess nothing more than their history, their heritage, to justify their claims to southernness. And, if we believe Woodward, that is probably enough. When all the evidence is considered and weighed against the characteristics of what my Alabama neighbors would have considered the "true" South, maybe most Ozarkers really should not be southern. . . . but from Madison County, Arkansas, to Madison County, Missouri, many of us are. This stubborn clinging to a regional consciousness in the face of opposition and change is perhaps our most southern attribute of all.

CHAPTER TWO

Fireworking Down South

A DOOR SLAMMED SHUT, startling me from a sleep too light and too brief. Struggling to get my bearings, I raised up on my elbows and peeked out the passenger-side window of my pickup truck. A yellow ball, brilliant and unrelenting, shot rays through a canopy of pine needles. It was already light, already hot, and I was already in a bad mood. The parking lot of Red Rocket Fireworks, the outskirts of Rock Hill, South Carolina, the Fourth of July.

I had spent most of the dark morning hours in descent, skimming the interstates from Beckley, West Virginia, to Rock Hill, fleeing the Alleghenies in a mad dash to the Piedmont, downing too many Mountain Dews and Chick-O-Sticks at seventy-five miles per hour, only to arrive two hours before opening time at the cavernous Red Rocket warehouse. A person in the fireworks business is rarely surprised by anything, and arriving at work to find a man in combat boots and a sweaty baseball cap sprawled in the seat of a pickup hardly qualifies as extraordinary. So I was invited in, offered coffee (which I declined in favor of a Mountain Dew), and given a seat on a vinyl chair the color of a ripe persimmon. The assistant manager, wearing a pink golf shirt and khaki Duckhead shorts, took my order, which I had scrawled on the blank side of a four-by-six note card. His subsequent phone call to an unidentified warehouse worker struck me as odd, even in a business as far off-center as fireworks. "I need a monkey driving a car, one hen laying eggs, two cuckoos, a fairy with a flower, one climbing panda, one cock crowing at dawn, and whatever we've got in the way of a Jupiter's fire or a thunder blast or a big bear." I could imagine the disconnect an innocent passerby might have experienced upon hearing such nonsensical spew. Fireworks speak is like the names of football plays, or

---

This essay was originally published in the journal *Southern Cultures* 10 (Spring 2004): 25–49. It appears here with only minor revisions.

Fireworks store in Huntsville, Alabama, ca. early 2000s.
Courtesy of Fireworks World, Inc., Batesville, Arkansas.

military instruction manuals, or the banter of social-science graduate students: it just doesn't make any sense taken out of context, and the context is so esoteric that explanation to the uninitiated is an exercise in futility.

My mission in South Carolina on this muggy Independence Day morning was a simple one: to load as many cases of fireworks as I could into my long-bed pickup so that the good folks of Beckley, West Virginia, would not have to celebrate the anniversary of our severance from the British crown in peace and quiet. I must confess that this was a noble mission, no matter how you look at it. Whether it was patriotic idealism or capitalism that fueled my quest, by early afternoon I was back in Beckley, and by nightfall most of the boxes were empty. All around Raleigh County, monkeys were driving cars, hens laying eggs, pandas climbing, fairies flowering, thunders blasting. A mighty good time was had by all, and I sat on the bed in my room at the Pagoda Motel, counting money and watching *SportsCenter*.

Today, just short of the Fourth of July, by the side of the road in the dancing shade of a cottonwood tree, she saw the stand with a banner that read: FIREWORKS FOR SALE. Gloria Turner slowed to a stop and read the smaller print underneath: BIG BANGS FOR LITTLE BUCKS. The words, blown out of a painted volcano, were sailing up and out of line.
—"The Cracker Man" by Helen Norris[1]

THERE IS NOTHING inherently *southern* about fireworks—they were, after all, invented by the Chinese some twelve hundred years ago—but southerners have long held an affinity for fireworks shared by few other American regional groups.[2] In the United States, fireworks are as ubiquitous as the flag. We use industrial-strength displays to celebrate everything from New Year's to ethnic holidays to political rallies, and few of us can remember the last time we saw a home-team home run that failed to light a spark or two. Sure, we all *watch* fireworks. In the South, though, we *use* fireworks; it's a hands-on affair. Teenagers stage bottle-rocket wars, farmers fight varmints of the air and of the ground with M-60s and whistle chasers, small children torment pets with backyard firecrackers, and toddlers wield sparklers like tiny light sabers.

Southerners like fireworks so much that for many years it was customary to shoot them off at Christmas, even more so than on Independence Day. According to the erstwhile Agrarian poet John Gould Fletcher, this practice stemmed from unrepentant Confederates who appreciated good fireworks but who were in no mood to celebrate what had become a Yankee holiday. White southerners, suffering the sting of defeat and the humiliation of military occupation, sulked and bristled on the Fourth of July in 1865 as their former slaves commemorated wildly their first true Independence Day. Mary Chesnut called it the "Black Fourth of July." Five months later the citizens of Atlanta celebrated Christmas with fireworks displays. Only after the end of Reconstruction would most white southerners revive their modest Independence Day celebrations, and only after World War II would the South truly rejoin the Union in unbridled Fourth of July merriment.[3] In some places in the South fireworks are still more popular for Christmas and New Year's. One can almost delineate the Deep South from the rest of the South by observing where you can buy fireworks for Christmas, and in recent years I have seen few for sale very far north of Tupelo.

Not surprisingly, southerners' affinity for fireworks has rarely been recognized in any conscious way. In his book *Fireworks: A History and Celebration*, George Plimpton found nothing worthy of mention below the Mason-Dixon Line. Plimpton's subjects were the Gruccis and other producers of industrial-strength, display-show fireworks, the kinds that ring in the New Year over New York harbor. Whatever sexiness and allure there is to fireworks is tied up in those larger-than-life extravaganzas and their creators, almost none of which are located in the South. The fact that fireworks are so easy to come by in the South renders the ostentatious displays a little less satisfying, a little too bystanderish in a region that not too long

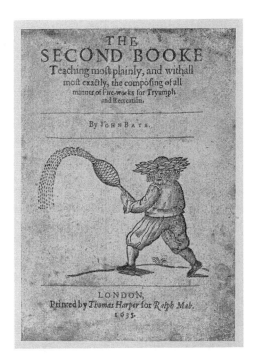

Title page of a 1635 fireworks guide and sketch of a 1749 fireworks show. *From* Pyrotechnics *by A. St. H. Brock, published by Daniel O'Conner in 1922.*

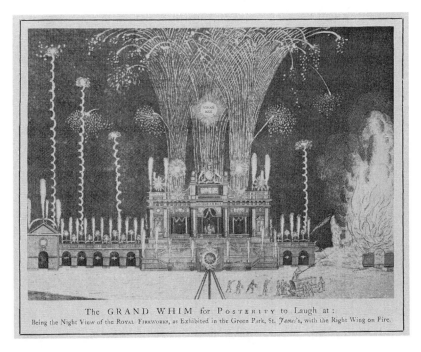

ago still celebrated special occasions by firing guns in the air and rocketing eighty-pound anvils into the black night sky.[4] In the South the fireworks business remains a populist and Protestant one, taking the goods, and the dangers, directly to the people, no interceders needed.

Like populist politicians and Southern Baptist churches, fireworks are plentiful in the South. Of the eight states that completely banned the sale and use of fireworks at the turn of the twenty-first century, only one, Georgia, was in the South. Seven of the eleven former Confederate states were among those with the nation's most liberal fireworks laws, which allow for the purchase and use of almost all Class C fireworks—firecrackers, Roman candles, rockets, aerial displays, and anything else containing no more than fifty milligrams of powder. If you throw Oklahoma into the mix, the South contained more than half the states that permitted almost unlimited Class C fireworks sales. In five southern states—Kentucky, West Virginia, Virginia, North Carolina, and Florida—laws permitted the sale of "safe and sane" fireworks—sparklers, fountains, smoke balls, noise-makers, and novelty items such as car-driving monkeys, spark-shooting chickens, and tanks and boats. And laws in some "safe and sane" states, such as Florida, provided loopholes that allow unlimited Class C sales to out-of-state customers and for agricultural and certain industrial uses. The prevalence of fireworks in the South may be a sort of chicken-and-egg question. Is the use of fireworks so common and popular in the South because they are legal and open to the general public, or are they still legal and open to the general public because fireworks are so popular in the region? I suspect the answer lies somewhere between the two and also has to do with the Jeffersonian tradition of hands-off government in the South, as well as the region's relative rurality and lack of a strong environmental movement—characteristics also true of the Plains states, which combine with the South to form a sort of "fireworks belt" strapped across the midsection of the country.

Certainly, the South's Jeffersonian tradition has contributed to the region's historical position outside the national norm—in the realm of fireworks legislation and many other things as well. Municipalities and states, reacting to both real and perceived dangers and spurred on by the efforts of the American Medical Association (AMA), first began banning the sale and public use of fireworks during the height of the Progressive Era in the early twentieth century. Not surprisingly, such laws were and are most common in the North and Northeast, where progressive government was at its most intrusive. (It is difficult to imagine a southern version of New

Fireworks tent near Kingston Springs, Tennessee, ca. early 2000s.
Courtesy of Fireworks World, Inc., Batesville, Arkansas.

York City's Society for the Suppression of Unnecessary Noise.) In spite of
a report stating that in 1909 deaths and injuries related to fireworks mis-
haps exceeded the number of casualties in the Battle of Bunker Hill, the
South's different brand of progressivism saw fit to leave such quotidian
matters as fireworks where they belonged, outside of statutory consideration. Nevertheless, a second anti-fireworks wave rushed over the country
in midcentury, and by 1953 more than half the states (including five in the
greater South) had completely banned all consumer fireworks. Still, the
South remained the most fireworks-tolerant section of the country. Of the
six states that passed no restrictive laws, five were former Confederate or
border-South states, and five additional southern states permitted at least
limited fireworks sales.[5]

In the years since the Consumer Product Safety Commission's failed
attempt to enact a nationwide ban on all firecrackers and most other
Class C fireworks in 1974, the trend has been toward a liberalization of
state fireworks laws—just another element in the "southernization" of
America in recent decades. In the years sandwiching the turn of the century, North Carolina, West Virginia, and Maryland, among other states,
lifted their bans on fireworks. When this essay was first published in 2004,

only obstinate Georgia remained outside the Dixie fireworks fold. In the Peach State's defense, there is no denying the danger in the fireworks industry. Fireworks factory explosions claim hundreds of lives each year; in December 2001 alone, fireworks manufacturing accidents killed almost two hundred workers in China, Peru, and Guatemala. Nevertheless, the fact that most of these accidents take place in developing nations and that fireworks-related deaths in the United States remain rare bodes well for the continued health of the American retail business. Despite continued lobbying by the AMA and other anti-fireworks organizations and despite the Consumer Product Safety Commission's claims that fireworks injure ten thousand persons each year, southerners (and, increasingly, Americans of other regions) cling to a tradition of loud, smelly, messy holiday celebrations. The nation's fireworks laws have followed a southernizing trajectory over the past two decades, leaving only four states that effectively ban sales—none of them south of the Ohio River.[6]

The proliferation of "official" municipal fireworks shows in recent years—a thinly veiled, neoprogressive strategy to take fuse-lighting out of the hands of the drunken riffraff—has done little to steer subdivision Gruccis and would-be warriors away from the tents and stands. Among the litany of rights cherished in the South is the right to endanger oneself and anyone else who happens to be in the vicinity. And few in the region are likely to take notice of statistical evidence until the casualty lists rival those of *real* battles like Chancellorsville or Chickamauga.

It seemed like maybe the fireworks stand was planted there to flag
her down. I guess this is where I was headed, she thought . . .
—"The Cracker Man" by Helen Norris

ALTHOUGH MOST OF US are blissfully unaware of it, at least until those clapboard stands and multicolored tents crop up around the Fourth of July, selling fireworks is big business in the South and in much of the United States in general, about as big as a seasonal business can get. Although the nature of the industry prevents thorough data-gathering, the American Pyrotechnics Association estimates that retail fireworks sales generated approximately $1.9 billion in 2020, an increase of 272 percent in two decades.[7] The fireworks marketplace is getting more crowded every year, as ambitious upstarts compete with church and civic groups and battle-tested veteran companies for the best locations and for the dollars of customers who come just about as close as people can to watching their money go up in smoke. Most fireworks are sold by licensed vendors who set up shop underneath tents or in small buildings, stands, and mobile homes. And almost all of the fireworks sold in these venues ultimately come from one of a handful of large wholesale/retail companies, all with strong southern connections: TNT Fireworks in Florence, Alabama; Fireworks Over America in Springfield, Missouri; Atomic Fireworks, headquartered in South Pittsburg, Tennessee, with distribution centers in Missouri and South Carolina; and Red Rocket Fireworks, which maintains warehouses in Missouri, South Carolina, and Louisiana. As competition has grown fiercer in the past quarter century, some larger retail companies have erected spacious, permanent buildings in suburban areas or on the outskirts of cities. These "superstores" are the Walmarts of the fireworks business—every item imaginable under one roof, air-conditioned, well-lit and clean, with greeters, check-out girls, and bag boys. Located in metropolitan areas like Houston, Shreveport, Little Rock, Montgomery, Knoxville, and Columbia, one of these superstores can generate hundreds of thousands of dollars in sales in little more than a week. Throwing subtlety out the window—who has time for it when your annual income rests on the earnings from a few days a year?—the superstores beckon interstate drivers with flags, banners, strobe lights, and giant Godzilla and King Kong helium balloons.

Among the most garish of the superstores are the border stops, convenience store/flea market/fireworks dealers in states with liberal fireworks laws who set up shop on freeways just across the lines from states that limit sales to "safe and sane" items. In some of these businesses, such as South of the Border in Dillon, South Carolina, fireworks are simply part of a full panoply of gewgaws and doodads. In other border locations, fireworks take center stage and lure would-be lawbreakers with giant Black Cat posters and ten-foot-tall red and white rockets, and with classic, friendly-capitalist business names like Wild Bill's and Jolly Joe's. The Georgia state legislature's decision to outlaw all fireworks in 1962—"All the firecrackers in the world are not worth one good bird dog," state senator V. E. Lindsey exclaimed in support of the ban—created a border-stop fireworks boom for Tennessee, Alabama, and South Carolina. Risking penalties of up to a year in prison and a fine of $1,000, for decades Georgians snuck away from the Peach State "to load up on rockets and firecrackers the way [they] used to go to bootleggers to load up on whiskey."[8]

Retail fireworks is an often disorganized, seat-of-the-pants business

Scene from *The Cracker Man*, a 1999 film based on Helen Norris's short story, photographed by Kent Eames. *Courtesy of Kent Eames and John DiJulio.*

that seems to attract mule-trader types who prefer a bit of adventure over the security of the nine-to-five world. It is a business that involves complex international trade on the one hand and monotonous haggling with countless low- and mid-level municipal bureaucrats of middle America on the other. Fireworks company executives blame some of the confusion and disorganization on language and international legal barriers that can muddle relations with the Chinese, who manufacture most of the fireworks sold in America.

But most of the disorganization inherent in the business comes from the seasonal nature of the enterprise and the challenge of dealing with an almost infinite variety of state and local fireworks laws. Few businesses swing so wildly from periods of frantic activity to stretches of virtual inactivity, and few businesses rely so heavily on an army of seasonal managers and laborers. And operating this seasonal enterprise within a complex web of overlapping and sometimes contradictory ordinances would seem to require each fireworks retailer to maintain its own legal department—at least, that is, if the laws were strictly and uniformly enforced. The willingness and wherewithal of local law enforcement officers to enforce

Strip mall converted into a year-round fireworks store in Houston, Texas,
early 2000s. *Courtesy of Fireworks World, Inc., Batesville, Arkansas.*

municipal and state ordinances varies from town to town, perhaps even
from neighborhood to neighborhood. Not infrequently, fireworks laws are
so convoluted as to be practically unenforceable. In Florida, for example,
the same state law that prohibits the selling of most Class C fireworks also
permits the "importation" of almost any Class C product for use in mining
and railroad work and for the purpose of scaring birds and other pests
away from farms and fish hatcheries. The curious result of this vague stat-
ute is a system whereby fireworks retailers sell just about anything to just
about anyone, provided that the buyer signs a form claiming the intention
to use the fireworks for one of their legal uses. Even the most suburban
Florida landscapes find themselves overrun with farmers and miners for
a few days each year in a scenario that one St. Petersburg reporter labeled
"the ruse before the fuse."[9]

Most fireworks operations fit into one of two categories: those operated
as fundraisers for local churches or civic groups and, more commonly,
those operated as a franchise for a larger retail fireworks company. Retail
fireworks companies often operate dozens, even hundreds, of shops (tents,
mobile homes, permanent buildings) by contracting them out to managers. One of the incongruities of the fireworks business is that, despite its
transient nature and carnival atmosphere, the folks running the cash reg-
isters and hanging the bunting are quite *normal*. Due to the timing of

the fireworks seasons, summer break and Christmas break, many of these managers are teachers or college students looking to supplement their too often meager incomes without sacrificing an entire vacation. The teachers may be locals or outsiders in their town of business. For instance, in its heyday Fireworks World of Batesville, Arkansas, hired a number of educators and other managers from around north-central Arkansas and sent them to run locations in Texas, Tennessee, West Virginia, and other states; occasionally they hired "local" managers who lived and worked in far-flung locations in Texas, Tennessee, or West Virginia. Sometimes a retail company franchises with a church or civic group. The companies generally cover permitting, ordering of stock, equipment, and supplies, tent rental, and shipping; managers generally receive a percentage of the gross sales, out of which they hire laborers and pay for food and lodging.

> *"It beats preachin' for gittin' folks high.*
> *And quicker than likker, I guarantee."*
> —Hank the fireworks salesman in Norris's "The Cracker Man"

IN THE PAST TWO DECADES, the fireworks tent has largely superceded the once ubiquitous stand as the symbol of the season. Every year, around the middle of June, colorful tents appear on parking lots and roadsides across the region. (Laws in Alabama, South Carolina, and Texas prohibit the sale of fireworks from tents, so semitrailers, wooden stands, and mobile homes generally do the trick in those states.) The tents range in size from 20-by-40 feet to 60-by-120 feet and come in a variety of eye-catching colors: red and white, yellow and blue, or, my favorite, red, yellow, and blue. They are of the same variety used in tent revivals, though the Lord's work usually calls for something a bit more understated—solid white is good for obvious reasons and blue and white works well in a dignified, Presbyterian kind of way. Most Presbyterians, or Southern Baptists for that matter, wouldn't be caught dead in a revival tent these days, but for fireworks peddlers, the gaudier the better.

The fireworks tent offers little in the way of eternal salvation. Far from it. Buying and lighting firecrackers and bottle rockets is about as ephemeral a pleasure as there is to be had. Only a Calvinist on the dark side of Calvin would find repose underneath the tent of blue, yellow, and red. But the idea of a dual-purpose tent remains appealing. Once, on a particularly slow day in Wilkesboro, North Carolina, after the third or fourth car sidled up to the tent to ask if we were holding a revival, a friend of mine wondered aloud, "Maybe we'd be better off having a preaching." We brainstormed a bit. "I'm pretty handy with *Heavenly Highway Hymns*," I assured him, "at least the choruses." Most anybody who has grown up in a rural Baptist church could summon up a tolerably powerful sermon, we decided; a passing of the plate, a couple lines from "Softly and Tenderly," and we could be in business. We sure did have the makings for a fine post-service show.

The connection between the fireworks tent and the tent revival hasn't gone unnoticed. In his 2002 song "Mission Temple Fireworks Stand," blues rocker and Tupelo native Paul Thorn sings about "a Black man with a bible and a sparkler in his hand" who "quit [his] job at a big church where the milk and honey flowed / to sell cherry bombs for Jesus in a tent beside the road." The dual-purpose fireworks/redemption tent might be anomalous in its lack of subtlety—"He said the end of the world is coming, so you better get on your knees / Today bottle rockets are 2 for 1, but salvation's FREE."[10] Nevertheless, the fireworks life is not without its spiritual dimension. While even the most brilliant fireworks display is not exactly awe-inspiring, in the sense of causing one to contemplate the wonders of the heavens and the majesty of Providence, fireworks themselves have served religious purposes. The Chinese inventors of fireworks used loud, colorful rockets to frighten away evil spirits, and in the Middle Ages Europeans incorporated fireworks into their own religious festivals.

In the South, fireworks sellers cater to a "spiritual" need—the need to blast away at the ghosts of the past, the need to salve the old wounds of defeat and dishonor with ever more fervent displays of patriotism, the need to escape the legacy of poverty vicariously through ostentatious jubilation. "The fiery brilliance of fireworks," historian Matthew Dennis observes, "seems to wash out historical memory, and the ephemeral pyrotechnics themselves leave little lasting impression in the sky, on spectators, or on the future." Fireworks marketers and designers have also recognized their products' relationship with southern civil religion. During my days in the business, the Confederate motif was a common one in the packaging and labeling of fireworks, as common as, perhaps more so than, the American Revolution motif. A shopper could buy a Dixie Blast, a Dixie Thunder, and a variety of other items sporting the Confederate battle flag. (In one Marjorie Kinnan Rawlings story, a fish fry and political debate in fictional Oak Bluff is capped off by a fireworks display whose finale is called the "attack on Fort Sumter.")[11] Southerners can honor the memory of Andy Jackson with the Battle of New Orleans display item, and the

Fireworks stand operated by the Cushman Assembly of God church, Cushman, Arkansas, early 2000s. *Courtesy of Fireworks World, Inc., Batesville, Arkansas.*

Battle of Gettysburg is a favorite among those who just don't care or don't know any better. In some cases it seems as if the Chinese have uncovered historical events of which even the Sons of Confederate Veterans were unaware; despite its dubious claim to historical accuracy, the Battle of Tennessee shot off the shelves in places like Cookeville and Henderson and Dyersburg.

Product naming is a study all its own in the fireworks business, a study that sometimes enlightens, often confuses, and never fails to entertain. Where else can you buy an Atlas IV Rocket, a B-52 Bomber, a USS Nimitz, an M-45 Tank, a Saturn Battery Missile, and a Megatron in one place, and stuff them all in the same plastic sack? Skeptics searching for a redeeming quality in the fireworks business can take comfort in knowing that beneath the hanging lights, perched atop the bunting-draped plywood tables, waits a veritable midterm examination in history and geography, not to mention a senior paper on the syntax of translated English. A quick perusal of the shelves will reveal such product names as Krakatoa, Mount Everest, Vesuvius, and St. Helen's Revenge, Galileo, Titanic, and Jurassic Adventure. For those looking to hit the town, there is Las Vegas at Night or the Sydney Opera. The animal lover enjoys an almost infinite selection: Black Cats and Flying Bats, Killer Bees, Red Dogs and White Tigers, Tasmanian Devils, Climbing Pandas, and Butterflies, as well as an entire reptile genre—Wild Snakes and Black Snakes, Mighty Cobras and Snake Pits. There is something to appeal to any taste: sadistic militarism (Crossfire, Firestorm, Screaming Fire, Nuclear Meltdown, and Survival Rival); old-fashioned patriotism (Rising Flag, 21-Gun Salute, Fly the Flag, and Cape Canaveral); and post–9/11 jingoism (Enduring Freedom, Cave Buster, and America Fights Back). And then there are plenty that seem to lose a little something in translation: Flying Ground Bloom, Shogun Smoke Crackers, Triangle Devil, Glitterati, and Knock Three Times.

"Bank on Hank for Fireworks"
—Business card slogan in Norris's "The Cracker Man"

I WAS FIRST DRAWN INTO the retail fireworks business in the late 1980s, in the summer after my high school graduation. My basketball coach "took a tent" with a then-small Batesville, Arkansas, operation called Fireworks World and hired me to work in the tent for a little more than two weeks. I was paid $600 and provided with meals and a hotel bed. One of my teammates came along as a night watchman. (Tents are unhandy when it comes time to lock up at night, so the flaps are rolled down and the low man gets to spend the night on a cot, fighting mosquitoes and listening to the radio until exhaustion obscures the cacophony of noises in the wee hours.) Our destination was a forty-by-sixty-foot red-and-white tent perched atop a barren knoll fronting a busy four-lane highway in Lowell, Arkansas, just north of Springdale in the burgeoning corridor sometimes referred to as "Northwest Arkansas City." Life in the tent was odd. You work like a dog for a day or so, hanging lights, running electrical cords, putting up tables (plywood boards on miniature sawhorses), hanging red, white, and blue bunting, and displaying dozens of different fireworks items. Then you sit. For the next ten or twelve days you sit and wait for a handful of customers to come by, you sit and read until your eyes hurt, you sit and count cars, you sit and listen to the Cardinals, and, sometimes, you just sit. You hope that people will see your red-and-white tent with its bunting and its red, white, and blue plastic flags. You hope that they will remember your tent and come back on the third or fourth of July, when 90 percent of the season's selling takes place.

It was as long a two-week span as I had ever suffered through. It was not unusual for me to spend fourteen to sixteen hours a day sitting under the tent, much of the time alone as my old coach ran errands, went sightseeing, and spent evenings scrimmaging with Razorback basketball players in nearby Fayetteville. But our time was not without event. The night watchman foiled a would-be theft with a flying tackle, and I learned to bluff my way through a sale by describing the brilliant displays of tubes and cakes (fireworks lingo for tall display items and short, fat ones, respectively) that I had never seen in action. The Fourth of July—the day that usually generates as much as half of a tent's total sales—was a disaster. A hard shower that morning sent streams rushing over the dirt and gravel floor; yet we noticed that lowering all the tent flaps (to keep out blowing rain) seemed to draw more customers than ever before, a testament to their love of fireworks and to the indomitable American spirit. By mid-afternoon a scorching sun had evaporated every drop of moisture, and my little brother—recruited for the Independence Day rush, placed in a bright-red Razorback hog suit, and stationed at the edge of the highway to wave at motorists—sweated out and finally deteriorated into a swoon. He recovered, but sales did not.

Over the following decade, as a college student and graduate student, I spent early summers and occasionally Christmas breaks selling fireworks or delivering truckloads of fireworks to tents and superstores across the South. By far the most alluring part of the job for me was the travel, not a sexy, cosmopolitan brand of business travel, mind you, but a priceless, anthropologically exhilarating series of journeys into and within the South's diverse subregions. I sometimes fancied myself a sort of scruffy Charles Kuralt whose penance for gleefully traipsing about the commoner's land was a few hot days peddling firecrackers beneath a carnival canopy. Over the years I worked my way up Fireworks World's very informal ladder to become first a tent manager and finally a kind of regional manager. And the opportunities for travel increased at every step.

My decade of fireworking eventually took me through the South's most identifiable regions: Appalachia, the Mississippi Delta, the Piedmont, the Carolina coastal plain, the Missouri bootheel, and the rolling hills and flat expanses of Texas. One summer season (about three and a half weeks) I logged more than seven thousand road miles, including a breathless, twenty-hour drive from my home in Arkansas to the North Carolina coast.

My seasonal work took me from Austin, Texas, to Kaiser, West Virginia, from Morehead City, North Carolina, to Cape Girardeau, Missouri. I spent three summer seasons in Morrilton, Arkansas, the hometown of the eminent historian C. Vann Woodward. Mostly uneventful tours they were, though one late night I did drive the boss's convertible Corvette faster than I'd ever driven a car, or ever will again. In Greenville, North Carolina, I sat through two local television news interviews while passing hog trucks left a lingering pungency more nauseating than any chicken house I had ever smelled back home in the Ozarks. In the winter season that stretches from Christmas to New Year's, I drove delivery trucks to Houston, Shreveport, Jackson, Mississippi, and Huntsville, Alabama. On a frigid December day, I drove from Little Rock all the way across northern Mississippi just to deliver a thirty-foot, inflatable Godzilla balloon to a couple of freezing old men running a tent in Tupelo. Once I stopped for dinner at the Bluebird Diner in Mount Airy, North Carolina—satisfying a serious *Andy Griffith Show* fetish—and then overheated my pickup trying to pull a loaded U-Haul trailer to the crest of the Blue Ridge. I saw the sights, haggled with local officials, and dealt with tent managers in places like Washington, North Carolina; Mountain View, Arkansas; and Lewisburg, West Virginia.

"You lookin' to blow up the world?"
—Hank the fireworks salesman in Norris's "The Cracker Man"

ALTHOUGH I NEVER lucked into a bonanza location, I sometimes made a decent profit and never came back home empty-handed. Business was good in Morrilton and Beckley and Rocky Mount, not so good in Greenville and Cape Girardeau. There were days so slow that I would read through an entire book, others so hectic that there was no time to eat. One mid-June day in Wilkesboro, North Carolina, my tent, which had mistakenly been erected on a parking lot *behind* the shopping mall, grossed $11. By the end of the week we had packed up fireworks, tent, and all and headed for West Virginia. Fireworks business folklore—and there is such a thing—is filled with stories, most likely apocryphal, of wealthy midnight shoppers buying a tent's entire stock. I never found such an enthusiast, though once I sold $500 worth of fireworks to a drunken construction worker who signed over his paycheck and who an hour later brought all of it back because he was afraid to go home and face his wife.

Like all business travelers, the fireworks salesman remains an outsider wherever he goes. But in the fireworks business there is an added dimension to one's outsider status, something I like to call the carny factor. With the exception of a few fireworks superstores in states that allow year-round sales, such as South Carolina and Missouri, the fireworks business is a

Ready for the Fourth of July. A stocked fireworks tent in
Batesville, Arkansas, early 2000s. *Photo by author.*

seasonal one. You drive by the Winn-Dixie on your way to work every day,
and then one morning in early summer you see a tent sitting on the parking lot, "as if it owned the world in sight."[12] The tents, stands, and fireworks are there for a couple of weeks, and in the Deep South a couple of
weeks again at the end of the year, and then they disappear. And the sellers of fireworks—like carnival folk and the guys who sell Christmas trees
or Confederate T-shirts on barren lots—are nameless, storyless transient
workers, drifters, probably crooks.

For a fellow who was solidly *from* somewhere, who had grown up on
the family farm surrounded by the farms and homes of aunts and uncles
and other kin, this role of the consummate outsider, the carny, was at once
the most difficult and the most liberating part of the fireworks life. In the
Ozarks we were always leery of outsiders, and an outsider was anyone not
immediately recognizable or kin to someone who was. We were especially
suspicious of those rootless carnival folk, even though we'd heard the story
of a boy who had gotten half his face blown off in a hunting accident and
had wandered off to run the Tilt-A-Whirl or tend the Shetland ponies or
operate the cotton-candy machine. That was the issue. Everyone knew

that only freaks or misfits went in for such things. So I had a pretty good idea what people thought of us fireworks peddlers. In the early years I tried to fight the stereotype whenever I could. Whenever someone "respectable"-looking would venture into the tent, I would tuck my shirt in, maybe turn the radio to NPR, and strike up a conversation in which I rarely failed to mention something about college or use an adverb.

And I quickly learned that carny folk are easy targets for ridicule. The Saturday night, town-cruising crowd never hesitated to hurl epithets, and heavier objects, from their Broncos and Camaros. The college kids home on summer break were probably the most abusive. One evening in Wilkesboro, a preppie, walking billboard for Tommy Hilfiger asked me if all our items were relatively benign, and then snickered to a friend, confident that I would have no idea what "benign" meant—and maybe even "relatively." And he was right. At that moment I had been awake for twenty-four hours, and my mind was doing well to process the word "items" correctly. So I just looked at the two young men blankly and said, "I reckon." The business had a way of doing that to you, dumbing you down to match people's expectations. I often wondered how much smarter I might have been had I spent my summers stocking shelves or gutting fowl. Luckily, I think the whole experience was pretty benign, or at least relatively so.

Fireworks tents also have a way of attracting local candidates for the carny folk lifestyle. Without fail, after a day or two of setting up shop in a strange town, the town's strange people, young and old, would drop in, and often linger. Winos, hobos, and the kinds of off-kilter, small-town characters populating the storyscapes of Flannery O'Connor and Carson McCullers, these comprised the local welcoming committees. Perhaps they sensed the presence of kindred souls, of visitors from far-off places who knew a thing or two about living on the margins, about being ostracized. Or perhaps it was loneliness or nosiness, or both, that brought them around. A fireworks tent is a great social leveler, an arena that almost demands humility. There was no escaping the odd or misfortunate characters who came in. Sitting in my lawn chair under the canopy, I listened to a West Virginian's exposition concerning the unappreciated merits of an obscure science-fiction author, an Arkansawyer's instructions for building a bomb using only duct tape and a box of sparklers, and more lectures on video game strategy than I care to remember.

More serious, from a business standpoint, was the disadvantage of an outsider label when it came time to get something accomplished at city hall or in the county courthouse. To fire chiefs and building inspectors, we were outsiders of the worst kind, transients and carnies who set up shop to rip people off and disappear into the night, taking a chunk of their neighbors' money with us. And, by and large, they were right. We certainly overcharged for our fireworks, though we never twisted anyone's arm, and we did eventually leave town with our money, often late at night. There are almost as many variations of local fireworks laws as there are local governments, and minor public officials and bureaucrats in small southern towns are notorious for being hard to deal with. In the business we sometimes called this the "Barney Fife syndrome." Give a fellow a modicum of authority and power and turn him loose on unsuspecting out-of-towners, and it can make for an ugly situation. In Cleveland, Mississippi, the manager of a tent (a college student) ran out for a bite to eat and returned to find his hired hand (a friend from college) handcuffed and being shoved into the back seat of a police car. Unbeknownst to the two young men, the fireworks company's management had failed to secure all the necessary municipal permits, and Cleveland authorities were taking no chances with this carny riffraff. In a North Carolina town, the local fire chief dropped in on the evening of July 3, just before the Independence Day rush, and threatened to shut the tent down because some of the items *looked* illegal.

Despite the derision and hassles, there was a certain freedom in being a transient. Cut loose from the moorings of community or family or any semblance of normality, the fireworker finds himself in no way beholden to the standards of the respectable element in the host town and sufficiently far away from the moral strictures of home ground. There is no way an outsider, especially a carny, is going to work himself into respectability and acceptance in three weeks, so why even bother? A fellow student who worked in my tent in Beckley took this to heart. A hard-working farm boy from a solid Church of Christ family, he nevertheless took advantage of the fact that the West Virginia coal-mining country seemed to be safely outside the Bible Belt and far enough away from Alabama that no one would tell his momma. A regular customer at all three strip joints in town, where the girls, he assured me, got "plum nekid," my friend had only one regret— that he had discovered Beckley's backstreet delights so late in our stay.

It was easy to step out of character. One afternoon in Springdale, Arkansas, in my eighteen-year-old-boy, just-for-the-heck-of-it stupidity, I drove through town wearing a navy-blue ski mask—in the coach's truck. Not long after, the police arrived at our tent. Someone had reported an attempted robbery at the filling station down the road, they told me, and the suspect had been driving a truck just like this one. I told them the owner of the truck was in the mobile home office next door, not knowing that the coach was at that very moment sitting on the office floor counting out the cash from the previous day's sales. Luckily for me (and the coach), they knocked. On another occasion I hauled a hitchhiker through the Ouachitas and enjoyed the brief life story, though not the smell, of an Indiana man who, it turns out, was *from* somewhere, too.

The fireworker learns a good deal about the South, about the different Souths, and about the people living in them. He gets a good feel for such things as the vague boundaries of the Bible Belt, the variations on an elusive "southern" dialect, and the Americanizing effects of fast-food franchises, chain stores, and the media industry. He also comes to appreciate the consumer-culture commonalities that defy boundaries of race and ethnicity. This last lesson is an important one for the seller of fireworks. There is a noticeable socioeconomic dimension to the fireworks crowd. While the fireworker may wait for those rare moneybags customers who can afford to squander a few hundred dollars to light up a cul-de-sac or impress friends at a barbecue, the most loyal customers are the poor and working-class folks who devote a considerable chunk of their income to this seasonal frivolity, the same class of people toward whom the Progressives' anti-fireworks laws were aimed more than a century ago.

From a marketing standpoint, then, the retail fireworks industry is somewhat like the lottery—it seems to draw its most devoted customers from the lower rungs of the economic ladder, regardless of race. With a power matched by few other things in American society, the allure of fireworks reaches across racial and ethnic divides. The whiz and bang of a bottle rocket appeals in equal measure to Texans of Hispanic heritage, to African Americans in the Delta, and to the white descendants of the Piedmont's mill towns. And the appeal is nowhere more prominent than among the poor and the working class of any shade. It was a circulating joke in the business that a "no shoes, no shirt, no service" policy in a fireworks tent would effectively cut business in half. And there was a little bit of truth in it. More often, though, observing poor folks spending every last cent in their pockets on items regularly marked up from 300 to 500 percent above wholesale proved a painful and bewildering experience. The Chinese poor labored by the thousands in sweatshops to produce these rockets and crackers and novelty items, and the American poor, rich by contrast, helped subsidize the whole enterprise. But I was a poor graduate student and just Jeffersonian enough to say, "It's their money. They can do

Interior of a fireworks super center in Channelview, Texas, early 2000s.
Courtesy of Fireworks World, Inc., Batesville, Arkansas.

whatever they want with it." And as we reminded ourselves on more than
one occasion, "If they don't spend it here, they'll spend it somewhere." I
reckon there was more than a little truth in that, too. As a result of this
fireworks business caveat, the prized spots for fireworks tents often flew
in the face of conventional retail strategies. A location on the parking lot
of a rundown mall in Rocky Mount, North Carolina, could outsell a prime
spot in a Raleigh suburb; two-bit burgs in West Virginia or Mississippi
could turn profits while upscale operations near Nashville and Greensboro
tanked.

All of these marketing conundrums seemed to converge in an unfortunate manner one memorable Independence Day season in Cape Girardeau.
Not exactly southern and not exactly nonsouthern, Cape Girardeau is one
of those hard-to-pin-down yet regional-flavored towns. Just a few miles
up from the cotton fields of the bootheel but closer to St. Louis than to
Memphis, and sufficiently "middle American" enough to produce a most
famous son like Rush Limbaugh, this Mississippi River town is just the
kind of place that can slam a fireworks salesman. The company assured
me I had a prime location, just north of town wedged in a busy intersection

with new subdivisions on three sides. But the crowds failed to appear, and when we did get customers, as often as not they were thirty-something übermoms who demanded to know every dangerous scenario posed by every single item and who usually left empty-handed, dragging two crying kids with them. Nothing spoils a good sale, or irritates a carny, quite like a concerned parent. Exhausted after a day of battling the lingering embers of Progressive public-safety consciousness through a campaign of general lying, I found myself staring longingly one evening down the river, thinking about the crowds in Dyersburg, West Memphis, and Clarksdale, and humming a bar of "Dixie."

I suppose that like a lot of things we in the South think of as southern, shooting off fireworks has a much wider appeal, in this case a global appeal. I am not really sure why we in the South love fireworks so. Perhaps the explanation lies somewhere in that martial spirit so often at the forefront of discussions of southern distinctiveness. Maybe the proliferation of and appreciation of fireworks is a sort of political creation—maybe southerners purchase and shoot off fireworks because they can, and maybe more Americans would if they could. Perhaps the working classes around the nation and the globe share a passion for shooting off fireworks, and maybe the South's popular culture and image has simply been more closely tied to the actions and tastes of its lower orders than have the images of other regions. It could be that southerners just love the smell of fried saltpeter. Whatever the reason, the South is, as anyone in the business would tell you, fireworks country. We southerners like our fireworks the same way my high school buddies liked their cars—big and colorful, loud and fast. And we'll light them ourselves, thank you.

CHAPTER THREE

The South According to *Andy*

"**B**OY, GIRAFFES ARE SELFISH! Just running around looking after number one, getting hit by lightning."[1] If you recognize this quote, you won't be surprised at what I am about to say. I will fight you over *The Andy Griffith Show*. I ain't kidding. Tell me something ridiculous like *Andy* is escapist drivel or nostalgic schlock, and we'll go at it. I'll be on you faster than Ernest T. jumped Malcolm Merriweather, quicker than Izamoto judo-chopped Fred Plummer. That's right. I'll tear into you like a windmill in a tornado. What'll it be? Biting and boots? Willow branches and whittling knives?

Where I come from, *Andy* is sacred, right up there close to the Bible. The King James version. Where I come from, we are on a first-name basis. It's just plain old *Andy* to us. We quote passages of *Andy* like Oxford dons quote Shakespeare. "Oh, shut up, Bernie, just shut up!" "I got a uvula. You got a uvula. All God's children got a uvula!" We know the song "Never Hit Your Grandma with a Great Big Stick" makes Charlene cry. We cherish the meteoric rise of Leonard Blush: "He just walked in here off the street one day. Two years later he was singing 'The Star Spangled Banner' at the opening of the county insecticide convention." We always know who said that—Floyd's Latin teacher at barber college, or Calvin Coolidge. So "put that in [your] smipe and poke it!"[2]

Andy works its way into casual conversations, family dinners, even sermons. My high school basketball coach's rendition of Barney's soliloquy from "Dogs, Dogs, Dogs"—whence this essay's opening quotation—could bring a tear to the eye. My niece at age five could answer all the questions from Ernest T.'s geography test. Preachers in the pulpit invoke the words and deeds of Saint Andrew Jackson Taylor, recount the parables of Aunt Bee's bed jacket and Opie's fishing pole. It is not completely ridiculous to claim that my family and friends share a reverence for *Andy* that borders on the religious.

There have been more sophisticated television shows. I'll give you that. And I will admit that being devoted to a program that's like catnip for the Cracker Barrel crowd sometimes gives me pause. But there is value in *Andy*, not just values. You may not realize it, but *Andy* has been teaching us about the South for more than six decades. I realize that *Andy* is bigger than the South, more than just a southern thing. After the death of Andy Griffith in the summer of 2012, no less a nonsoutherner than Jerry Seinfeld admitted that his legendary sitcom used a subtle and "secret tribute" to *Andy*.[3] The show has not been off the air since it came into existence more than sixty years ago, rerunning nationally and in local markets from one corner of the US to the other.

Yet *Andy* holds a special place in the hearts of many southerners. It occupies a position in the South's pop-cultural landscape that has never been—and likely will never be—matched. Many southerners view *Andy* as authentic—as innately, palpably southern—in a way that eclipses other popular regional television shows like *The Waltons*, *In the Heat of the Night*, and *Designing Women*. Much of that, obviously, has to do with the man whose name is in the title. A native of little Mount Airy, North Carolina, Andy Griffith parlayed a hick standup comedy routine into a starring role on a popular and successful Broadway play in the mid-1950s. In 1957, his powerful portrayal of mercurial and narcissistic Lonesome Rhodes in Elia Kazan's critically acclaimed *A Face in the Crowd* raised the baby-faced, pompadoured actor's profile to heights no one could have predicted. But stardom and success are fickle creatures. By the end of the decade, a box-office flop and a poorly received television film had taken the starch out of the thirty-three-year-old actor's collar. His decision to take on the role that would cement his legacy may not have been one of utter desperation, but becoming Andy Taylor was at the least an admission that the second-class world of television was his last best hope.[4]

Though Griffith bristled at the prospect of playing yet another southern hayseed, a positive response from the Mayberry sheriff's first appearance on a backdoor pilot of *The Danny Thomas Show* in early 1960 launched *The Andy Griffith Show*. But Andy was no bumpkin in real life. In fact, according to Daniel de Visé's dual biography of Griffith and Don Knotts, the shrewd Tar Heel may have been closer in temperament and personality to Lonesome Rhodes than he was to the good-natured, benevolent sheriff. While his name would never appear among the producers or writers of the series, Griffith's retention of half-ownership in the show would make him a wealthy man in no time. It also granted him a level of creative control and showrunner input enjoyed by few other stars. *The Andy Griffith Show* may have emanated from southern California. Its producers may have been New Yorkers. Its directors and writers may have been Hollywood veterans who understood the South as deeply as they understood the steppes of Kazakhstan.[5] But it was Andy Griffith's world; it was his vision that shaped eight years of television storytelling. That vision was molded by an upbringing in the Depression-era, small-town South.

Southerners recognized in Andy Griffith one of our own. He talked like us, sang like us. He rhymed can't with ain't, like God intended. He understood that funny doesn't come from one-liners. It isn't manufactured but grows organically from personalities and familiarity and affection. With the help of a bona fide native, Hollywood got it right for a change. That is not to say that a future civilization could reproduce an "authentic" mid-twentieth-century southern world using the DNA of a television show. As with all long-running series, there were missteps along the way and lapses in which Hollywood southernism trumped genuine southernism. (And need I even mention Aunt Bea's accent? What part of the South was she from anyhow? The part north of the Adirondacks?) But, all in all, the South according to *Andy* rang true for viewers in the sixties and still strikes southerners as fundamentally accurate.

Just what, then, did *The Andy Griffith Show* tell us about the South? Perhaps more crucially, what messages did it convey about an American region to Americans, of the sixties and for generations to follow? And what do those images and our reactions to them say about us?

The *Real* South Is in the Past

A few years ago, one of the most popular shows in Branson, Missouri, was *Lost in the Fifties*. The musical tributes to Elvis, Buddy Holly, and the Everly Brothers were interspersed with the harmonica stylings and comic routines of a Barney Fife impersonator. Odd, considering that the first episode of *Andy* premiered in 1960. Then again, Mayberry's time-traveling deputy may not be as anachronistic as this would suggest when you consider that the show was only nominally set in the sixties. On a 1996 *Today* show interview, Andy Griffith fessed up: "Though we never said it, and though it was shot in the sixties, it had a feeling of the thirties. It was—when we were doing it—of a time gone by."[6]

Anyone who has spent much time watching *Andy* recognizes that the fictional world of Mayberry, North Carolina, bore little resemblance to the reality of the sixties, even in a small southern town—an observation that doesn't necessarily challenge the show's fundamental *authenticity*. Mayberry had one long-distance line and a local phone exchange that depended upon the diligence of a lone unseen operator, Sarah. Residents still listened to Sunday afternoon radio shows featuring organ music and parlor songs. Mayberrians went for Sunday drives and dropped by the soda fountain at the drugstore. Automobiles and an occasional pop-cultural reference reminded viewers that Andy and Opie lived in the atomic age, but the spirit of *Andy* was unmistakably pre–World War II. Mayberry was a reflection of Andy Griffith's childhood, his own romantic evocation of a world that had slipped away. Viewers at the time responded to this nostalgia. For hundreds of thousands of Americans (especially southerners) who were raised on farms and in small towns but now found themselves in metropolitan areas, Mayberry was indeed a romantic idyll, an escape into a past that never existed in such innocence and harmony. Similarly, television viewers of the 1980s crowded around the set each week to absorb and applaud fifties-style family values on *The Cosby Show*, a nostalgic-in-its-own-way antidote to *Hill Street Blues*, *Miami Vice*, and other edgier fare of the era. In this sense the creation and appeal of Mayberry—and of *Cosby*'s Brooklyn—demonstrated the human spirit of romance, the primitive spark struck by a remembered life and world. For Andy Griffith and most viewers of *Andy*, the *real* South existed only in memory, and perhaps only in clouded, selective memory.

Sorry, My City Friend, but You Ain't Southern

Okay, I will admit that my first lesson from *Andy* was more about the human condition than about the South per se. It is time to taut this ship—a sentiment dear to the heart of a certain overeager deputy.

We all know there are multiple Souths—different ways of defining the South and its subregions, contrasting concepts of southernness. *Andy* shows us a variety of southerners, but the show is quite clear on one point. The South—the *real* South—exists only outside of metropolitan areas. We hear it in the accents. Real southerners come from small towns and rural places, like Mayberry and its environs, not from the city. In her study of Hollywood's portrayal of the South during the civil rights era, Allison Graham observes of Mayberry, "Trouble occurred usually when outsiders—from the North or from California—came to town with nefarious schemes for bilking the citizens or introducing some kind of modernizing plan."[7] More often than not, though, the outsiders were from inside the geographic South, usually from inside North Carolina. Invariably, escaped convicts from the state penitentiary were streetwise toughs with accents that suggested their crime careers started in New Jersey or Chicago—anywhere but the real South. Most any visitor from Raleigh or another southern city evinced no audible evidence of southern heritage. Even Mount Pilot, the bigger town nearby, was suspect. It served at one time or another as home or home base to Otis's oily attorney, the shady entrepreneurs behind the Miracle Salve Company, and *Andy*'s two most sexually liberated characters, "Fun Girls" Skippy and Daphne. None of them sounded the least bit southern.

The best examples of these non-southern southerners were officers of the state police and other government employees who occasionally traveled the dusty backroads to Mayberry. The show's second episode set the tone. In "The Manhunt" a troop of state policemen in search of an escaped convict commandeer Mayberry's courthouse, the condescending captain (played by actor Ken Lynch) dismissing Sheriff Taylor's suggestions in rapid-fire, Irish-cop staccato—until, of course, Andy's unconventional, common-sense methods save the day. Most any state bureaucrat—whose big city ideas and attitude rendered him the Outsider (and de facto Yankee) in opposition to Mayberry as the stand-in for the South—sounded as if he had stepped off the set of *Dragnet*. In one of many episodes that championed localism and decentralized decision-making over authoritarian, "Organization Man" efficiency, a young trainee from the state attorney's office shows up in Mayberry bearing graphs, charts, and statistical analyses of crimes.[8] In true *Andy* fashion, he comes to appreciate the unquantifiable values of the personal touch and intuition in police work but leaves town with his non-region-specific accent intact.

An extension of *Andy*'s small-town focus is one of the show's overarching themes: New South modernization ain't all it's cooked up to be. Time after time *Andy*'s plotlines champion the virtues of town hall democracy over federalism, human inefficiency over impersonalism, tradition over science and rationalism—the "wisdom of rural mindedness" over the "folly . . . of urban thinking," according to two scholars' analysis.[9] The show's classic endorsement of this small-town, preindustrial southern philosophy shines through in two similar episodes: "Man in a Hurry" and "The Sermon for Today." In both instances, cosmopolitan outsiders serve as catalysts. In "Man in a Hurry" big-city businessman Malcolm Tucker, whose accent marks him as an outsider even more clearly than does his

fancy car, experiences engine trouble on his way through town to a meeting in Charlotte. A frenetic man who expects the locals to jump to attention at his plight, Tucker is repeatedly stymied in his attempts to overcome his predicament. It being Sunday, Wally, Mayberry's lone mechanic,
refuses to work on the car, and his assistant, Gomer Pyle, is too green to
undertake a major repair. Two elderly sisters tie up the long-distance line
discussing their health problems. Even Andy and Barney's leisurely, front-
porch banter sends Tucker into a rage. Ultimately, the man in a hurry gets
his car fixed, but only after imbibing a dose of Mayberry's alternative universe that makes him appreciate this little slice of anachronism.[10]

Conversely, in "The Sermon for Today" the outsider, a visiting minister
from New York, inadvertently disturbs the bucolic balance of Mayberry
by preaching a sermon more fitting for his parishioners back home. "Slow
down. Take it easy. What's your hurry?" he advises, unaware that his lis-
teners are less burdened than most Americans by modern distractions.
Mayberry's subsequent frenzied effort to revive the defunct Sunday afternoon town band concert ends in failure and exhaustion. The advice had
never been for them.[11]

Just as the non-southern-sounding southerners have no impact on
the local dialect, Mayberry survives its brushes with outsiders without
adopting their newfangled ideas. *Andy*'s South thus remains the South of
front-porch visits and intimate acquaintances, a place where bureaucracy
is almost always wrongheaded, where the specific always trumps the general. Whether motivated by insecurity or egalitarianism, it doesn't get too
small to matter in Mayberry.

The South in Black and (Mostly) White

In recent years the academic debate on *The Andy Griffith Show* has generally revolved around race, an issue that for some critics besmirches *Andy*'s
legacy. The authors of a piece on "Mayberry as Working-Class Utopia," for
instance, conclude that Griffith "perpetrated a dishonesty toward African
Americans." How could a show set in the South, such critics ask, blindly
and intentionally portray a place that is lily white? Especially in the sixties? The answer is an easy one, says Allison Graham. "Reconstructing the
Depression as a kinder, gentler time for white America," writes Graham,
"The Andy Griffith Show offered the tantalizing spectacle of a southern
Shangri-la." Most important for the show's producers, this Shangri-la—
bothered by no hint of controversy—posted top-ten Nielsen ratings year

after year. Mayberry's mono-color cast was typical of the era. The latter half of the 1960s may have ushered in the age of color television, but even in the 1967–68 season, the final one for *Andy*, eighty-two percent of American television shows featured no Black character, and most African Americans who appeared on the small screen in those days did so in token roles.[12]

Andy was not completely devoid of color. Black people appeared as extras in some episodes, and episode 215, in the seventh season (1967), featured the first and only speaking role for an African American. Rockne Tarkington is the answer to that trivia question. He played a former professional football player who volunteers to help coach Opie's team and encourages the sheriff's son to continue his piano lessons. We do not know exactly what role Andy Griffith played in the segregation or desegregation of the show. Given his significant influence over the show, it is natural to assume that Griffith at the very least acquiesced to the era's lack of racial diversity on television. We do know that in later years he expressed regret for not having cast more African Americans on *Andy*, and his hit series in the 1980s and 1990s, *Matlock*, featured a Black actor in a prominent role.[13]

How crucial was the absence of racial diversity to the South according to *Andy*? The answer probably depends on who you are and where you're from. In the wake of Griffith's death, a number of Black journalists expressed admiration both for Andy and *Andy*, without denying the troublesome nature of the show's almost complete whiteness. Rochelle Riley, a small-town North Carolina native writing for the *Detroit Free Press*, admitted feeling great sadness over the loss of "our sheriff." Recalling her reaction to the death six years earlier of Don Knotts, who played bumbling deputy Barney Fife, Riley reminded readers that "*The Andy Griffith Show* was about our lives, regardless of color or background. . . . My family didn't watch *The Andy Griffith Show* to count black people."[14] Others have been less willing to give the show a pass. Though no longer available at the time of this book's publication, a YouTube video accompanying a 2008 blog post entitled "Why Come There Ain't No Black People in Mayberry?" mined laughs by using green-screen technology to insert an African American man into footage from various *Andy* episodes. The Black man was apparently gunned down, however, insinuating that Mayberry is "perhaps just another sundown town for black America." Similarly, Black columnist Elijah Gosier suggests the potentially foreboding image of all-white Mayberry: "Might I drive into Mayberry and never be heard from again?"[15]

For many critics the issue boils down to simple demographics. One scholarly study of the show found *Andy*'s lack of African Americans "disturbing given the important role they play in America's working-class history" and the fact that they account for over 20 percent of the population of North Carolina.[16] By such a measurement, the show and its one African American guest star over the course of eight seasons came up woefully short. As a southerner raised in one of the region's whitest areas, however, I'll admit that Mayberry's whiteout was something that I remained unconscious of for years. Like me, Griffith was also from the upland South. Though he repeatedly denied having based Sheriff Taylor's idyllic community on his North Carolina hometown, it is obvious that his experiences growing up in Mount Airy shaped his sensibilities and thus influenced the creation and development of Mayberry. In 1960, the year *Andy* hit the airwaves, more than 95 percent of Mount Airy's 7,055 residents were white. *The Andy Griffith Show* reminds us that the South is not monolithic and that, in true populist, *Andy* fashion, the one-size-fits-all model doesn't work for every place. Whether its lack of racial diversity reflects the demographics of a specific place in the South or an intentionally segregated "southern Shangri-la" of whiteness, the mere exercise of remembering *Andy* reinforces the centrality of race and diversity in Griffith's home region.[17]

Mountain Folks Are a Different Breed

While racial minorities may not play any meaningful role in *Andy*'s South, the show is replete with characters representing the fringes of southern society—moonshiners, alcoholics, cow thieves, and other *Others.* "The type of Other portrayed in Andy," according to James Flanagan, "is a social Other rather than a racial *and* social Other."[18] No southern Other is more crucial to *Andy*'s universe than the mountaineer. And no character type falls victim to stereotype on *Andy* more than the mountaineer. This should come as no surprise, given Hollywood's long tradition of both comic and sinister hillbilly caricatures. The mountains outside Mayberry contained a stable of characters who collectively accounted for practically all the leading hillbilly stereotypes: moonshining, feuding, banjo-playing, superstition.

The Wakefields and Carters were Mayberry's contribution to the oeuvre of hillbilly feudists. Rafe Hollister was a mountain moonshiner with a heart of gold and tenor pipes to match. Undoubtedly, though, *Andy*'s most memorable hillbillies were the Darlings and Ernest T. Bass. The Darlings and Ernest T. appeared in only a handful of episodes, yet the characters play a much more important role in fans' memories.

The Darlings—dad Briscoe, daughter Charlene, and four silent, bluegrass-playing sons—first appeared in Mayberry near the end of the third season. Over the course of the sheriff's interactions with the clan, we learn that they practice an archaic sort of patriarchal chivalry; they are beholden to a complex set of superstitions; they only rarely leave their humble mountain home; and the brothers (played by the Dillards, a popular sixties bluegrass band with roots in the Ozarks) perform an impressive array of original songs. The Darlings appear to be poor, though not destitute, and aside from vivacious Charlene they're a little standoffish, though ultimately harmless. The same can't be said for their neighbor Ernest T. Bass, an illiterate simianesque character with a short fuse and a penchant for throwing rocks through windows. Like many an unbridled hillbilly, Ernest T. can't go anywhere without getting into a scrape. He picks a fight at an army recruiting station, jumps on a fellow guest at Mrs. Wiley's party, and challenges Englishman Malcolm Merriweather to a fight to honor his Irish ancestors. Ernest T. is a walking id, generally motivated by a desire for female companionship.[19] Even Sheriff Taylor, who orchestrates goings-on in Mayberry as if he were a deus ex machina in a lawman's uniform, finds civilizing Ernest T. an impossible task.

I suppose I should be offended at *Andy*'s portrayal of rural mountain dwellers. They are, after all, closer to being *my* people than anyone else on the show. How is it conceivable that a television show featuring a guy from the Bronx (Howard Morris) playing the quintessential Appalachian hillbilly would not be offensive? That a fictional place in which the hills are more thickly populated with moonshiners than with cows would not breed resentment? But I'm not offended, and I don't know anyone else who is. Perhaps it is a testament to my low self-esteem, maybe even to a low collective self-esteem among rural and small-town southerners. It's a complicated reaction that Appalachian writer Jeremy B. Jones captures with a repeated confession in an essay otherwise deconstructing mountaineer stereotypes: "I loved Ernest T. more than any character on *The Andy Griffith Show*."[20] Many of us did. How does *Andy* get away with obvious regional and cultural stereotyping? We trust Griffith to be judicious, to never allow stereotype to overwhelm a character's humanity. It is obvious that Griffith and the show's producers loved these characters, and that appreciation shows through the layers of caricature. Andy Griffith was, after all, one of us.

But which one of us? *Andy*'s portrayal of mountain folks reminds us of something else. Even in the upland South, there were levels of society. There were and are different *us*-es. In *Two Worlds in the Tennessee Mountains*, historian David Hsiung traces the origins of hillbilly stereotypes to the towns of Appalachia, where aspirants to the middle class mocked and criticized their own hinterlanders, reminding respectable society outside the mountain South that they were different from and better than their country cousins.[21] "They're the hillbillies. Not us." Representing as it does the small-town South—a sort of middle ground—*Andy*'s Mayberry seems to be telling Americans, "We may not be cosmopolitan sophisticates, but we're way yonder more uptown than our hillbilly neighbors." This was a reflection of Griffith's small-town, middle-ground upbringing. I understand this, but I'm still not offended—and, like Ernest T., still raring to fight.

Unto the Least of These

Is it possible that Griffith's own self-esteem issues played a role in another of *Andy*'s statements on the South? In an interview conducted years after *Andy* went off the air, Griffith admitted that his family came "from the wrong side of the tracks" in Mount Airy. While Griffith likely exaggerated the depths of his socioeconomic ostracism to improve an already impressive rags-to-riches story, his upbringing was undoubtedly working-class. His father supported Andy and his mother on wages earned at a furniture factory, and high school classmates remembered Andy working afterschool jobs to help supplement the family's income. Being called white trash by an elementary schoolmate "stuck with me my entire life," he recalled.[22] If *Andy* was indeed a reflection of Griffith's experiences and philosophies, it is no surprise that in Mayberry the lower class was the heart and soul of the South. Now, *Andy*'s populist spirit was no television anomaly. For ages the entertainment world has gotten mileage out of vilifying the upper crust and championing the underclass. But this theme recurred often enough in Mayberry that it became a defining characteristic of the show. In the South according to *Andy*, the salt of the earth were not only the region's most populous class; they were the true bearers of southernness in the nation's consciousness and the inheritors of whatever it was that made the South distinctive.

This is not to suggest that *Andy* granted the poor and the despised the agency to claw their way out of their predicaments. Sheriff Taylor almost always effected their redemption—secretly, of course, so as to retain their dignity. He allows incarcerated Sam to celebrate Christmas with his family in the jailhouse, over the protests of miserly department-store owner Ben Weaver. Sheriff Taylor stands up for singing moonshiner Rafe Hollister after Mayor Stoner dismisses him as "seedy." He comes to the rescue of town drunk Otis Campbell on numerous occasions, helping sober him up when the snooty genealogical society has second thoughts about presenting Otis a plaque in honor of his distinguished ancestor. The sheriff even belies his own class-based insecurities when he distances himself from a love interest after discovering that her father is a wealthy industrialist.[23]

In Mayberry *downtrodden* and *dignified* are not mutually exclusive terms. We do not know if the celebration of the commoner was motivated by a desire to redeem the white South that was most prominent in the era: the racist rednecks hurling epithets and bricks at civil rights demonstrators, the poor migrants peopling hillbilly slums in Chicago and Cleveland, the misfortunate, coal-country Appalachians whose plight attracted increasing media attention and generated federal government response. Perhaps it was just a reflection of the region's almost un-American tradition of poverty and the nation's subsequent tendency to define the South through its lower orders. Whatever lay behind *Andy*'s populist spirit, the message was clear. The heart of the South rested in the breasts of the common folks, even the poor and disfranchised. And if Sheriff Taylor respected them, so should we.

"That haircut of your'n may be city style," Briscoe Darling tells the sheriff, "but your heart was shaped in a bowl."[24] Sheriff Taylor represented humanity's dearest ideals and intentions: kindness and decency, fairness and tolerance, resolute justice and unflinching integrity. They are ideals rarely captured in one human heart, even a bowl-shaped one. They are ideals few Americans associated with the white South in the sixties. Behind its escapist facade, underneath its nostalgic Americana sheen, beyond the romantic alternate universe that Mayberry offered viewers in that turbulent decade and still offers fans in the complex and troubling twenty-first century, *Andy* and its sheriff created a vision of the South.

Andy's South was a vision not of the South of the six o'clock news, nor of the South of the war on poverty. *Andy*'s South was in large measure Andy's South. Mayberry may not have been Mount Airy, but *Andy*'s South was a projection of Griffith's working-class raising in a small town in the upland South. Mayberry's strengths and weaknesses were the strengths and weaknesses of that world. Its prejudices, insecurities, hues, and values were those of the South that Griffith knew best. *Andy*'s South was not *the* South. It was *a* South. If Mayberry seems real today, more than half a century after the *Andy Griffith Show* ended its run, it is because it was a projection of something quite southern, even if not a complete portrait of the South.

CHAPTER FOUR

Where Everything New Is Old Again

SOUTHERN GOSPEL SINGING SCHOOLS

HE LOOKS LIKE he should be in pads and a helmet, protecting a quarterback on some manicured Southeastern Conference field. But his massive hands and fingers frolic along the keyboard with the dexterity and unpredictability of mice in a hayloft. He sits grinning through a goatee at the main piano, romping away at a tune he had never seen before yesterday, a new melody branded with the echoes of jangling strokes on pine walls and sunburned voices in two-door meeting houses. Twenty feet away, perched formally atop the second piano's bench like a downy owl peeking from his nest, a wisp of a boy accompanies his massive partner. The lad's eyes burn a hole in the songbook. His petite hands move effortlessly across the keys—a waterbug on a summer eddy. No wasted movements, no change of expression on his face. Two masterful musicians, bound to be ignored.

The voices in this auditorium are what matter most. That becomes clear when the singing starts. The silver-haired song leader peers over tiny spectacles, chops the air with her right arm, swings it to her left, to the right and back up to its starting point, and we are off. Six-year-old sopranos, eighty-year-old tenors, teenage wannabe basses hold their paperback songbooks as instructed—out from the body in one hand (the other is for "leading")—and follow their respective parts. The tenors lead: *mi, mi, do, mi*. Half a beat into the second measure, everyone else joins in, each section following its own line. Shape notes the first time through, followed by three verses of a newly minted song called "A Godly Man." It will likely never appear in another songbook; once the new books arrive for next

---

This essay was originally published in the journal *Southern Cultures* 22 (Winter 2016): 135–49. It appears here with minor revisions.

Students "leading" songs at the final program of the Brockwell Gospel
Music School, 2018. *Courtesy of Glenda Small/Beverly Meinzer/
Brockwell Gospel Music School.*

year's school, it may never be heard or sung again. But on this day, "A Godly
Man" reverberates throughout the cinder-block auditorium, one hundred
voices in four-part harmony—or something approximating it. This is, after
all, only the second day of singing school.[1]

People have been doing this on North American soil for the better part
of three hundred years—and with shape notes for two hundred. The gospel singing school melds two American musical traditions—the singing
school and shape notes. Designed to improve congregational singing
by imparting the rudiments of musical education, singing schools date
to early eighteenth-century New England. Near the end of that century,
William Little and William Smith published *The Easy Instructor,* which
introduced the concept of replacing standard round notes with shapes that
correspond with tones or pitches on the musical scale. Though denounced
as "dunce notes" by traditionalists, Little and Smith's four-note system
gained widespread popularity among the untutored Christian masses,
especially those stimulated by the revivalist fires of the Second Great
Awakening. This four-note system, in which three of the shapes were re-
used to complete the seven tones on the diatonic scale, reigned nearly half
a century until the publication of Jesse Aikin's *The Christian Minstrel,*

The campus of the Brockwell Gospel Music School, Brockwell, Arkansas.
Courtesy of author.

which added three additional distinctive shapes and thereby created the seven-note system. Aggressively marketed by southern songbook publishers like Aldine S. Kieffer and A. J. Showalter, the seven-note system was adopted as the common language of a pliable and adaptive sacred style that gradually emerged as "gospel" in the late 1800s.[2]

Shape-note singing schools appeared soon after shape notes came on the scene. The earliest schools were held in the Northeast, but it was below the Mason-Dixon Line that they would be "preserved . . . as in no other region of the country." By the late nineteenth century, itinerant singing-school teachers roamed the South, offering the basics of shape-note musical training to young and old alike. Most often held in church houses on winter nights or in the summer after crops were laid by, singing schools also provided opportunities for socializing and became much-anticipated annual events in many communities. By the early twentieth century, singing schools constituted one leg of gospel's three-legged stool, working in unison with singing conventions and songbook publishers to support an increasingly popular form of vernacular sacred music.[3]

The singing school may not have been a southern creation, but its proliferation in the post–Civil War years was largely a phenomenon of the South. Its survival, and revival, in the twenty-first century is almost exclusively a southern story. Today, there are at least twenty annual shape-note gospel singing schools, almost all of them located somewhere in the greater South. They are relics of a bygone era, holdovers from the days when a Coca-Cola cost a nickel and the family vehicle had wooden spokes.

Though steeped in tradition, singing schools and the seven-note gospel singing community, in sharp contrast to their trendier and more historically conscious four-note, a cappella, Sacred Harp cousins, are not backward looking, at least not in the sense of revering sacred musical texts. Their methods and sounds may evoke the aural past, but they spend little time dwelling on it. A willingness to adapt and change has served southern gospel well, ensuring its survival and its numerical superiority over Sacred Harp singers and other more rigid traditionalists of the four-note sound. Ironically, though, this same penchant for ahistoricism and its disregard for memorialization have ensured gospel singing and singing schools an unusual anonymity. "Southern gospel music might well be the best kept secret in America," observes historian James R. Goff Jr. Even amid a dynamic-yet-primitivist resurgence, singing schools remain among the most unlikely off-the-radar southern institutions.[4]

Going Back to Brockwell

In the summer of 2011, my daughter and I attended one of the oldest of the gospel singing schools. Only a seven-mile drive from the family farm in Arkansas, the Brockwell Gospel Music School has instructed generations of children (and adults) in the do-re-mi's. My father and aunt attended in the 1950s. My aunt plays a solid gospel piano, and her strong alto still stands out at the rural Missionary Baptist church my ancestors founded in 1878. Dad followed a different musical path—which is to say no musical path. With little discernible talent and even less interest, he and a buddy played hooky and threw rocks at pop bottles underneath the highway bridge near the one general store in Brockwell. He learned to sing his do-re-mi's through and back—always falsetto and off-key—but, in general, singing school didn't take with him. He deemed it a torturous experience, one he spared my brother and me by never sending us to singing school, while various cousins became skillful singers and musicians.

Most of those gospel-singing cousins were Pentecostals, for in the days of my youth in the 1970s and 1980s our little Baptist church maintained a pretty traditional stance when it came to congregational music. *Traditional* in those days and in that place didn't mean southern gospel, a rousing style that most old-timers deemed unsuitable for proper services. Thus, Sunday mornings (and most Sunday nights) found us singing nineteenth-century hymns out of the old hardback Baptist hymnal with standard round notes, but one Sunday night a month we would circulate the tattered, tan paperback *Heavenly Highway Hymns* and sing four numbers. These were upbeat, rollicking songs that we didn't find in our staid hymnal. Other than those once-a-month Sunday-night singings, our brushes with southern gospel were rare. The Decoration Day singing that followed dinner on the grounds each year drifted toward gospel congregational songs and "specials." On occasion, during those informal singings, Orgel Mason, the founder and director of the Brockwell Gospel Music School, would take the floor to promote the school, tout the beauty of shape notes, and lead the house in a gospel standard or two. His passion for the music and the gospel style was palpable.

Like almost all the young men of his era and place, Mason came of age during the Depression, facing little more than the prospect of following in his father's footsteps as a poor scratch farmer on the rocky hillsides and narrow creek bottoms of the Ozarks. A singing school at the rural Methodist church his family attended opened up a new world to young Mason. Eventually, he found a mentor in Luther G. Presley, a songwriter and singing-school teacher who maintained an Arkansas office for one of the nation's leading gospel songbook publishers, Texas-based Stamps-Baxter, the company that would publish *Heavenly Highway Hymns* two decades later. Mason completed Stamps-Baxter's normal school in Dallas before launching his own career as a singing-school teacher in the late 1930s. Assisted by members of the Izard County Singing Convention, Mason organized the first Brockwell Music School in the summer of 1947.[5]

Today, the focus of the singing school remains the same as it was in 1947—the rudiments of reading music and singing the do-re-mi's. The creekside campus has expanded from a single "tabernacle" in the early days to a cluster of five buildings, the length of the school term has been reduced from three weeks to two, and the school has shifted from its original July-after-the-crops-were-laid-by scheduling to mid-June. But much remains the same at Brockwell. Like generations of students before them, children at recess and lunchtime continue to wade the shallow creek in search of crawdads. The youngest ones delight in being chosen to tramp the campus grounds, ringing the cowbell that signaled the end of lunch break back in the days when it was called dinner.

Singing school is no summer vacation. If it were, it would be much more

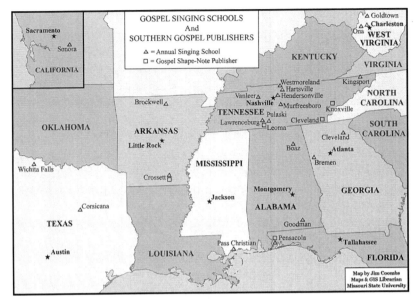

Map of annual singing schools, ca. 2016.
Courtesy of Jim Coombs.

expensive. No one is in this business for the money, as Brockwell's two-week tuition fee of $50 attests. Despite the informal atmosphere, leisure is in short supply. Even beginning students spend about five hours per day in classrooms and in the auditorium. Beyond the seven shape notes, there is intensive morning instruction in music theory. In addition, each student learns how to direct songs ("keep time" or "lead") in various time signatures and spends part of the afternoon engaged in "ear training," learning to recognize the different pitches simply by hearing the notes on a piano. The more difficult lessons, such as chords, chromatics, and songwriting, are left to intermediate and advanced students. These students, often from families with deep roots in gospel and long connections to the school, return year after year. It is from their ranks that the next generation of singing-school teachers and singing convention leaders will emerge.

Of course, it wouldn't be singing school without singing. Three times each day—first thing in the morning, before noon, and at the end of the day—everyone in the school gathers in the auditorium to practice what they've learned, singing their parts on songs in the new songbook. Students and teachers turn practice to performance in the traditional closing-night program, during which parents and community members are invited to watch the various "specials" performed by voice and instrumental pupils and participate in congregational songs led by groups of students. If you think you will breeze through school because you've sung the tenor line to "I'll Fly Away" three hundred times, think again. One of the peculiarities of the gospel tradition is its reliance, even insistence, on new songs, and the annual adoption of a new songbook is a time-honored gospel practice, one that dates to the rise of gospel singing conventions in the nineteenth century and the paperback songbook publishers who competed for convention business. It is a point of pride for gospel singers to have the "ability to pick up an unfamiliar piece of music and sight-read it perfectly." "You give me a brand new song today," explained Orgel Mason. "I look to see what time it's written in. And, if it's shape notes, I get my pitch . . . even without instruments 'cause I've sung 'em so much on that staff. And then after I get my pitch, I take off from there."[6]

Three Notes and a World of Difference

Perhaps you've heard the joke that there are more books and documentaries on Appalachian snake handlers than there are actual snake handlers. It is a safe bet that Sacred Harp singers outnumber snake handlers, but the number of publications and films focusing on this most revered four-note tradition may be gaining ground on its practitioners. Perhaps nothing illustrates the divide between southern gospel and Sacred Harp more clearly than their reception and treatment by academics and the American intelligentsia in general. Since its "discovery" during the folk revival of the 1950s and '60s, Sacred Harp has inspired academic studies, articles in national magazines, PBS documentaries, and NPR features. Even more tellingly, Sacred Harp has attracted thousands of educated, middle-class Americans into its hollow square. Many of these Sacred Harp converts come from outside the South and share little religious connection with traditional southern singers. By contrast, southern gospel has rarely attracted participants from outside the narrow world of evangelical Protestantism. Its mostly Baptist and Pentecostal practitioners live on the periphery of American popular culture "in a kind of academic blind spot."[7]

So, why the divergence between Sacred Harp's intellectual trendiness on one hand and southern gospel's disquieting conservatism and cultural anonymity on the other? Certainly Sacred Harp reflects a gritty, noncommercial authenticity—an "ancient, exotic, primitive" quality—that its more malleable and commercialized cousin lacks. More important is the disconnect one might expect outsiders to experience in the world of southern gospel. Whereas the "cosmopolitan spirit" of Sacred Harp singing generally welcomes outsiders, many in the gospel community would have reservations accommodating the intellectually curious. In contrast to the gospel sentiment "that religious songs should only be sung by people who are sincere about what they are singing," secular singers find in "the very act of Sacred Harp singing . . . a secondary expression of sacrality." It is this spiritual buffer zone in Sacred Harp that allows outsiders and nonbelievers to "venerate the singing . . . but not the evangelical worldview of the rural south."[8]

Beyond appeals or deterrents to ecumenical sensibilities, the two shape-note traditions differ in other ways trivial and monumental. Along with the pounding pianos and occasional guitars you will find at a gospel singing, songbook philosophy is one of the chief contrasts between seven-note gospel and its older relative. Sacred Harp singers, inheritors of "a sacred 'heritage' to be jealously guarded," rarely deviate from their tune books. Gospel singers do not completely discard older songs—for example, singing conventions and congregations regularly launch into Depression-era classics such as "Victory in Jesus" and "On the Jericho Road"—but neither do they approach their favorite songs or songbooks with such sacred and jealous regard. The process may be cherished as a sort of holy tradition, but ultimately the songs and songbooks are nothing more than vessels through which the process is realized.[9]

This presentist-bordering-on-ahistorical philosophy of gospel provides a fundamental contrast with Sacred Harp and other four-note traditions. For instance, a four-day singing at Camp Fasola in rural Alabama in 2011 featured lessons on the history of shape-note hymnody, on the one hundredth anniversary of the publication of a major *Sacred Harp* revision, and on the story of a family of nineteenth-century composers. Such historical self-consciousness and adoration for movement heritage is much less pronounced, if even present, at a gospel singing or singing school.[10]

For the underpinning of this shape-note divide, we need look no further than one of Protestantism's oldest soteriological debates. Sacred Harp tradition rests most fully in the small world of Primitive Baptists, who remain among the staunchest believers in the Reformed doctrine of limited atonement, or predestination. These Calvinist Baptists rejected the unlimited atonement of Arminianism, which in the decades following the nineteenth century's Second Great Awakening swayed ever greater numbers

of Baptists and others to follow the lead of their free-will Methodist neighbors. Primitives considered the missionary efforts and Bible tract societies
of an increasingly mission-minded Baptist majority unnecessary and even
unscriptural. Almost two centuries later, personal piety and an intense
devotion to the Bible constitute unifying Baptist traits, but when it comes
to the issue of individual salvation, Primitive Baptists remain miles apart
from their more numerous Baptist brethren and other evangelical (and
evangelizing) Protestants.

So what does this mean for shape-note singers? An agnostic, a Catholic,
or someone from a non-Christian faith heritage is not likely to be "witnessed to"—of having a play made for her conversion—at a Sacred Harp
singing, for as far as the Primitive Baptists are concerned salvation is completely in God's hands. The same visitor would stand a far greater chance
of being witnessed to at a gospel singing. And even if the proselytizing isn't
overt, the evangelizing tone of the songs, prayers, and stage banter remind
the visitor that her soul is a subject of communal concern.

Although ethnomusicologist Drew Beisswenger found that singing-
school teachers in south-central Kentucky who did not proselytize on
occasion aroused suspicion among their clientele, evidence suggests that
the proselytism level at most singing schools is quite low, comparatively
speaking. I found this to be the case at the Brockwell Gospel Music School.
Aside from a brief "devotional" each morning, a handful of public prayers,
and the lyrics of a few cross-centric hymns, any evangelization at singing
school depended more on subtle atmospherics than verbal pleading and
altar calls. (I grew up in a fundamentalist Baptist Church, so admittedly
my assurance that the proselytizing was minimal might be akin to your
Laplander hunting guide telling you that you'll never notice the cold.)[11]

For Orgel Mason, it was about the music. "We don't talk church or politics," he told me. "We just talk singing and learning how." This would
seem to be a pretty common philosophy among singing schools—at least
if the dozen or so that maintain websites can be taken as representative
institutions. "One will find that the study of gospel music instills confidence, creativity, competence, and the love of God." This statement, found
on the home page of the Alabama School of Gospel Music, is typical—not
secular but never sectarian and rarely overtly evangelical. The website of
Ben Speer's Stamps-Baxter School of Music, held each July on the campus
of Middle Tennessee State University, makes only the vaguest references
to religion, none of which reflect the tradition's evangelical roots. "This
school is dedicated to the furtherance of Southern Gospel Music," reads

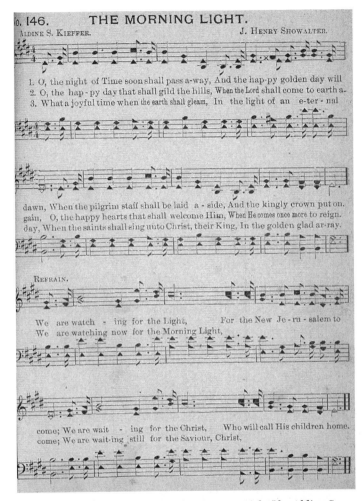

Shape-note sheet music for "The Morning Light," by Aldine S.
Kieffer and J. Henry Showalter, from the 1899 hymnal *The Highway
to Heaven*, published by the A. J. Showalter Co. of Dalton, Georgia,
and the Showalter-Patton Co. of Dallas, Texas.

its mission statement, "and to raising the standard of musical excellence
in our art form." Like Ben Speer's, the Texas Southern Gospel School of
Music, held annually on a community college campus in Corsicana, promises to improve its students' singing abilities. But when it comes to evangelizing, the Texas institution makes only the broadly Christian claim that

"the study of gospel music instills confidence, creativity, competence, and love for God."[12]

The few schools whose online statements evince a more aggressively evangelistic mission are not affiliated with institutions of higher education and tend to be located far from the nearest metropolitan center. Among the core values of the Do Re Mi Gospel Music Academy, located in Tennessee's Cumberland Plateau region, are "seeking and following the leadership of the Holy Spirit . . . and winning the lost to Christ." Clearer still was the mission statement of the Leoma Music Company, which operated a singing school at a youth camp near Lawrenceburg, Tennessee, but whose website had gone inactive by the time this book was published: "To spread the word of Jesus Christ's saving grace to each and every lost soul that we can possibly reach by way of writing, singing, publishing and promoting shaped-note style Southern Gospel Music." The values and missions of Do Re Mi and Leoma most clearly illustrate the divide between the seven-note and four-note traditions, between the evangelizing impulse of Arminianism on the one extreme and the predestinarian acceptance of old-style Calvinism on the other. Both would welcome the hipster, but only the latter crowd would feel comfortable leaving the destiny of his soul solely in the hands of God.[13]

The Great Revival . . . of Singing Schools

While Leoma may have been an outlier in its vigorous proselytism, singing schools in general reflect the cultural and theological conservatism of the gospel music world. The folk revival's discovery of Sacred Harp singing introduced it to appreciative practitioners who have maintained it and grown it in urban, intellectual enclaves. Anyone anticipating a similar folkie embrace of southern gospel is likely in for a long wait. Nevertheless, the gospel singing school has experienced its own rebirth in recent decades. It's a rebirth that seems to have caught everyone off guard. When folklorist William Lynwood Montell published one of the first scholarly studies of southern gospel back in 1991, his section on singing schools—which "virtually vanished in the 1950s"—was a documentation of a dying tradition. By the time Montell was studying the phenomenon, singing schools seemed destined for the dustbin of history, threatened in the immediate post–World War II years by the rising popularity of quartet concerts and commercial gospel records and challenged in the 1970s and 1980s by the emergence of Contemporary Christian Music (CCM),

Singing school at Lunenburg, Izard County, Arkansas, date unknown.
*Courtesy of the Garlich Collection, Old Independence Regional
Museum, Batesville, Arkansas.*

a catchall category that includes pop-, rock-, and mainstream country-inspired sacred music.[14]

But stories of the singing school's imminent demise have been greatly exaggerated. Of the eighteen current gospel singing schools whose dates of origin can be determined, only three were in existence when Ronald Reagan took office in 1981. No fewer than eight were founded in the current century. Beyond the obvious goal of spreading shape-note literacy, two primary causes are behind this resurgence: a backlash against the rise and dominance of CCM and a more conscious, politicized rejection of what many conservative Christians consider to be the declension of American society. Southern gospel, a genre that built a massive following by co-opting vernacular musical styles in the late nineteenth and early twentieth centuries, became increasingly identified with a Depression-era, "old-timey" sound, one whose appeal to younger generations declined in the decades after World War II. The growing popularity of CCM's modern sounds and sensibilities marginalized traditional gospel by the end of the 1980s. The *Gaither Homecoming* series of televised concerts and videos,

Singing school certificate signed by noted publisher, composer, and teacher Luther G. Presley, 1923. *Courtesy of White County Historical Society Collection, Old Independence Regional Museum, Batesville, Arkansas.*

launched in 1991, worked to regain some of southern gospel's lost relevancy by binding "an increasingly diverse and fractious coalition of evangelicals . . . to an idealized vision of the past." It seems likely that the post-1980 proliferation of gospel singing schools served a similar symbolic and practical function.[15]

Undergirding the conservative resistance to CCM's power play is a broader cultural and political trend: the emergence of an increasingly activist evangelical conservatism. The rise of the religious Right as a force in modern American politics triggered a resurgence in the gospel singing school movement, at least indirectly. It would be presumptuous to suggest that each of the singing schools founded within the past forty years was the product of anxious fundamentalists fretting "a loss of cultural clout in mainstream America," and of the four singing school directors I interviewed only one identified "moral decline in society" as an impetus for the recent singing school revival. There remain those within the gospel singing school world who, like Orgel Mason, put music before partisan politics or sectarian religion. Yet, southern gospel responds to and inculcates an "underlying anxiety about the sustainability of a fundamentalist, white evangelical monoculture in contemporary American society," an anxiety that manifests in a "renewed concern with history and urgent efforts to create . . . a usable past." For many fundamentalists and other conservative evangelicals, there may be no better, more tangible symbol of the past than shape-note southern gospel and the singing schools that once sustained it. Even if the vast majority of gospel singers remain unselfconscious of their own history and traditions, the modern singing school revival clearly reflects just how much the past weighs on southern minds. Anchored in the past and heavily motivated by history, even if not obsessed with a reverence for its own heritage, the singing school promises to maintain southern gospel's traditions for future generations.[16]

What we are witnessing in this revival of gospel singing schools is a budding historical consciousness among members of a group once known for their eager adaptability and disregard for the past. Effectively marginalized for a generation or more, within American society as well as its evangelical subculture, increasing numbers of southern evangelicals and fundamentalists find in traditional gospel an expression of regional, spiritual, historical distinctiveness. Whatever their cultural and political implications, gospel shape notes appear to be making a modest comeback, or at the very least holding their own. The rural Baptist church of my boyhood—the one that pulled out the *Heavenly Highway Hymns* one night a month for variety—now uses nothing but shape-note hymnals. The specialized industry of singing-convention and school-songbook publishers, down to three companies in the 1980s, has added two new publishers in the past twenty years, their names—Gospel Heritage Music and Southern Legacy Music—reflecting a newfound historical consciousness. Like Sacred Harp, the gospel singing school is finding a new lease on life secured in large part by the self-consciousness of marginalization. Unlike Sacred Harp, the filiopietistic self-consciousness reinvigorating southern gospel is generated from within. Mirroring the worldview of its revivalists, the revival will be fervent, perhaps sustainable, but not inclusive.[17]

There is, after all, an ambivalence at the heart of the enterprise—the backward-looking tendencies of conservatives in general, and more specifically of fundamentalist Protestants who face modern challenges, versus the forward-looking, ahistorical tendencies of commercialized, seven-shape gospel tradition and the otherworldly outlook of evangelicals with their eyes on the prize. It is this churning, often contradictory bundle of impulses that keeps the twin pianos pounding, that keeps the arms waving in time with the rhythm, that keeps generation after generation coming back to a place like Brockwell, Arkansas, to learn the do-re-mi's and sing the new songs in an old way. It is this intriguing, frustrating, enrapturing harmony that makes everything new old again.

CHAPTER FIVE

Against the Current

LANDOWNERS AND THE FIGHT
FOR OZARKS STREAMS

MY MATERNAL GRANDPA was an avid outdoorsman. If it loped, flew, or swam, he loved to shoot it or catch it. He had a passion for quail hunting, and for longer than I could remember he raised and trained English setters, selling many of them for good prices to affluent sportsmen in Arkansas and Missouri. He relished a crisp fall morning in a deer stand, and that fading old stuffed buck's head on the wood-paneled wall next to the fireplace is emblazoned in my memory. There may have been nothing he liked to do better than wet a hook. Fishing in Current River, in Spring River, in the Eleven Point, and in White River, for years he pursued fish of many species. His favorite was the walleye—jack, as he called them, from the antiquated jack salmon of the old-timers. But there was one fish I never knew him to seek out, the trout.

Despite the popularity of trout fishing in the White River Hills today, trout are not indigenous to the Ozarks. Only in rare circumstances does the rainbow trout reproduce in our waters. While perhaps not your classic invasive species—they were introduced to Ozarks streams as early as the late 1800s and continue to be stocked today—trout simply do not belong in the Ozarks, like the more reviled armadillo and feral hog. Their popularity in the region today is a byproduct of a twentieth-century dam-building frenzy and the ecological change it wrought. The cold, lake-bottom water used to turn the hydroelectricity turbines at the Army Corps of Engineers' dams altered downstream ecology on the White, the Osage, and their tributaries, making miles of streams uninhabitable to native warmwater species. The solution was the establishment of government-operated hatcheries that have provided trout fingerlings for the cool tailwaters for more than half a century.

My grandpa was no environmentalist, no eco-warrior taking a stand against nonindigenous species. For him the decision to ignore the trout in favor of native fish was at least in part a personal one. In the last months of his life, Grandpa began—even as the most reticent among us do—to relate stories from his childhood and young adulthood, both of which had been unmercifully brief for a boy whose mother died when he was eight and whose father tramped the Plains to find work and to forget in the suffocating days of the Depression. Separated from siblings and shuttled from farm to farm in an extended network of kinfolk, the boy labored in the fields and the woods for his room and board, finding contentment only at the home of his elderly grandparents just a few miles north of Mountain Home, Arkansas. His grandpa, Elijah Trivitt, had been born on this place on Pigeon Creek before the Civil War and was still here more than eighty years later. Old Lige and his wife, Arminda ("Armindy" in the hill country dialect), had also taken in another grandchild, a young woman named Sarah, and Sarah would become both confidant and caretaker of my grandpa, more like a beloved aunt than an own cousin.

But stability just wasn't to be for Grandpa. Not long after he arrived on the old homeplace on Pigeon Creek, the papers announced that some outfit called the Army Corps of Engineers was going to build a dam on the North Fork of the White River. His grandparents lived only half a mile up Pigeon from the North Fork; much of their land would be underneath the reservoir created by the dam. They and hundreds of other families in the area to be inundated would have to go. Grandpa never said much about those times, about the family's removal from their home and farm. The only story he ever related was a sort of farewell journey he took with a couple of other boys after the floodgates had been closed, after the people were gone. Paddling out to a hilltop—now an island formed by the rising water—they marveled at the transformation, a lake aborning before them, all because of a concrete wall miles away. They camped the night on this hilltop island, awash in memories and surrounded by the barren loneliness of a human place with no humans.

Representative Clyde T. Ellis, the ramrod behind the Army Corps's dams in the White River basin, proclaimed, "In my district there is not a single person opposed to these projects that I know of." And he may have been telling the truth as he understood it. That's the way these reservoir projects worked in those days—if you weren't affected personally you tended to be for it, neighbors be damned. Ellis could not, then, have been acquainted with old Lige and Armindy. In the days after my Grandpa's death, I found

Norfork Dam with Norfork National Fish Hatchery in foreground.
Photo by Springfield News-Leader. *Used by permission.*

out that he had a pen pal. I'd never taken Grandpa for a letter writer, but in the last year or two of his life he and Sarah—his beloved cousin and caretaker—had managed to reconnect after almost seventy years. I got Sarah's address in Oregon, wrote her a letter to tell her Grandpa had passed away, and later called and had a long conversation with her on the phone. Though well into her nineties, she could hear like a bat and possessed a razor-sharp mind. Her grandparents, old Lige and Armindy, had received a rocky, glady piece of land on a hillside south of Mountain Home in exchange for their farm on Pigeon Creek, but they didn't want to leave. Sarah remembered the day when the authorities came to force her grandparents off the farm where old Lige had been born eighty-three years before. Who these authorities were she wasn't sure—federal marshals, Army Corps personnel, the local sheriff's department?—but they had to physically carry the two octogenarians from their house to a waiting automobile. Not because they were too feeble to walk but because they were too stubborn to leave. This display of defiance didn't make the local paper—not surprising when you consider that *Baxter Bulletin* editor Tom Shiras was perhaps Norfork Lake's biggest promoter.[1]

Grandpa wasn't there that day, either. But he certainly inherited Lige and Armindy's stubbornness. Those old-timers would both be dead within two years. At their age it could have just been their time, but the family was convinced the trauma and heartache of dislocation hastened their demise. Their remains lie beneath the soil on high ground on the side of a highway, the spot the Army Corps of Engineers chose for the reinterred graves of their ancestors, one of twenty-six cemeteries that had to be relocated before the dam flooded twenty-three thousand acres. Grandpa eventually had to make his peace with the loss of the old homeplace, the site of a rare period of stability and happiness in his youth. As a young man with a new family of his own to support, he even found work as a laborer for the company that built Bull Shoals Dam, an even larger impoundment on the main channel of White River a few years after World War II. The only stories he ever told about his days on the Bull Shoals project stressed the hazardous working conditions but the inability of desperate workers like himself to do anything about it. Poverty has a way of tamping protests and derailing stands on principle. And he probably would have partaken of a little slab of trout in those uncertain times. But in later years, that alien species of fish—whether brown or rainbow—became the symbol of the federal government's appropriation of the family farm, the inundation of a landscape filled with cultural and personal significance, a reminder of citizen powerlessness in the face of eminent domain, even perhaps a product of the ecological transformation wrought by those cold tailwaters turning the turbines of the dam's hydroelectricity plant.

So, despite the fact that the Bull Shoals and Norfork Dams created trout-friendly waters all the way downstream to my native Izard County, we were not trout people. But this isn't an essay about the damming of Ozarks rivers. It's about the region's famously un-dammed rivers. The tale of my family's brush with the era of damming serves as a reminder that the story of the Buffalo, the North Fork, or any other river is a human saga. The rivers were here before we were, of course, but as long as we're here their fate is in our hands. The competing visions for the fate of rivers are ours. The political squabbles over dams and parks are of our doing. The people who find themselves uncomfortably stuck in the middle of sniping interest groups—the landowners and residents most intimately affected by federal and state legislation—are us. Like us, the story of Ozarks rivers in the twentieth and twenty-first centuries is a complex one. It's a story whose multiple layers wait to be explored, a story whose complicated nature too often eludes our comprehension.

Let's take a look at three aspects of the efforts to prevent the damming of the Buffalo River in the 1960s and its nationalization by the National Park Service (NPS) in the 1970s. The first is a reminder that the tale of the Buffalo River is part of a broader story of Ozarks rivers from the 1930s to the 1970s—of dam builders and canoeists, of politicians and landowners, of government agencies and competing visions. And the Ozarks story was, of course, part of a much bigger national story playing out over those same two generations. The second is a look at the people most likely to be overlooked in these stories of dams and national parks, the displaced landowners like my great-great-grandparents and like the families in the Buffalo Valley who either lost their homeplaces or brokered scenic easements with the NPS that restricted land usage and building. These contentious episodes involving eminent domain and other federal govern-ment proceedings contributed to a burgeoning property rights movement among a rural population increasingly distrustful of government, espe-cially federal government—a movement harboring right-wing, conspira-torial elements that have come to exercise a surprising amount of political clout in the twenty-first century. And my third point focuses on the thing on which so many right-wingers concentrate their fury, either consciously or unconsciously. That thing is a movement or a force deeper than a story of dams and artificial lakes, broader than the story of national rivers and free-flowing streams. Whatever we call that thing, it is, ironically, the source not only for those who wanted to preserve the Buffalo but for those who wanted to dam it.

The First National Streams

The earliest significant damming projects in the Ozarks were private affairs carried out by power companies—most notably Powersite Dam on White River, just downstream from Branson, that created Lake Taneycomo in 1913, and the much more massive Bagnell Dam on the Osage River, which created the monstrous Lake of the Ozarks in 1931. The Army Corps of Engineers—the federal agency that has done more than anything else to alter the physical landscape of the Ozarks and many other places around the nation—was not in the dam-building business before the Great Depression. It was the Flood Control Act of 1938—capitalizing on

the momentum generated by the New Deal's Tennessee Valley Authority—
that launched the Corps of Engineers on its forty-year frenzy of dam building. When war came, only two of the many Ozarks projects authorized
by this bill were underway. The Corps finished Wappapello Dam on the
St. Francis River in the hills of southeastern Missouri—necessitating the
complete relocation of the county seat town of Greenville—and Norfork
Dam, but the great age of reservoir construction in the Ozarks came in
the postwar years. Subsequent flood control bills pumped tens of millions of dollars into massive dam projects in the watersheds of the Ozark
region's two primary rivers. In the sixties and seventies, the Corps of
Engineers dammed the upper Osage, above the placid waters of the Lake
of the Ozarks, and placed impoundments on two tributaries, the Pomme
de Terre River and the Sac River. The larger White River watershed saw
even more action. Beginning with southeastern Missouri's Clearwater
Dam on the Black River in 1948, the Corps completed five dams in an
eighteen-year span. Greers Ferry Dam stopped up the Little Red River
near Heber Springs, but the other three were built on the main channel of
White River—Bull Shoals in 1951, Table Rock in 1958, and Beaver in 1966.
All of these postwar dams except Clearwater were built with the capacity
to generate hydroelectricity.

Most of the dams completed in the fifties and early sixties generated
little public protest or outcry, beyond the hundreds of families displaced
from farms and homes. Even if displacement generated dozens of letters
to politicians, the displeasure of this small and powerless set of constituents was almost always outweighed by the hearty support of those not
immediately harmed by the reservoirs. And almost to a person the politicians were avid backers of the Corps's damming mission and the millions
of dollars it pumped into their states and districts. This was especially
the case in northwestern Arkansas's third congressional district, where
Claude Fuller, Clyde T. Ellis, and James Trimble provided three decades
of dam cheerleading. The latter, elected to congress during World War II,
staked his career on the benefits of flood control and hydroelectricity, and
nothing ever pulled him away from that position.

But there were many more dams on the Corps's drawing board, smaller
dams that didn't always carry the promise of electricity generation. And
it was some of these proposed dams that first drew public opposition.
Among the dams authorized by the 1938 Flood Control Act were one on
the Current River near Doniphan, Missouri, and another on the lower
Eleven Point River in Randolph County, Arkansas. In 1949, Gov. Forrest

Smith of Missouri and the Missouri Conservation Commission came out in opposition to the Current River dam and two proposed dams on the Meramec River, a position shared by the chief of the Corps of Engineers. Gen. Lewis Pick agreed with the governor not out of any conservation ethic but because the proposed dams were deemed non-cost-effective. But the notion of federal involvement on the Current had wedged itself into the minds of dam opponents and state bureaucrats, prompting several Missouri state agencies to cooperate with the National Park Service on a study of the Current River watershed. Completed in the fall of 1956, this interagency report recommended the creation of a massive wilderness recreation area of some 350,000 acres in the Current and Eleven Point watersheds. Buried in the middle of the report was a statement calling for the "eventual elimination of all private land use" on more than one-hundred-thousand acres of this proposed reserve, as well as scenic easements of up to a quarter mile from the rivers on the rest of it.[2]

In 1956 the National Park Service wasn't yet in the river business, and NPS officials believed that any park development should be the work of the state of Missouri. But that soon changed. That very year the NPS launched a new initiative called Mission 66. The goal was to improve and expand the agency's recreational capacities by the time of the NPS's fiftieth anniversary in 1966. In the late fifties the NPS was already looking into expanding into the management of lakeshores and seashores, and the Cape Cod National Seashore became the first of many such properties in 1961. By this time NPS officials were already hot on the trail of what they hoped would become the first national monument based on a river system, and it was in the Ozarks. It wasn't the Buffalo. It was the Current River and its tributaries, most notably the Eleven Point and the Jacks Fork.[3]

The impetus for this hopeful move into river management may have been quickened by the efforts of some boosters in the region to put the two dams back on the Corps of Engineers' drawing board in the late 1950s. But more than anything, it was interagency competition in the beltway that goaded the NPS into action. In late 1958, the US Forest Service (USFS)—whose Clark National Forest encompassed extensive acreage along these streams—announced plans to establish recreation areas on the Current and Eleven Point. Interpreting the USFS's plans as a shot across the bow, the NPS began formulating its own plans for the Current. The relationship between the Forest Service and the Park Service had long been an adversarial one. It would grow more heated in the fight for control of the clear, swift streams of southeastern Missouri. The Missouri state legislature passed a resolution in 1959 supporting the concept of a national recreation area, which resulted in a congressional appropriation for further study by the NPS. Released in early 1960, the report proposed the creation of an "Ozark Rivers National Monument," which would of course be managed by the NPS.[4]

By 1961, any push for dam building had died away, but it was clear that the people of the Current River country were not going to be left alone. That year two different Current River bills were introduced into the US House of Representatives. One, sponsored by St. Louis Republican Thomas Curtis, called for USFS management of the river system. The other, sponsored by Democrat Richard Ichord (whose district encompassed the upper Current), recommended the establishment of a national monument largely based on the 1956 study and under the jurisdiction of the NPS. Two opposing citizens' groups were in full swing by this time. One was led by a St. Louis timberman and conservationist named Leo Drey, whose massive forest holdings included thirty-five miles of river frontage; this group, which included most other landholders in the proposed recreation area, favored the USFS bill and its less-intrusive, multiple-use policies. The group supporting the NPS bill was made up primarily of St. Louis–area canoeists and conservationists, with a smattering of Current River region business owners. Its leader, popular and influential St. Louis outdoors writer Leonard Hall, was an Aldo Leopold disciple who had recently published a best-selling book about floating the Current River. Soon a third group emerged. The Missouri counties bordering Arkansas were represented by a different congressman, Paul Jones, and his landowning constituents along the Current and Eleven Point had better and more extensive agricultural lands and wanted no part of either plan.[5]

Claiming that NPS control of the recreation area would overrun the rivers with tourists and remove the valleys' best lands from agricultural production and local taxation, Drey and his supporters in the Current–Eleven Point Rivers Association traveled to Washington, DC, to denounce the Ichord/Park Service bill and support the Curtis/Forest Service bill at House and Senate hearings in the summer of 1961. Representatives from the pro-NPS Ozark National Rivers Monument Association showed up to do the opposite, arguing that the USFS was ill prepared to promote and cultivate the kind of recreational tourism southeastern Missouri so desperately needed. While neither bill made it out of committee, the hearings hit a sour note for Drey and other backers of the USFS plan. Forest Service officials received a shock when their boss, Secretary of Agriculture Orville

Freeman, testified against the Curtis bill and told the house committee that the USFS would willingly turn over its monument lands to the NPS should the Ichord bill make it into law. Drey and Curtis suspected this fatal blow was a product of political pressure applied by powerful Missourian Stuart Symington, cosponsor of the NPS bill in the Senate.[6]

Missouri's other senator, as well as Governor John M. Dalton, also favored the NPS bill, and, when the USFS backed off its support for the Curtis bill, it was the Park Service act that eventually made its way through Congress. President Lyndon Johnson signed the Ozark National Scenic Riverways (ONSR) into law in August 1964, designating the Current and the Jacks Fork the country's first national river system. The ONSR covered a much smaller area than the 1956 report had recommended. Congressman Jones managed to extricate his constituents in Ripley, Oregon, and Howell Counties from the bill, though the Eleven Point would come under limited USFS management following passage of the Wild and Scenic Rivers Act of 1968. The bill signed by Pres. Johnson represented something of a compromise for the Park Service. The NPS had rarely utilized the scenic easements that were common in USFS management—agreements that allowed landowners to maintain ownership of and residence on their land with certain building, farming, and forestry restrictions. But the 1964 ONSR law provided for scenic easements and a limited lease-back program through which some owners could sell their property to the government and lease it back for lifetime residence. Yet the NPS continued to prefer outright purchase when it could be had, and government-paid land buyers were not always eager to explain the various options to landowners. Furthermore, much of the park's territory was considered so essential that owners had no option but to sell and leave. The government obtained more than two hundred tracts via eminent domain condemnation. Ultimately the NPS gained ownership of some sixty-five thousand acres that had been in private hands, much of it in the form of old homeplaces and family farms. The bitterness engendered by the removal of families continues to breed anti-government suspicion and mistrust among many descendants more than half a century later.[7]

Battling for the Buffalo

The creation of the Ozark National Scenic Riverways was obviously an essential precursor to the establishment of the Buffalo National River by federal law eight years later. The various facets of the Park Service's

Outfitters such as Ernie Middleton's Scenic Rivers Canoe Rental in
Eminence, Missouri, (1985) benefitted from increased tourist traffic.
Photo by Springfield News-Leader, *used by permission.*

land use and land purchase strategy in the Buffalo Valley had been mostly
worked out in the 1964 bill. Furthermore, the brief effort to fight pro-
dam advocates in the Current River region and the subsequent lobbying
for a riverine national park proved a training ground for a few people
who would become essential players in the drama that played out along
the Buffalo. None of these were more important than canoeists Harold
and Margaret Hedges, whose Kansas City–based Ozark Wilderness
Waterways Club was instrumental in generating national publicity for the
fight to keep the Buffalo free flowing in the early 1960s. The Hedgeses
remained active in efforts to nationalize the Buffalo and eventually settled
on the river in 1968.[8]

The fight over control of the Buffalo shared much in common with the
overlapping struggle taking place on the Current in Missouri, but they
weren't carbon copies. For a variety of reasons, the damming of the Current
was never a serious prospect, leaving the NPS, the USFS, and their respective supporters to fight for the prize. The impoundment of the Buffalo was
a much more serious possibility—at times even a likelihood. By the 1950s
the Army Corps of Engineers had identified locations for as many as five
dams on this small Ozarks stream. And, unlike in southeastern Missouri,

the political support was in place to get at least one of them built. Despite a strong heritage of Jeffersonian democracy in the Land of Opportunity—and the poor schools and underfunded social services that flashed that heritage to the world—Arkansas politicians eagerly supported public (more specifically federal) funding for flood control and power generation. And nowhere in the state was this support stronger than in the northwest's third district.[9]

Though the fight for control of the Buffalo ended in 1972, the struggle's origins went back at least fifteen years. In the late 1950s, Congress passed a bill authorizing construction of two dams on the Buffalo River, one near its mouth and a second upstream near the community of Gilbert. But President Eisenhower vetoed the bill, pointing toward the Corps's own study questioning the dams' cost-benefit ratio. The election of Democrat John F. Kennedy to the White House revived hopes for dam supporters in the Ozarks, and early 1961 saw the introduction of Buffalo-damming legislation in the House and Senate, sponsored by Rep. James Trimble and Sen. J. William Fulbright, respectively. Dam boosters in the nearby town of Marshall—desiring an economic facelift similar to the one just then transforming the new twin lakes area around Mountain Home—organized the Buffalo River Improvement Association (BRIA), pledging support for the efforts of Trimble and the Corps. But Fulbright, trying to cover all his bases, had also met behind the scenes with Stewart Udall, a wilderness and conservation advocate appointed Secretary of the Interior by Kennedy. At this point Fulbright seems to have believed that plans for dams and a national park could coexist, and Udall sent a team from the Park Service to prepare a report on the Buffalo Valley in the fall of 1961.[10]

By early 1962, when Trimble presented his new House bill, the battle for the Buffalo and the fight for public sentiment were on. The BRIA dominated the Corps of Engineers' first public hearing at Marshall. The anti-dam folks countered with a highly publicized float trip by US Supreme Court associate justice William O. Douglas. The creation of the Ozark Society, led by Bentonville physician Neil Compton, gave the anti-dam forces a focal point. The almost simultaneous establishment of the Buffalo River Landowners' Association—a group that wanted no part of a dam or a national park—lent the battle a third side. Despite the efforts of Trimble and his local backers over the next few years, no Buffalo damming bill made it out of congressional committee. In mid-decade Trimble's opponents seemed to be winning the battle. At the very least they were fighting the BRIA to a draw. The National Park Service issued a favorable report

Supreme Court associate justice William O. Douglas and wife
flanked by Margaret and Harold Hedges, 1962. Neil Compton
Papers (MC 1091), Box 31, File 2, Image 1124. *Special Collections,
University of Arkansas Libraries, Fayetteville.*

for a prospective national recreation area on the Buffalo, a proposal supported by the Ozark Society and endorsed by many newspapers around the
state of Arkansas. From a symbolic standpoint, no endorsement carried
more weight than the one from Tom Dearmore. A budding star in the
state's journalism fraternity, Dearmore edited Mountain Home's *Baxter
Bulletin*, the paper his grandfather, Tom Shiras, had long used to advocate for the building of dams. The environmentalists could even turn to
economic impact studies. A report issued by a University of Arkansas
researcher projected that the amount of tourism spending generated by
a national park in the Buffalo region would equate to the wages of more
than 1,700 manufacturing jobs—a powerful argument in an era of state-
sanctioned smokestack chasing.[11]

But the reservoir champions were not finished. Trimble and the Corps of Engineers streamlined their efforts to focus on only one dam, at Gilbert, a strategy reflected in a new House bill as 1965 dawned. Trimble received endorsements from the three other Arkansas members of the House, one of whom, Wilbur Mills, was at that moment pushing his own dam project. Senators J. William Fulbright and John L. McClellan backed off their earlier pro-NPS stances in deference to Trimble. On the local level, intense pressure from the BRIA effectively quelled overt opposition to the dam, while the same brand of hardball politics silenced state agencies that had previously favored a free-flowing Buffalo. The situation was promising enough that damming advocates feted Trimble at a celebration in Marshall in August 1965. But an unlikely environmental champion emerged at the eleventh hour. In December Gov. Orval Faubus made public a long and eloquent letter imploring the chief of the Corps of Engineers to leave the Buffalo alone. Within a few months the Corps shelved its plans for a dam at Gilbert, and Republican John Paul Hammerschmidt's surprise defeat of Congressman James Trimble in 1966 drove the final nail in the coffin containing the blueprints for a Buffalo impoundment. Hammerschmidt promptly filed a bill for a national recreation area in 1967, and Arkansas's senators offered a similar bill in their chamber. It would take five more years and a good deal of political wrangling in both Little Rock and Washington, but on March 1, 1972, Richard Nixon's pen created the 95,000-acre, 135-mile-long Buffalo National River.[12]

Hammerschmidt's insistence secured continued hunting and fishing privileges in the park, as well as other regulations deemed beneficial for landowners, most notably the prerogative for many to sell scenic easements. Residents in three areas designated private-use zones were given the option to sell scenic easements and continue to use their land within certain restrictions. But no amount of massaging the technicalities of land transfer was going to assuage long-time residents (some of them of multiple-generation vintage) required to sell to Uncle Sam. And that was no surprise to anyone who knew anything about the situation. In *The Battle for the Buffalo River*, Neil Compton quoted the original leader of the Buffalo River Landowners Association, who warned Compton that his members were "'as violently opposed to a park or recreational area as they are a dam.'" In fact, opposition to the park proposal did turn violent on occasion—or at least belligerent and threatening. A few landowners felled trees into the river to block canoeists. Some canoeists even reported being shot at.[13]

Dueling bumper stickers in the battle for the Buffalo.
Neil Compton Papers (MC 1091), Box 80, File 13. *Special Collections,
University of Arkansas Libraries, Fayetteville.*

In the 1960s canoeists were almost always outsiders and therefore received the brunt of antipathy as reminders of local powerlessness. In fact, the actual residents of the Buffalo Valley played practically no role in the tug-of-war between advocates of the dams and those supporting the national park proposal. "The real Buffalo River landowners, the people who owned property in fee in its valley and on its banks, were totally ignored by the businessmen, newspaper people, and real-estate developers in towns like Marshall and Yellville," observed Ozark Society president Neil Compton. It wasn't just the dam supporters of the BRIA who paid little attention to them. At a November 1964 Marshall hearing sponsored by the Army Corps of Engineers, the speaker for the Buffalo River Landowners Association (BRLA) was relegated to last place on the itinerary, by which point all but one of the reporters in attendance had already left.[14]

Not surprisingly, the landowners' legacy has been just as overlooked. At the time of this book's publication the BRLA didn't even merit a single mention in the *Encyclopedia of Arkansas*'s online entry on the history of the Buffalo National River. Natives of the valley remain conspicuously silent and scarce in accounts of the decade or so leading up to the nationalization of the river. Most of the advocates for landowners' rights identified by Compton were relative newcomers to the area, including mouthpiece of the BRLA, Charles McRaven, a native of Little Rock and graduate of Ole Miss. Perhaps the most visible native was Orphea Duty, an articulate septuagenarian storekeeper and mail clerk from Boxley who traveled to Washington, DC, with the Ozark Society in 1969 to speak before a Senate subcommittee hearing. "Most of the people in the valley 'heired' their land and their roots are deep," she told the senators. "Like all proud farmers, they wish to retain their land to pass on to their children. If you can bring a park that will not disrupt the citizens, that will keep the river free of factories and taverns—a park that will allow reasonable use of the land, then we see eye to eye." But Duty was in the minority among her neighbors when it came to her support (however conditional) of the park proposal. Most reacted to the idea of a nationalized river with the exasperation of St. Joe resident Lunce Cash, original vice president of the Landowners Association. "Doc, if they are not going to get those dams, why don't we just draw off and leave the Buffalo alone?" he asked Neil Compton.[15]

The issues of landowner opposition to and resident resentment toward the National Park Service have rarely made it into the story of the Buffalo River. Compton's book concludes with the passage of the park bill in 1972. Theodore Catton's solid historical account of the valley—the NPS's current official history on the subject—observes only that the hearings on the park bill exposed "the fact that landowners . . . did not generally favor a national river either." The "Buffalo National River" entry on the *Encyclopedia of Arkansas* website, authored by a former NPS employee, concedes that there were "unwilling sellers" of land in the valley, but it maintains a clearly park-centered perspective when it recalls that "the staff . . . had to face the emotional turmoil in the community regarding the disruption of life for the Buffalo River residents." This absence of conflict in the official record is especially surprising when one considers that accounts of the region's first national streams—the Ozark National Scenic Riverways— contain numerous instances of landowner defiance and resentment. In fact, a few studies of the Current River country focus on almost nothing else. The greater number of eminent domain condemnations in Missouri's national riverways almost certainly contributes to a more thoroughly chronicled lingering animosity in the eastern Ozarks. And from my own limited observation, it seems likely that this animosity toward the NPS has not only been better chronicled in Missouri but has in fact been more intense and persistent.[16]

Yet there is plenty of evidence that resentment and bitterness lingered in the Buffalo Valley in the years after the NPS acquired its land. Much of this bitterness stemmed from just how much land the NPS acquired. The bill creating the national river set aside three private-use zones in which residents were given the option of maintaining their property through scenic easements or remaining on the land by selling it and leasing it back from the government. As one of those zones consisted of a Boy Scout camp, the only private-use zones of home- and farm-owners were the small agricultural settlements in the Boxley and Richland valleys, together constituting 8,560 acres—only 9 percent of the park's total land area. Anyone living outside of these zones had no choice but to sell out and leave. Within the small private-use zones, the "aggressive" tactics of government land buyers and general confusion over the particulars of the bill resulted in the NPS obtaining about 84 percent of the land in fee simple. Of the fifty landowners in the Boxley Valley, only six secured scenic easements and retained full ownership of their property—and only half of those were longtime residents with family roots on the Buffalo. "By the end of the land acquisition period," observes a former NPS historian assigned to the Buffalo National River, "Boxley Valley had become a 'crazy-quilt' of private and federal ownership. Families left. Farms were abandoned. Community businesses ceased." In 1982 only about forty dissatisfied and isolated people remained in their homes in the entire park.[17]

In the summer of 1983, interviewers from the Center for Ozarks Studies at Southwest (now just) Missouri State University in Springfield descended on Newton County, Arkansas, to conduct an NPS-supported oral history project.[18] The vast majority of questions and responses dwelt on the old ways and old days, but often interviewers asked their subjects for opinions on the NPS and the process of creating the park. Even several years removed from land transactions, the responses by valley natives were almost always negative. And the vast majority of interviewees were among those who might have been expected to offer the most positive assessments of the situation. Most of those interviewed by historians resided in the private-use zone of the Boxley Valley—so these were the ones who were still there in 1983, the ones who were for the most part still in their homes and on their land, either through scenic easements or the sell-and-leaseback program. With only one exception, the interviewees were not the truly displaced. The latter were gone—and the interviewers didn't go looking for them, as far as we know.

Given the era, it should come as no surprise that popular points of contention were the perceived prevalence of marijuana-growing in the area (often laid at the feet of the NPS) and the hippies who must certainly have brought the weed with them. (As Jared Phillips has illustrated in *Hipbillies*, not all old natives took such an anti-counterculture stance, but positive commentaries on "longhairs" were in the minority among these interviewees.) Some of the complaints were typical of stories involving forced relocations and government restrictions on private land use. A few residents pointed to stories of elderly people being evicted from lifelong homes. "They took everything that I had that was any count is what it amounted to," Hurchel Fowler of Boxley told interviewers. Lynn Emmett, denied a permit to build a house on land her family had once owned but now leased, worried that the park's restrictions on home building and land use were incompatible with sustaining community life in Boxley. "I understand that they don't want people moving in and building there and I don't want that either," she lamented, "but I think . . . when your family has always lived there and you've always lived there—as I explained to them, I would never do anything that is harmful to the land there. I would never want any industry to come in there. I wouldn't want a lot of commercialization or anything. But young people just can't live there and if younger people can't live there, eventually there won't be anybody there. . . . You don't want to invest a lot in something that's not really yours and never will be yours."[19]

Lynn Emmett also noted the widespread opposition to the park among her family and neighbors in the 1970s. "Most of the natives, most of the people who had always lived here, they didn't want the Park comin' in. They felt, 'We've made it fine for a long time without this and we don't need anything. Why can't Boxley just continue as it is?'" Newton County's county judge at the time, Alton Campbell, echoed the notion that the Park Service had been an unwelcomed arrival. "If they'd had a vote when the Park first come in, if they'd a had a vote for the people," Campbell assured interviewers, "they'd have voted ninety-nine to one against it. It might even have been more than that. . . . I don't know of no one that's really for it unless it's someone in that Park . . . that's wantin' to leave the country . . . and that would give 'em a chance to sell and move out." Bertha Sparks, an eighty-one-year-old former teacher who became something of a pioneer-woman Yoda for back-to-the-landers in her neighborhood, was convinced that massive recreation on the river would do more damage than anything the locals had ever done. The tourists "use our area for their own pleasure. They don't care for people. They're selfish. They litter. They throw things in the river. They litter the banks with their beer cans. . . . We took pride in it. . . . Why did they need anything?" Sparks inquired about the creation of the park. "I think leavin' it like nature and God made it is the best. It was prettier, we took care of it, it was clean, go in swimmin' without any fears, and you could do anything you wanted. I think leave it as it was is what ought to be done."[20]

One thing that many interviewees made clear in 1983 was that they enjoyed a much better relationship with current NPS personnel than they had in the earliest days in the 1970s. The most serious problems for land-owners in those early days in the proposed park area stemmed from the park's land acquisition process, which was confusing at best and deceitful at worst. When interviewers asked middle-aged Ponca postmaster and farmer Waymon Villines to comment on the park, he warned, "Now, you're fixin' to get in a long conversation with me on this"—and he was right. "The federal government infringed upon the rights of others when he come in here," Villines declared. "They could have done it different. We tried to get 'em to do it different. We tried to get them simply to pass a law to restrict commercial development on the river as you would on an open market basis . . . but if someone didn't want to be bothered, let him alone until that generation passed. . . . But the federal government don't do things like that. They're still usin' the old redman tactic. Push out the redman and bring in the new." "It's the Acquisition Department that put the pressure on the people and cooled the people towards the government," he told interview-ers. "Then the rangers come in here with what they got and had to try to get along with the people." Villines, a veteran of World War II, assigned much of the blame to "a retired Army man" who ran the acquisition pro-cess out of an office in Harrison. "Now the Army . . . man's attitude is, 'Let's play war. Let's take it. No use a dallyin' around with these people—these idiots over there. Let's take it.'"[21]

And it wasn't just disgruntled natives who chafed under the NPS's hard-ball acquisition tactics. Among the interviewees that summer of 1983 were Hubert and Mary Virginia Ferguson, a well-educated and affluent couple who had been charter members of the Ozark Society and active support-ers of the Buffalo National River bill. The Fergusons had bought land in Boxley Valley shortly before the NPS began its acquisition process and were nonplussed when land buyers tried to convince them to forego the scenic easement process that had clearly been spelled out as an option for their area in the 1972 bill. "When they came in and talked to you," Hubert recalled, "they said in effect, 'Look, you don't want to sign this easement. . . . The government will be tellin' you what to do and this and that and what you really need to do is just deal with us in fee [simple] and then we'll rent it back to you for twenty-five years, cheap!'" The Fergusons complained to Sen. Dale Bumpers, and the hard-sell tactics subsided. By this point, however, many landowners in private-use areas had sold their farms and leased them back, instead of maintaining ownership of their farms and selling the NPS a scenic easement, as did the Fergusons and a few other savvy and stubborn landowners in the valley.[22]

Those who lived outside of the designated private-use areas generally had no option to sell a scenic easement or to sell and lease back, especially if their property lay within one of the areas in which the NPS planned to develop recreational and visitor facilities. These were the properties that the Park Service acquired through a declaration of taking, or eminent domain. And it was these stories—people who were given a limited amount of time to vacate the property—that still circulated in 1983 as examples of NPS ruthlessness. In the absence of any public meetings or announcements in the local weekly paper, Roy and Katy Keaton were shocked when they were served papers instructing them to move within ninety days. The park service then proceeded to bulldoze their old house and three barns and bury the refuse in a landfill. "What I can't understand," a resentful Katy told interviewers from their new home at Marble Falls, is that "they took our place and took the buildings off and everything and now it just sits there." To which Roy added, "They ain't done a blame thing with it." If Boxley Valley residents like Waymon Villines felt fortunate to have come through the confusing ordeal with land leases and still living in old homes, Roy Keaton's bewilderment had settled into bitter complacency. "It's just so doggone big you can't see the head of it. It's a whole herd of 'em, a whole herd of Congressmen and things like that appropriated the money for this."[23]

A Matter of Property Rights

People like the Keatons may not have known how in the world this snowball was formed and what hill it came rumbling off, but they knew it had rolled slick over them. They were the unfortunate casualties of someone's version of progress, just as sure as old Lige and Armindy had found themselves in the crosshairs of a very different kind of progress thirty years earlier. They didn't matter to the Army Corps of Engineers. They didn't matter to the environmental activists. They didn't matter to the National Park Service. They didn't matter to their elected officials. They were as powerless as driftwood on a sandbar. So why do their stories matter? Why dwell on the misfortunate few when the preservation and nationalization of the Buffalo has provided joy for the many? These were after all the descendants of westering white Americans who generations earlier had benefited from their government's removal of previous natives—real natives. What's good for the goose is good for the gander, right?

I won't pretend that my interest in a topic like this isn't motivated by my own family's experience. But that's not all there is to this. Part of what historians do is tell the stories of the dispossessed, of those who didn't or can't tell the stories themselves. Part of what we do is shine light in the dark areas of the past so that we might get a clearer, fuller view of what happened and why. By doing just that, this particular story can provide an entryway into something much bigger than displaced Ozarkers, Grumman canoes, and scenic easements.

In the spring of 2011, I went to a public meeting held in the community center at Mountain View, Missouri. On the docket that evening was a discussion concerning the efforts of a West Plains nonprofit organization to have a multicounty region of southern Missouri designated a National Heritage Area. The building was packed to standing-room-only capacity, and the discussion turned out to be an ambush. The three representatives from the nonprofit were almost alone in their support of the National Heritage Area program, and it quickly became clear that the two speakers representing landowners' rights organizations were the fan favorites. In one particularly heated moment of the program, two henchmen physically accosted and carried out a middle-aged man who too loudly questioned the conspiratorial warning being woven by these two activists. It was my first brush with henchmen, and, having no horse in this race, I started studying the layout of the community center and planning my escape should the gathering devolve into chaos.

Had the West Plains non-profiteers done their homework, they probably could have seen something like this coming. Though the National Heritage Area program involved no eminent domain or scenic easements—no land acquisition or zoning whatsoever—it was a project of the National Park Service and, as such, was automatically in the crosshairs of a segment of people in the Current River country still ill about the creation of the Ozark National Scenic Riverways. Probably more importantly, the program and its government overseer were anathema to a boisterous and seemingly growing cadre of ultra-conservative landowners' rights advocates and various other right-wing, anti-government subsets. To tell the truth, I'm not sure if there was a bona fide Ozarks native among the conspiracy theorists and flannelled henchmen who denounced the National Heritage Area that evening. Most of the accents were decidedly un-Ozarkian, and I can still hear the older man who proclaimed, "I moved here from Pennsylvania to get away from this kind of nonsense"—not the nonsense of surreal, potentially violent public meetings but the nonsense of meddling federal programs with roots in some shadowy United Nations (UN) cabal. Had the non-profiteers done their homework, they would have discovered that an actual UN initiative called Ozarks Man and the Biosphere had been derailed fifteen years earlier by a similarly vociferous outcry over questions of land rights and the loss of private owner autonomy. Had they done their homework, they would have discovered that the NPS's plan to remove a herd of feral horses from the Ozark National Scenic Riverways in 1990 sparked a vehement protest that was not so much pro-equine as it was anti-Park Service.[24]

The modern-day property rights movement wasn't a byproduct of the birth of national rivers in the Ozarks, but conflicts in Missouri and Arkansas certainly aided its growth in its youthful days. In *The Battle for the Buffalo*, Neil Compton noted the activities of early zealots in the cause (almost all of whom were newcomers to the Ozarks) and suggested that the intrusion of the radical, out-of-state American Landowners Association served to alienate some of the very people it claimed to assist. Compton's assessment of the role of outlanders in the Buffalo's property rights debate may have been accurate, but developments in the Missouri Ozarks indicated a much wider embrace of landowners' rights, as the struggle for control of streams began to reflect a definite urban-rural splintering. It was in the Missouri Ozarks, in the late 1960s and early 1970s, that the property rights movement experienced one of its earliest bursts of activity. In the wake of the creation of the Ozark National Scenic Riverways, prominent Missouri politicians collaborated with state agencies, environmentalists, and outdoor recreationists in one of the nation's first attempts to designate a statewide system of protected scenic streams. Yet the fallout over eminent domain land takings in the ONSR and rising cultural tensions quickly changed the game.[25]

In 1967 a statehouse bill in Jefferson City proposed placing more than eight hundred miles of twenty Ozarks streams under the jurisdiction of the Missouri Conservation Commission (MCC), which would be able to utilize both eminent domain and scenic easements to guarantee "permanent enjoyment of wilderness type recreation." A nascent protest movement engineered by a Madison County Farm Bureau leader convinced rural representatives to prevent the bill from leaving the house's parks and recreation committee. When a 1969 scenic rivers bill met the same fate, environmentalists and canoeists in St. Louis and Kansas City coalesced around a proposed statewide voters' initiative. Though watered down to remove the MCC's right of eminent domain—considered the most objectionable element of the house bills—the scenic rivers initiative "annoyed nearly every landowner along the rivers in the Ozarks, arousing some to threats of violence." Most simply joined one of the growing number of landowners' rights organizations springing from southern Missouri's soil, an assemblage that came together under the banner of the Sho-Me State Heritage Association. When an unknown assailant bombed the car of the suburban St. Louis junior high teacher spearheading the scenic rivers campaign, supporters shelved the initiative.[26]

The introduction of yet another scenic rivers bill by a suburban St. Louis legislator in 1971 stoked temperatures beyond the boiling point. A March hearing in the chamber of the state house of representatives attracted a throng of "shouting and hand-waving rural landowners . . . with ruddy, windburned faces." One of them, a Steelville farmer and presiding judge of Crawford County who had also been a state legislator, warned his former colleagues that "the people of Crawford County are ready to take up arms to protect their property. We're not going to take this laying down." While a negative house committee vote once again buried the proposed legislation, this fourth battle in a four-year span paved the way for the rise of the most vocal, hardline property rights advocates to positions of leadership within Sho-Me and other similar organizations. By the time the federal Bureau of Outdoor Recreation recommended national protection of stretches of the Gasconade and Big Piney Rivers in 1975, the voices of opposition were so loud and vociferous that Gov. Christopher "Kit" Bond and other prominent Missouri politicians rejected federal designation, closing the book on the scenic rivers fight.[27]

An Ever-Flowing Force

The initial instinct for most anyone on the moderate to progressive stretch of the political spectrum is to dismiss property rightsers and their right-wing cohorts as kooks, maybe even dangerous kooks. But sociologists J. Sanford Rikoon and Theresa L. Goedeke remind us to take a step back. "Conflicts between environmentalists and their opposition reveal attempts to impose and to privilege particular social agendas," observe the sociologists. "The spoils of victory include not simply a particular form of environmental protection, but the imposition of one type of cultural system on others." The loudest and most extreme property rights advocates undermine their own cause with the stale old chestnuts of tin-foil-hat, padded-room, slide-whistle lunacy—internet diatribes, anti-Semitism, UN conspiracies. But at the core of anti-environmentalism, Rikoon and Goedeke argue, "is a social critique . . . against a scientific and managerial elite claiming to represent the higher interests of a cause often beyond the opposition's understanding and a solution to environmental problems beyond their individual capabilities."[28] In short, it's a resentment toward a class of people who think they're better and wiser than those who happen not to be in their group, a class of people whose goodness and wisdom (so goes their own narrative) positions them to make decisions binding for all of us. In this sense, anti-environmentalism or anti-Park Service sentiment is but a manifestation of a much broader populist fear and mistrust of conventional authority.

Despite the silliness and cartoonish nature of so much fear-based protest, there is a sort of common force that lurks behind the objects of the protestors' ire. And we see it on full display in the fight over Ozarks streams in the twentieth century. We've given the manifestations of this force of the modern world many names: the impersonal capitalism that Max Weber both admired and feared; the gospel of industrial efficiency found in Taylorism; absolutism, perfectionism, bureaucratic rationalism, progressivism, world systems. They're all expressions of a force wielded by people with power, with money, with expertise, with self-granted prerogative—all the ingredients for hubris. It is a force built on sameness and bigness and togetherness, a force whose nightmare extremes are represented in popular culture by the Borg and the Matrix, the very same force the Hipbillies declared war on half a century ago. I'll call our particular manifestation of this phenomenon "planning," a popular catchword in academia and government throughout the middle decades of the twentieth century. Born in the Progressive Era, groomed in the Great Depression, and let loose to roam the nation in a postwar era of comparative consensus and self-satisfaction, planning is a rationalist, capitalist compulsion to maximize national (ultimately world) efficiency at the expense of local control and prerogative. There were those who condemned the creation of our national rivers as communism, that dirty word of the Cold War. They weren't wholly off base, as communism and planning were both offspring of a larger, unrelenting, intangible ghost of a thing that sweeps through time and across human space, bearing all of us toward some unseen future like so many grains of pollen on a rolling river. But communism was only a more unblushing, straightforward, unimaginative form of this force, and as such it was and is destined to fall by its own earnestness. Planning in the twentieth-century American imagination was more complex. It provided the backbone for corporate consolidation, economic and cultural globalization, and cultural homogenization.

The narrative that we've all come to accept about the Buffalo River saga is that it was a battle between the dammers and the free-flowers—it was the Army Corps of Engineers and its supporters against the National Park Service and its supporters. In the case of Missouri's Ozark National Scenic Riverways, there was also the US Forest Service and its supporters. But there's only one big philosophical root sustaining the whole herd, to borrow from Roy Keaton. The Park Service, the Corps' Board of Engineers for Rivers and Harbors, the Forest Service—they're all products of the search for order and efficiency and conformity and unassailable faith in expertise that defined the epoch we call the Progressive Era, which was but a particularly Protestant American manifestation of what Hegel might have termed the *Weltgeist*, the world spirit. And that Weltgeist is but an expression of humanity, of our own internal struggle, our own psychic desires for order and control and stability. They were all fighting (and supporting) the same faceless, nameless force. They were all raging against (and embracing) little cogs on the machine of planning. If anyone grasped the big picture, it was those people in the valley. If home was Pruitt or Tyler Bend, you were damned if you dammed and damned if you didn't. Resistance may not have been futile, but it was purt near close.

To their credit, director Alec Gould and other personnel at the Buffalo National River in the early 1980s recognized the "deterioration of the Boxley community, both in morale and in maintenance of the cultural landscape." It is what prompted the 1983 oral history project and the appointment of an assistant director whose primary job was to improve relations with valley residents convinced that the federal government's goal was to evict them all. Looking to avoid another Cades Cove—the depopulated Great Smoky Mountains National Park community where only sagging old barns and houses serve as reminders of the once vibrant human neighborhood—the NPS instituted a limited buyback program in the Buffalo National River in 1985, providing an opportunity for those who had stayed in the valley on lifetime or limited-time leases to reacquire fee-simple ownership of their homes and farms. By 2005 thirteen property transactions transferred 815 acres back to private ownership with scenic easements. The effort didn't appreciably impact the tiny population of Boxley Valley, but it did stabilize a community that would have been on life support before the turn of the millennium. Lynn Emmett and her husband, Skip, even received permission to build the community's first new house since the Eisenhower era. In the late twentieth century, one old-timer predicted that at some distant day there will be no valley descendants left in Boxley, only back-to-nature types who want to live in a national park. That may come to fruition, but at the very least some of those descendants will have the choice to stay or go.[29]

However modest and overdue it may have been, the National Park Service's recognition of humans' integral role in a cultural landscape and in the maintenance of the semi-wilderness that enchanted visitors was an important step—even if one necessitated by ill-advised federal actions and still subject to overwrought federal bureaucratic procedures. Perhaps it is fitting that such a "radical" program was hatched deep inside this middle American highland region called the Ozarks. Our whole social construct, after all, revolves around defiance of whatever it is that homogenizes and sucks the singularity out of people and places, whatever it is that made damming the North Fork seem like a swell idea, whatever it is that puts tract housing on old dairy farms and a polo field in a Goshen pasture, whatever it is that assures the wealthy and powerful and the experts that they have the authority and the duty to make life-altering decisions for the rest of us in the process of their planning. Vance Randolph, Otto Ernest Rayburn, Charles Morrow Wilson, May Kennedy McCord, Donald Harington . . . they all found in the hills and hollers a people who were not going gently into that homogenizing, modern world. Regardless of the degree to which that cussed nonconformity was a projection of the observers' own desires, the Ozarks in the very process of its social construction in the twentieth century became a refuge for those who didn't want to queue up and be stamped by the Weltgeist. The Ozarks became a refuge for those who would resist—those who would bring about revolution and those who would hunker down in case they had to defend themselves from revolution.

———

BERTHA SPARKS WAS in her mid-seventies, and the changes were coming fast and furious. Her husband died, and then the National Park Service moved into the Buffalo Valley. A retired teacher and native of Newton County, she made the decision to change her future by returning to the past. She started living like the old days—churning butter, curing hams, relying on garden sass for her sustenance. In the process, she became a shamanic presence for the many back-to-the-landers in her area, teaching them how to grow and can and preserve, instructing them in the fine art of herbal remedies. What made Bertha an even more effective guru for the counterculture crowd was her understanding of human nature. She knew the quest of youth was something universal. "They always seeked something better," she observed of the rural Ozarkers with whom she'd spent her life. "They'd go and look, be disillusioned and then they would come back." She knew that's exactly what a lot of her young charges were doing. When asked by interviewers in 1983 if there were other people like her, other people following the old path, she responded, wryly, "No, there's not any of 'em living that way, only a few deadheads like me that are trying to prove a point. Not because I have to, but just because I want to." Though not happy with the nationalization of the river, Bertha Sparks had made her peace with it, a peace that innervated her existence and shone through in her endorsement of a life of simplicity, a life lived locally. "You'd be healthy, you'd be happy, you'd have what we've lost—contentment."

Bertha's Buddhist response to the disruption and discord in the wake of the nationalization of the Buffalo was likely atypical, but it may have been the most Ozarky response of all. Make the best with what you have and in whatever place you find yourself. As for me, perhaps I owe it to my grandpa to resent and resist the planners for as long as I can. They might be swimming in different currents, but chances are they were spawned in the same stream.

CHAPTER SIX

The Country Store

IN SEARCH OF MERCANTILES AND
MEMORIES IN THE OZARKS

THERE'S NOTHING quite like going back home. If, like me, you're a child of the rural South, you'll know that feeling, see and smell and hear and *feel* that feeling. The smell of tilled earth or freshly cut hay, the crackle of a gravel road beneath hard rubber, that old whiff of red oak and varnish in the church house, low clouds of wood-stove smoke on winter mornings, jar flies on sultry summer days, lightning bugs and a chuck-will's-widow in a dusky holler. You can even taste it. Well-water from a faucet, Momma's cornbread and pinto beans—cappuccino and a slice of Arrezzio's Chicago-style with black olives and banana peppers from the country store. Takes you back, doesn't it? Nothing reminds me of dear ol' nineteenth-century-born Aunt Nellie quite like pizza, espresso, and frothing milk—except for maybe a Harley-Davidson do-rag, lemongrass soap, and a fifteen-minute bake in a tanning bed, all of which you can get at the country store, too. You know, back there next to the hoe handles and saw blades and pig shorts—the kind for feeding, not wearing.

A couple of generations ago, a traveler in the rural South encountered a general mercantile every five miles or so. Most were simple establishments, combining the functions of filling stations, groceries, feed stores, hardware shops, and community centers under one roof. They were family-owned and operated, with the owners often occupying living quarters in back, upstairs, or in a house next door. Sometimes the country store was also home to the community post office, all the more reason for people to gather on the front porch or huddle around the potbellied stove inside.

This essay was originally published in the journal *Southern Cultures* 18 (Winter 2012): 43–60. It appears here with minor revisions.

This country store of yesteryear no longer exists. Even in the most remote nooks and crannies of the South—Appalachia, the Ozarks, the Delta—the nostalgia seeker will come up short in the quest for mercantiles reminiscent of *Lum and Abner*'s old Jot-em-Down Store, with its hand-cranked telephone, its cracker barrels and nail kegs, its Bull of the Woods tobacco and Red Top snuff, its hardwood floors and creaking screen door and wooden cash register. Yet the essence of the country store, its immutable *country storeness*, has survived, even as the symbols by which it was once identified have faded into the past.

In the face of a succession of challenges—parcel post and mail-order houses, automobiles and the good roads movement, dime stores and supermarkets and Walmart—the country store survives, albeit in scarcer quantities and with an evolution over time that has kept it relevant to its rural clientele. The survivors—and there are more of them than you might imagine—are models of adaptation. Country merchants no longer buy much of anything from their customers, no cream or eggs, apples, or hickory handles. They no longer furnish sharecroppers and small landowners in exchange for 10 percent per annum interest rates and liens on crops either. Instead, you will find in the Ozarks dozens of stores that serve their local customers in many of the same ways that their predecessors served rural communities generations ago, by providing feed and fertilizer, gasoline and farm diesel, tools and local gossip, groceries and tobacco products, overalls and work boots, benches and a warm stove. The country store has evolved to meet the changing needs of a rural clientele more likely to drive thirty miles to work in service jobs in the county seat than to spend all day plowing the back forty, gathering eggs, and milking cows.

They also continue to provide a glimpse into life in the modern-day rural South, just as what remains of their predecessors, the yellowed photographs and musty ledgers and daybooks, provide an invaluable window into the region's past. As we are all susceptible to the pull of nostalgia, the country store's hallowed position in our collective memory seems secure. Nostalgia responds to an almost inexhaustible variety of impulses, most of them removed from the "authentic" item sparking our romantic spirits. As Thomas D. Clark observes in *Pills, Petticoats, and Plows: The Southern County Store*, "The modern American in search of local color regards these anachronisms in present-day chain-store glitter and commercial rivalry as sources of antique merchandise, antiquated human relics, and rural wit and wisdom." Cracker Barrel understands that impulse, and understands as well that we'll take our nostalgia fix however concocted and packaged we can get it. So do the Amish country stores—not the ones the real Amish patronize but those in tourist meccas that snooker the "English" into over-paying for rocking horses and cake mix. But longing of any kind is a pow-erful emotion, and, as Clark poignantly observes, "The square box front, narrow front porch, rusting signs, and pungent smells all represent what most people believe was a better day." Maybe it was and maybe it wasn't a better day, but it wasn't the last day for the country store.[1]

When my uncle and aunt started talking a few years ago about selling the little store that they owned and operated for several years in my home community, it got me to thinking about the future prospects of stores like theirs. So I decided to study the current state of the country store in an appendage of the South with which I am most familiar, my native Ozarks. As a trained scholar I was certain that I could do so in an objective manner, free of the nostalgic tendencies that color the visions of travel writers and other lesser mortals. My sober search for the modern country store would show no favoritism for potbellied stoves and heirloom seeds; it would not look askance at cinder-block buildings and stores peddling take-out pizza and burgers. This would be no quest for anachronism, no escapist journey into memory and myth. Or so I thought.

In the past few years I've traveled thousands of miles of roads in the rural Ozarks, and rarely have I missed an opportunity to stop and visit in the stores, old and new, that one finds scattered across the landscape of flyover country still today, almost eighty years after Thomas D. Clark declared the country store a relic of the past. What follows, then, is a sur-vey of the modern country store in the Ozarks.

In most cases, the country stores cited here are the only stores in town, often the only centers of retail commerce of any kind. As such, they gen-erally offer a wider variety of products and services than the typical mod-ern convenience store. Very few are to be found in incorporated villages, and all are in towns with populations less than one thousand. With few exceptions these stores do not have the physical appearance of the modern convenience store, and "convenience" or speedy service doesn't top their list of priorities.

Not included in the survey is any store that is not open year-round (canoeing outfitters, for example), any rural store that relies essentially on the sale of one line of products (the feed store), and any store that has been a victim of gentrification, which means that, this essay's introduction not-withstanding, "country stores" peddling espresso and lattes get the boot. Sorry, exurbanites, but a fellow's got to have standards. In deference to

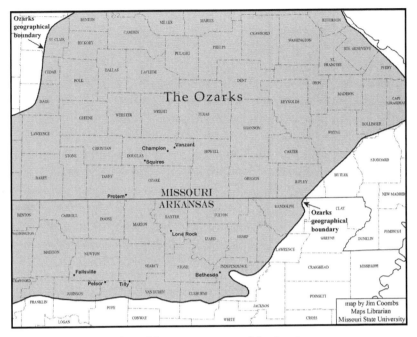

A few of the country stores of the Ozarks.
Courtesy of Jim Coombs.

what might be termed the "Maw and Paw Principle," I've excluded rural convenience stores that are part of corporate chains, though I realize in a few instances these establishments continue to serve as community gathering places where old men teach younger men the art of lying convincingly. And, because we all like our natives unselfconscious and "natural," I tend to thumb my nose at any store that seems a little too self-aware of its countryness. It was a general rule where I grew up that any place that advertises itself as a farm—Pleasant Valley Farm, Happy Hill Farm, any other place whose subtext shouted "I'm Retired and from Chicago so look at my goats and guineas!"—is no farm. Likewise, it's a pretty safe bet—though not a foolproof one—that any store with the words *country store* on the sign has partaken of the fruit of knowledge and thus forfeited its authenticity.

Perhaps the most foolproof method of judging a country store's bona fides is the old sensory test. If it looks like a country store and feels like a country store, it probably is a country store. So that's settled. They may share an essential *country storeness*, but not all country stores are of a kind. Herewith, a taxonomy of the Ozarks country store.[2]

The Country Superstore

The country store that Thomas D. Clark would have proudly claimed was one that provided an almost endless variety of products and services for its customers. There remain a few rural superstores that provide good, old-timey service to customers lucky enough to live nearby. One such business is Spurlock's Store in Squires, Missouri. Third-generation owner Randy Spurlock recalls the perhaps apocryphal story of his father's encounter with a then-unknown Sam Walton. It was 1968 when the founder of Walmart stopped by Spurlock's Store on Missouri's well-traveled Route 5. Randy's parents, Fred and Dorothy Spurlock, had just completed their new building. It was a massive structure by country store standards, so big that Walton offered to buy it on the spot, according to Spurlock family memory. Fred and Dorothy declined, however, and now, more than five decades later, the Spurlock family can claim well over a century of store ownership in their tiny community. When Fred's father, Charles M. Spurlock, arrived in town and opened a little trading post shortly after 1900, there were at least two other stores to compete with. But Squires has been a one-store town for as long as anyone now can remember, and Spurlock's long ago developed its wide-ranging services to make sure it stayed that way.[3]

I'm pretty certain you can't buy an actual mule-drawn plow at an Ozarks store nowadays, but if you ever chance across one, it will probably be at Spurlock's. For sheer volume of stuff—dizzying and seemingly endless rows and piles and mounds of stuff—no country store in the Ozarks can hold a candle to Spurlock's. Hay hooks, electrical switches, coloring books, pocket knives, fishing gear, ammunition, PVC pipe, pork and beans, work boots—it's all here. At one point—perhaps when Sam Walton ventured into the store those years ago—the clothing section was separate and distinct from the hardware section, the farm tools clearly demarcated from the plumbing supplies and auto parts. But no one remembers that time. Spurlock's merchandise has spread kudzu-like across the scuffed tile floors, along walls unseen by man for decades, over and under buried wooden shelves whose contents reveal time capsules hearkening to "good old days" that Professor Clark could not yet imagine in 1944. Just as transistor radios and dust-covered Key overalls have taken the place of an earlier generation's antique merchandise, one era's old-timers have replaced another's on the church pew up front and at the visiting table with its red-and-white-checkered wax tablecloth. And surveying the whole scene on the day I visited was octogenarian Dorothy Spurlock, a former one-room schoolteacher who gave up her profession to join Fred in the family business when he returned from World War II. She spent practically every day after in this store, dispensing advice, giving directions, making anything from sandwiches to ropes, and keeping tabs on local goings-on.[4] But even a woman of Dorothy's mettle was bound to slow down, and only Randy's timely retirement from his job at a prison in the next county over provided the new blood necessary to keep Spurlock's in business.

"These are my roots," Randy explained, "and I just couldn't leave." If running a country store is in the blood, it has to be in his. Even family outings as a child seemed to involve country stores. As a boy in the 1950s and '60s, he often accompanied his elderly grandfather, Charles Spurlock, on auto excursions into the surrounding hills. One of his grandfather's favorite destinations was just south of the state line in Three Brothers, Arkansas, where a little old lady operated a tiny roadside store. Wooden cash register, icebox, hand-cranked cheese slicer, a solitary lightbulb hanging above the counter—a *real* country store, his grandpa thought. It's all relative.[5]

The End-of-the-Line Store

Country stores like Spurlock's manage to hang on in comparatively well-traveled locations because of traffic flow and their versatility. Traffic flow is a key ingredient in the survival of the End-of-the-Line Store as well, only not in the same way. In a few isolated nooks and crannies of the Ozarks, little country stores open their doors six or seven days a week because they almost *have to*. Far away from the nearest county seat or town of any size, often at the end of a state-maintained highway, a few remote Ozark communities continue to generate just enough isolation-induced commerce to keep a storekeeper in business. There's remote, and then there's pee-on-the-side-of-the-highway-in-broad-daylight remote. It's at the end of some of the latter ribbons of blacktop that you'll reach the end of the line and its store.

And remoteness, regardless of the degree, is one of the factors accounting for the survival of country stores in general. Most twenty-first-century country stores exist outside of the "Walmart perimeter," an invisible force field emanating in all directions from your nearest "Everyday Low Prices" behemoth. Distance-from-Walmart has long been a measure of

The long-closed Old Nail Store at Nail, Newton County, Arkansas, 2009.
Courtesy of author.

remoteness in the Ozarks, and nowadays throughout the entire South. My admittedly unscientific field research suggests that the Walmart perimeter extends at least twenty miles, sometimes farther depending upon ease of travel. Rarely will you find a real country store within a thirty-minute drive of the nearest blue-and-gray retail giant.

The multiple generations of storekeeping at Spurlock's is not unusual, and few people had a stronger family connection to the country store than Sandy Deckard. Sandy and her husband Kelly owned and operated one of those end-of-the-line stores for more than a quarter of a century. Deckard's Grocery (and its present-day successor) is the only store in Bethesda, Arkansas. The state highway comes to an end in front of the store. Beyond Deckard's and Bethesda lie several miles of back roads and eventually the White River. In the nineteenth and early twentieth centuries, a ferry crossing west of town made Bethesda a popular resting place on one of the roads leading to Batesville. But the ferry is a distant memory, and not a soul just "passes through" Bethesda nowadays. That was just fine with Sandy Deckard, whose father, Gene Matthews, bought the old Bethesda store, which once stood behind the location of Deckard's Grocery, in 1953. Sandy all but grew up inside a country store; both sets of grandparents were storekeepers, and her father operated a "rolling store" before finding his way to Bethesda. Sandy, who fondly recalled the thrill of cranking her father's hand-operated gas pump as a child, supplied just about anything in demand in the community, from livestock feed and farming supplies to groceries and fuel.[6]

Like Sandy Deckard, a few other country storekeepers found their way to the end of the line. You'll find little stores in out-of-the-way Arkansas places like Rea Valley and Mount Judea (pronounced *Judy*). You'll also find a sampling of a close relative of the end-of-the-line store, the Middle-of-Nowhere Store. This depends, of course, on just how you define nowhere, but you can find such stores, with a good map, in places like Witts Spring, Arkansas, and Thornfield, Missouri. For years Chuck Riley has operated such a store in the blink-and-you've-missed-it community of Lone Rock, Arkansas. Local farmers can assure you that the community's name is a damned lie, and Riley's Crossroads Store is only a partial truth. The dirt road that runs into the state highway at the store doesn't go anywhere else, though there may have been a crossroads here before the Arkansas Department of Transportation built and paved serpentine Highway 341 through this remote stretch of the Ozark National Forest. The old Crossroads Store burned in the 1990s, so Chuck Riley's twentieth-century cinder-block incarnation isn't likely to land on a "Scenes of the Ozarks" calendar, at least not for another hundred years. But if you like your stores gritty and basic, your storekeepers of the surviving kind, stop in for a visit.

Though the Crossroads Store may represent an extreme of remoteness, Chuck Riley's challenges are familiar ones to all country store owners. One of the biggest headaches for modern country storekeepers is procuring merchandise and getting it delivered. Faced with recurring fuel price spikes, during the current century many wholesalers dropped little country stores from their delivery routes. Country stores buy merchandise in small amounts, and, like the Crossroads Store, they're often far off the beaten path. PepsiCo, for instance, won't deliver to Lone Rock. Like most store owners I've talked with, Riley buys a good share of his merchandise from the same places everyone else in the rural South buys stuff—Walmart and supermarkets. From Lone Rock that means a thirty-five-minute Sunday drive to the nearest market center. Riley and other storekeepers read the grocery store advertisement supplements in local newspapers for bargains and sales and then resell the products they've bought at retail prices. Gas companies still deliver to even the remotest stores, but the combination of higher wholesale prices for smaller bulk orders and Environmental Protection Agency fees and fines for outdated tanks and pumping systems renders fuel sales a money-losing proposition for Riley. To make matters worse, per-use fees on credit card purchases often eat up the slim profit margin on typically small country store purchases. Like some other rural store owners, Riley couldn't get by on store business alone, so he supplements a meager and unpredictable store income by operating a lawn-mower repair business on site.

The Feels-like-Old-Times Store

Chuck Riley's Crossroads Store might not look the part, but there are still a number of more photogenic country stores in the Ozarks that evoke the spirit of the old-timey store. Occasionally, the exterior will do the trick for stores in old buildings, the more dilapidated the better, but our search takes us on the inside. In this genus—*Mercantilae nostalgicus*, I believe, in its Latin rendering—we find two separate, but not mutually exclusive, species: the store with the post office inside and the store with a wood-burning stove. Neither of these should be confused with a distant relative, the Ye Olde Countrye Store (*Mercantilae imposterus*), a creature of cunning camouflage whose chief aim is to lull the visitor into a nostalgia-induced trance that inevitably ends in overdose on saltwater taffy and sarsaparilla. *Mercantilae imposterus* will likely feature a potbellied stove (nonfunctioning, of course) and other relics of old-timeyness (those top-lid coolers filled with real glass bottles of soda pop), but don't be fooled. The preacher always said the devil can take on a pleasing form.

Perhaps nothing illustrates the changes in the country store more than the scarcity of wood stoves and post office/stores today. A couple of generations ago, practically every rural post office was housed inside a country store, and the potbellied stove was such a ubiquitous ornament of the old store that it must have been included in the country storekeeper's start-up kit. Most rural communities, regardless of how small and how remote, have stand-alone post offices nowadays, but the Ozarks still features a few hamlets where Uncle Sam pays rent to the storekeeper. The Missouri citizens of Scopus, Protem, and Hardenville still buy their stamps in the only store in town, though the old country store in the last was converted into an antique shop some years ago.

Even rarer than the post office/store today is the postmaster/storekeeper, which makes Marilyn Hurley of Tilly, Arkansas, something akin to the last of a breed. Hurley's post office/store sits beside Arkansas Highway

The Pioneer Store at Protem, Taney County, Missouri, 2009.
Courtesy of author.

27 atop a ridge of the Boston Mountains, the Ozarks's most rugged and inaccessible subregion. Beneath the modern metal roof and vinyl siding is a seventy-year-old store called Fountain's Grocery. Marilyn's post office is little more than a walk-in closet occupying the northwestern corner of the store. Marilyn's parents, Alfred and Avis Fountain, established the family's first little store in Tilly more than eighty years ago. On the day of my first visit to Tilly in the spring of 2009, my local history informant was Marilyn's sister, Charlotte Fountain, a straight-shooting retiree who keeps an eye on the old family business from her home next door. "If you tried to depend on the store for a living, you'd go broke," Charlotte observed. Even as far back in the hills as Tilly is, local residents find their way to the nearest Walmart or supermarket for serious shopping, buying only "what they *have* to have" from Fountain's.[7]

It is a familiar lament among country storekeepers but a cold fact of life. With no economy of scale, the country store can never hope to compete with the Walmarts and supermarkets of the world. Remoteness is a two-edged sword, however. The same deep hollers and rows of ridges that keep wholesalers off the backroads hem in the residents of places like Tilly, at least to some degree. At some point the higher-priced groceries, feed, and fuel at Fountain's becomes more economical and convenient than a daily drive to the nearest big town. It's that conundrum of isolation that keeps many country stores in business.

The passerby who happens upon Tilly's little mercantile isn't likely to ponder the financial vicissitudes of the country store. Instead, she'll be taken with the obvious *country storeness* of the scene: the neatly arranged wooden shelves, the homey décor of family photos and community mementos, the old white metal scales, and the iron wood-burning stove sitting in the middle of the store's gray-painted concrete floor. It turns out that Fountain's Grocery is the rare and almost extinct double-threat of country store nostalgia—the kind with a post office *and* a wood-burning stove. A tourist intent on the woodstove experience will find what she's looking for in a smattering of other Ozark hamlets as well, like Kingston and St. Paul in Arkansas and Davisville in Missouri. On occasion the stove's function is more atmospheric than climatologic. In most cases, stoves do what stoves have always done—keep people warm and, when surrounded by chairs, spark conversation about weather and livestock and times past.

The Not-Your-Grandpa's-Country-Store Store

In rare cases, the country store's adaptability has resulted in odd mutations in the rural Ozarks, businesses that look and sometimes even feel like a country store but with highly unusual characteristics—the two-headed calves of the country store universe. I've encountered a couple of these establishments, and I expect there are others in the Ozarks and elsewhere—or at least there will be. Like a lot of rural southern locales—especially those sporting more than a few granny singers and white oak basket makers—the Ozarks attracted its fair share of back-to-the-landers and other counterculture types in the 1960s and '70s. A trickle of this self-generating subset continues to flow into the region to this day.

If these neophyte hippies are in search of a guru, they could have done worse than Ray McCall, who for more than four decades ran his own unique country store on a lonely stretch of Missouri Route 76 in eastern Douglas County. A generation or so into the worldwide web era, it is still unusual to find an Ozarks country store with a website. More unusual? Finding one that referenced Martin Luther King Jr. and Rudolf Steiner in the same sentence, as Ray's did until it disappeared after his death in 2021. To pronounce the late McCall and his Ray's Country Store "different" is a gross understatement. A Kansan by raising and trucker by training,

McCall, a self-described "rainbow person," was looking for a place that would fit his personality and philosophy when he discovered the Ozarks. We don't know how many of his rural neighbors believed he had found the right place, but in 1980 he bought the little white-frame building that locals still referred to as the "Holt Store," after the family who built it in 1932.[8]

In subsequent years, McCall and his wife, a Mexican immigrant who had converted to Pentecostalism before heading north, turned Ray's into Douglas County's oddest attraction: a country store that served authentic tamale suppers, specialized in anything related to the Grateful Dead and Harley-Davidson, reddened the faces of unsuspecting patrons who ventured into the only peek-a-boo room of pornographic magazines I've yet to encounter in an Ozarks country store, and featured full-moon sing-a-longs and jam sessions with an occasional display of belly dancing. Ray's was an acquired taste for neighbors in Douglas County, though in the live-and-let-live Ozarks his eccentricity was generally tolerated. He kept long and steady hours, after all, and you never know when you might be in need of something at the country store.[9]

Mercantilae authenticus

Like Appalachia, the Delta, Cajun Country, and other southern regions assumed to be the bearers of distinctive local cultures, the Ozarks has been attracting travel writers and photographers for the better part of a century. Unless commissioned by *High Times*, they're not likely to turn to Ray's Country Store for a photo spread. Instead, they will find their way to one of a handful of country stores in old buildings with antique furnishings, and sometimes antique proprietors. A few months into my travels I found myself, despite my scholarly intentions, searching for this store—the one we might call *Mercantilae authenticus*. I had already encountered examples of a less satisfying store that nevertheless delights the photographer and tickles the travel writer—the country store that exists somewhere within the metaphysical conjunction of *Mercantilae authenticus* and *Mercantilae imposterus*. They are stores that wink at tourists and revel in the conscious display of country, while maintaining a tenuous link with a past incarnation that continually replenishes the supply of *country storeness*. As opposed to the intentionally anachronistic Ye Olde Countrye Store, they are stores that were once plain country but have adapted and survived as self-conscious country.

Ray's Country Store in Douglas County, Missouri, 2009.
Courtesy of author.

But my search for something more meaningful—for real *contact*—seemed hopeless. Of course, the country store of legend doesn't exist. Or does it? The premise undergirding my search, after all, had been not that the country store of yesteryear lives in modern America, but that the country store has changed with the decades into something still country, but country by today's standards. When it came to the anachronistic survival of yesteryear's country store, I would sadly have to follow Thomas D. Clark's lead and declare *that* country store extinct. But what if there were such a place, and what if my earlier condemnations of such fantasy were exaggerations if not outright lies? It wouldn't be the first time a country store nudged a fellow into stretching the truth.

It was on one of my early country store searches that I first got wind of what sounded like the white buffalo of country stores, a place so timeless, so anachronistic, so *spiritual* that it would make grizzled travel writers weep—so nostalgic that it would render travel writers grizzled, *then* make them weep. An acquaintance gave me three leads, two of which turned out to be stores that had been closed since before I was born. The third he had never seen but had only heard the legends. It was in a neighboring county, he thought, but his description was short on specifics: "They say it's the real deal," he intoned, like a weary Sherpa recounting campfire tales of the Yeti. "Potbellied stove, wood floors, all that stuff."

I was skeptical. Probably another abandoned old store peeking out of an overgrown thicket on some twisting back road. Or some Ye Olde Countrye Store that had fooled my friend's source into believing he had stumbled on a modern-day Jot-em-Down, where all the drinks are Nehis and all the candy hard as rock. Either way, this wasn't much to go on. But the possibility of such a place was intriguing. The ivory-billed woodpecker had allegedly reappeared in an Arkansas swamp a couple years before, after all, so why couldn't your grandpa's country store have survived for half a century in some Ozark backwater that not even the travel writers and regional photographers could find. At the very least, I had to see the store in order to catalog it or personally dismiss it as an imposter.

Using a detailed topo map of Douglas County, Missouri, I set out one day to roam the back roads in search of this mythical mercantile. Having already visited Spurlock's Store and Ray's Country Store in the same county, I knew remote and rugged Douglas was ideal country store habitat. I traveled just about every state-maintained highway I could find in and around Douglas County, stopping on occasion to describe the object of my quest, but with no luck. Adventure and romance slowly getting the best of me, a couple of days later I decided to try again. Arriving at the county seat first thing in the morning, I stopped to gas up at a convenience store. (Did I mention the price of country store gas is *high*?) Once again, I described the country store I was looking for to the cashier. "You mean the Champion mall?" she replied with a laugh. It wasn't a laugh of derision, a good sign. It was real, she assured me, but not the easiest place to find. I already knew that.

Thirty minutes and three turns later, I was there. The legends had not deceived. On a bursting spring morning I found myself staring at the ivory-billed woodpecker in all its wooden glory, at a faded board-and-batten passenger pigeon with a sagging tin roof and gravel-and-dirt driveway. How could it be? A decade into the twenty-first century—an age when science fiction writers of old were convinced that their descendants would be decked out in tin foil jumpsuits while driving their hovercrafts to the moon—here sat a country store that even a teenaged Thomas D. Clark would have recognized as representative of the family *Mercantilae*. It was enough to make a grown southern historian cry.

Intoxicated by the sight of the hand-cranked diesel pump on the rickety front porch, I stumbled through the open doorway and came face to face with the thing that brought me to my knees: the potbellied stove. Once I'd learned that the rusted white enamel pan at the base of the stove— the spitting image of my grandma's old pea-hulling and bean-snapping pan—was there so that the old men wouldn't get peanut shells all over the floor, I was overcome. A quivering mound of flesh rendered immobile by a nostalgia-addled brain, I writhed on the hardwood floor worn smooth by generations of foot traffic for what must have been minutes, I'm told, mumbling incoherently about crop liens, Ike Godsey, and worm candy. I won't swear to it, but I'm pretty sure at one point in my moonshine-peyote visionscape I talked crops over cornbread and buttermilk with a great-great-grandfather, the one whose portrait my old-maid cousin kept covered up with a picture of a Coca Cola-drinking flapper girl. I will swear to it that I saw John-Boy—or at least some barefooted local with a nickel-sized mole on his cheek—barter two hens and a side of bacon for a carton of Pall Malls and a tank of gas.

As a scholar, you strive for levelheaded moderation, the discernment of the sober and rational mind. As a historian, you leave the quaint and extraordinary to the travel writer. You play down exceptionalism. But occasionally even the best of those in pant suits and tweed jackets gets blindsided by a long-repressed romanticism, and it is at moments like these that

Gatlinburg and Branson make a little more sense to us. Although it was in no way typical of the modern country store, Henson's Grocery & Gas did indeed evoke romantic images of yesteryear. The lush greenness and budding fragrance of that crisp spring morning only added to the mystique. The beauty of Henson's was its utter unselfconsciousness. It was the rare store that appeals to our nostalgic tendencies while still functioning as a genuine country store. Henson's seemed to beckon from the past because it didn't beckon at all. No website, no advertisements. There was not so much as a single sign pointing the way to Henson's from the various highways I navigated to find it. The blacktop ended at the store's driveway. Beyond lay miles of gravel roads.

Betty Henson, proprietor and sole employee of Henson's Grocery & Gas, has spent most of her adult life at the end of this road. Running a country store in the Ozarks was most assuredly not what Betty dreamed of as a child in small-town Iowa. But it is a destiny that seems to fit her. Betty made her way to south-central Missouri after she met and married a young soldier named Duane Henson, whose parents had been in the store business all his life. Ed and Anna Henson bought this little store in 1940, and even on the cusp of World War II it already had an old-timey feel to it. Hastily constructed in the 1920s of rough-sawn lumber on a fieldstone foundation, the store building was never a model of architectural integrity. For as long as anyone could recall, the hardwood floor sloped noticeably toward the northwest, and the roof sported a visible sag that, in this case, just added to the ambience. For years Ed Henson ran a little gas-powered gristmill for local farmers and maintained a small garage on the premises, but he and Anna changed almost nothing on or in the store. Betty and Duane Henson began helping Ed and Anna with the store a few years before Anna died in 1983 and took over sole management of Henson's Grocery & Gas a couple of years later.

With Ed's death in 1998 and Duane's just a few years later, Betty Henson had been running the store solo for the better part of a decade when I first met her. She still kept pet and livestock feed in a back room and provided off-road diesel for local farmers and one gasoline pump for anyone who couldn't make it to the cheaper convenience stores twenty miles away. The local post office shut its doors years ago, but Betty continued to sell stamps and collect outgoing letters from patrons, which she gave to the rural mail carrier on his daily visit. She still stocked everything on wall shelves behind the dark, wooden counters that ringed most of the store and inside the glass-covered display cases of the counters themselves. And, of course, there was the potbellied stove in the center of the room, with a long stovepipe that snaked its way to the back wall.

If the average Ozarks country store has trouble getting merchandise delivered, Betty Henson doesn't stand a chance. Almost everything Betty sells comes from the shelves of Walmart or supermarkets. And still the soda pop I bought that day was cheaper than those at the checkout-aisle coolers at Walmart. As you might expect of someone who devotes long hours, six and sometimes seven days a week, to this little store, greed is not something that motivates Betty Henson. This may be an adopted community, but it is without a doubt her home (her house sits just up the hill a stone's throw away), and her customers are like family. She provides them with a convenience that no other such remote Ozarks community enjoys in the twenty-first century, and in return their patronage keeps her in business. Betty's reasoning is more succinct: "I need the people, and they need the store."[10]

Betty Henson displays another of the essential elements of successful country storekeeping: a deep commitment to place and neighbors. If you don't have it, you become just another tiny, overpriced dollar store, and you eventually go out of business, depriving the community of a piece of its heritage and of an institution that remains surprisingly integral to healthy village life in the twenty-first century. The rural covenant works both ways. Garrison Keillor's fictional Minnesota town Lake Wobegon "survives to the extent that it does on a form of voluntary socialism . . . and it runs on loyalty." If the community's residents cease to hold up their end of the bargain by at least occasionally paying a few dollars more for groceries, gas, and feed in order to ensure the store's solvency, the covenant collapses, the store closes, and the community finds itself more isolated than before.[11]

Of course, no country store this anachronistic, in a place as crawling with tourists as is the Ozarks, can forever fly under the radar. Betty Henson is no stranger to curiosity seekers and motorcycle touring clubs. She has seen her share of photographers and travel writers. Even *National Geographic* found its way to this sparsely settled cranny of Douglas County decades ago. She has taken all of us gawkers and picture-snappers with a grain of salt and has helped dust us off when the smell of oak flooring and kerosene made us light-headed. Despite her no-nonsense humility, it was obvious that spring morning that she knew what her little store did for people, what it meant to visitors. She's been told too many times not to know. But for her it was still what a country store has always been: a living, even a calling. No need to be ostentatious. No need for billboards with

Henson's Grocery & Gas, Champion,
Douglas County, Missouri, 2009. *Courtesy of author.*

Old English font or misspelled hillbilly slogans. The people she catered to knew where to find her, and that's what really mattered.[12]

Yet it was difficult to visit this little place, nestled in a grove of trees on a creek bank beneath a hill at the end of a blacktop road, and not be touched in some way, not be moved to ponder loss and perseverance, the impermanency of our stubborn creations, our desperate, fleeting existences, amid the patient inattention of the earth itself. Like all country stores, Henson's will survive until it doesn't matter enough to the community and people it serves, or until there is no steward left. That may be in five years, or it may be in fifty years. The country store itself, in one form or another, will survive as long as there is country, and in my mind as long as there are people there will always be country. There is something in us that makes us seek out the past even as our world leaves it behind, even as we ourselves declare it dead and gone. Like so much of life that we have dismissed to the past, the country store, both the old and the new of it, waits to be found. So get off the four-lane highways and find *your* country store.

As for your grandpa's country store? Well, there's good news and bad news. The bad: A couple of weeks after submitting the first draft of this essay to *Southern Cultures*, I found out that Betty Henson had demolished

the old store in the summer of 2010. A painful reminder of the impermanency of our creations. The good: The picturesque old store building may
be gone, but Henson's Grocery & Gas isn't, not yet anyway. Betty's store
now operates out of a new, larger building that sits on the exact spot occupied for more than eighty years by its predecessor. The new building even
resembles the old store, calling to mind the "bigger house" that replaced
the Johnsons' sharecropper shack in the closing scene of Steve Martin's
The Jerk. What the new store lacks in charm and anachronism it more
than makes up in stability and safety. That, after all, is why Betty Henson
made the change. "One of these days somebody was going to drive up and
say, 'Oh, the old store fell in. Where's Betty?'" she explained on my first
post-demolition visit. "And I'd be in it."[13]

And that's what makes Betty Henson a true modern-day country storekeeper. Practical by nature, appreciative of her store's connection to the
past but not tethered to it, she looks into the same future that beckons
her rural neighbors. I hope Henson's Grocery & Gas is still there and still
in business when you read this. *National Geographic* is unlikely to stop
by again, and the nostalgia-seekers will disappear, which is just fine with
Betty Henson. But the little brown store at the end of the blacktop is still
worth a visit. How do you get there, you ask? Let's just say it's at the end
of a journey.

CHAPTER SEVEN

Rethinking the Scots-Irish Ozarks

DIVERSITY AND DEMOGRAPHICS
IN REGIONAL HISTORY

N HIS *History of Randolph County, Arkansas*, Lawrence Dalton describes an early Independence Day celebration on the American frontier. This one took place in 1821, when the author of the Declaration of Independence, Thomas Jefferson, still walked the earth. The location of this celebration was somewhere in the vicinity of the long extinct Arkansas community called Fourche a Thomas, or Fourche de Thomas. I don't know exactly whence Mr. Dalton derived his information—for his book is blissfully free of citations—but "according to information handed down to us," he relates, settlers erected a liberty pole taller than the trees and staged a military-style parade. Jacob Shaver, a veteran of the War of 1812 whose father had fought in the Revolutionary War, served as grand marshal, while his brother-in-law, Matthias Mock, presided over the picnic dinner. As was the custom in those days, an esteemed community member was tasked with reading aloud the Declaration. On this day the honors went to storekeeper, farmer, and amateur doctor Daniel Plott.[1]

Other than the shuddering thought of an "amateur" doctor, there was really nothing extraordinary at all about this Independence Day celebration—except that it took place on the edge of the frontier, far from Philadelphia and the thirteen colonies that had opted for rebellion forty-five years earlier. Nothing extraordinary at all, unless you've been raised—as have almost all of us—on stories of the Scots-Irish Ozarks, the region so populated by the Protestant sons and daughters of Ulster that it should glow orange on the map. Shaver, Mock, and Plott, the three biggest wigs at our Fourth of July gathering, were all Germans—or, more precisely, Americans of German descent. Three Dutchmen—as other Americans often erroneously labeled immigrants from *Deutschland* and their descendants—commemorating America's independence in a region still populated by thousands of Native Americans representing perhaps as many as a dozen different languages, living on a creek with a French name, surrounded by other settlers from Tennessee and Kentucky and Illinois and Missouri whose ancestors came from England and Wales and France and Canada and sub-Saharan Africa.

If you've read anything about the historical or cultural Ozarks (or the greater South, for that matter) published within the last forty years, chances are you've encountered what we might term the Scots-Irish thesis. I would summarize the thesis like this: in the nineteenth century, the Scots-Irish and their descendants made their way across the southwestern frontier that stretched from the Carolina Piedmont to the trans-Appalachian plateaus and, either because of a predilection for occupying hilly, rugged lands or because they were unable to compete with more skillful and progressive farmers in the more fertile areas all around, they settled in the backcountry of the Ozarks, an isolated place that for generations incubated the cultural characteristics of the Scots-Irish—a fierce independence, a willingness to fight with the least provocation, a taste for moonshine, a devotion to fiddle tunes and ancient ballads of old-country origin, a love of the outdoors and the hunt, a preference for the leisurely life of the herder over the rigorous existence of the tiller of the soil—and in the process warded off potential pioneers from other backgrounds and produced one of the country's peculiar cultural strongholds. So persistent and pervasive has the thesis become in the last generation that, according to a recent statement of one historian, "the historical Scots-Irish have come to stand today for gun ownership, property rights, anti-tax movements, economic deregulation, Christian evangelicalism, moral conformity, minimal government, and a militaristic foreign policy."[2]

But before the 1970s, there was little mention of the offspring of Ulster in the various writings on the Ozarks—and in the days when the nineteenth-century pioneers were actually settling the region, the phrase "Scots-Irish" was never uttered. So, who were the Scots-Irish? How did they come to play such a key role in the story of the Ozarks? And how accurate or inaccurate is the Scots-Irish thesis?

The first question has the most straightforward answer. In the early 1600s, in an attempt to subdue the so-called "wild Irish," or the stubborn and uncooperative Roman Catholics of the emerald isle, the English began establishing "plantations" in the northern part of the island using Protestant settlers who hailed primarily from the border country of southern Scotland and northern England. The plantation system failed to conquer the Irish and replace the Catholic Church with the Anglican Church, but the Protestants were able to establish a formidable beachhead in the area that we know today as Northern Ireland, or Ulster. A century later, in the early 1700s, a variety of push factors—mostly of the economic kind—sparked a flow of emigration from these northern Irish counties that continued in fits and starts until the outbreak of the American Revolution, and for generations after. Tens of thousands of these Irish Protestants made their way to the American colonies, and especially to Pennsylvania, where many of them headed to the backcountry, large numbers of them trekking southward up the Shenandoah Valley of Virginia and into the Carolinas. As early as 1800, some of these immigrants—more often their descendants—ventured beyond the Mississippi River and into the eastern fringes of the Ozarks.[3]

These were the Scots-Irish, and if you have roots in the Ozarks you almost certainly have a family connection to this mass movement of peoples. If they were so central to our story, then, why did it take us so long to recognize them? Some of this boils down to semantics. The nineteenth-century settlers of Ulster descent did not use the term *Scots-Irish*. In fact, the label is an American creation that gained widespread use only near the end of the 1800s, largely as a result of efforts by Protestant Irish immigrants to differentiate themselves from the more numerous Catholic Irish immigrants of the post–potato famine era. In Goodspeed's *Reminiscent History of the Ozark Region*, an 1894 book that concentrated on nineteen counties in Missouri and Arkansas, of the 282 biographies that listed ethnic or national origins only twenty-five (or less than 9 percent) claimed Scots-Irish ancestry—not surprising when we consider that the term had only been in common use a short time. More than one-third of biographies claimed Irish ancestry, and, given the relatively few Catholics in the biographical sketches, it is probable that a great majority of the Irish ancestors were in fact from Northern Ireland. But even if we assume that 90 percent of those claiming Irish ancestry were descended from Irish Protestants, we are still left with the curious fact that fully 60 percent of the featured biographies with allusions to ethnic heritage made no claim on Ulster forebears.[4]

In the late nineteenth and early twentieth centuries, there was a gradual ramping up of recognition of the allegedly unique cultural contributions of the Scots-Irish. One of the earliest writers to identify the centrality of the Scots-Irish to the American frontier experience was Theodore Roosevelt, before his days as a military hero and US president. In his sweeping and heroic account of the white man's conquering of North America, *The Winning of the West*, Roosevelt argued that the "dominant strain" of the American backwoodsman was "the Presbyterian Irish—the Scotch-Irish as they were often called." Flooding the backcountry from Pennsylvania to the Carolinas, these "Roundheads of the South" not only won the West but were the first to take up arms in the cause of American independence. While the Scots-Irish more than any other group "impressed the stamp of their peculiar character on the pioneer civilization of the West and Southwest," Roosevelt avoided the reductionist tendencies of later scholars. Noting the heavy German migrations to the same locales, the future Rough Rider admitted that the "Presbyterian Irish were . . . far from being the only settlers on the border." And unlike later observers, Roosevelt put little stock in the survival of ethnic folkways and cultural markers beyond the Appalachians. Embracing the melting-pot image, he argued that "long before the first Continental Congress assembled, the backwoodsmen, whatever their blood, had become Americans, one in speech, thought, and character."[5]

It didn't take long for writers to dispose of Roosevelt's caution and find the "peculiar character" of the Scots-Irish among the post-Revolutionary generations of the southern backcountry. One of the most influential examples was Horace Kephart's 1913 book, *Our Southern Highlanders*. Finding evidence of cultural transmission among the early twentieth-century denizens of the Smoky Mountains, Kephart, a St. Louis native who cut his outdoor writer's teeth in the Ozarks, suggested that the descendants of the Scots-Irish were culturally preadapted to life in the rugged and unforgiving wilderness. Kephart's views (as did Roosevelt's) derived from Romantic-era nationalistic and racial theories, perhaps most strongly identified with German scholar and cleric Johann von Herder. Herder's *Volksgeist* theory stressed the idea that distinct populations or nationalities shared more than morphological and physiological traits. They also shared a unique group culture consisting of a sort of composite psychology, intelligence, and character. Like the French philosopher Montesquieu before him, Herder believed that human beings were the products of the lands they inhabited and that the result was a shared genetic character. This genetic character was, Herder suggested, expressed in society through language, literature, religion, the arts, and folklore. So Kephart's ideas were not new ones, but his linking of Scots-Irish cultural attributes with the people and lifeways of the southern mountains was a novel approach at the time. Within a few years, scholars—especially those at the center of the burgeoning American Studies movement—took up the cause of white ethnic cultural impact on the American story, and the Scots-Irish, "our great pioneering race," emerged triumphant as the ultimate frontiersmen of Manifest Destiny.[6]

The Scots-Irish label lent many old-stock Americans a unique ethnic identity—even if one partially or even largely contrived—and one ultimately free of the cultural and political subversiveness of more exotic groups in an age in which much of the country was suddenly awash in national and ethnic distinctiveness. In other words, the "myth" of the Scots-Irish granted many mainstream white people an exoticism that a "superior" race could not normally claim. Despite the fact that most modern scholars dismiss racially charged philosophies such as Herder's, the idea of the survival of immutable, static lifeways among a people such as the Scots-Irish, according to historian Warren R. Hofstra, holds "a continuing fascination for devotees of ethnic heritage in an age in which fixed identities and their ancestral embodiments have become ever more powerfully linked in the American character."[7]

Nonetheless, armchair anthropologists and historians who studied the Ozarks in succeeding decades made few direct references to the Scots-Irish. The region's most prolific chronicler, folklorist Vance Randolph, seems never to have warmed to this ethnic explanation for Ozarks uniqueness. Many others, including Randolph's prolific friend Otto Ernest Rayburn, preferred touting the Anglo-Saxon bloodlines of the hill people in thinly veiled celebration of pure whiteness in an age of eugenics-inspired racism. But Ulster would soon have its day in the Ozarks and across much of the greater South. The revival of the Scots-Irish thesis (or myth?) began with publication of James G. Leyburn's *The Scotch-Irish: A Social History* in 1962. In the 1970s historians began to reimagine southern and Ozarks history as a long product of Scots-Irish cultural transmission, for good or bad. Leading the charge were two historians whose surnames suggested a personal and familial connection to the topic, Grady McWhiney and Forrest McDonald. McWhiney and McDonald's "Celtic thesis" attempted to reframe the story of southern history by contrasting the lifestyles and philosophies of the Scots-Irish and other Celtic immigrants to the southern colonies and states with those of the English farmers who settled the northern colonies and states. The traits of the Celts—including a preference for animal herding over tilling, clannishness, the cultivation of a leisure ethic instead of a work ethic, and an affinity for oratory and spoken language over writing—shaped the South in distinctive ways, argued the two historians.[8]

Influenced by Leyburn and especially by the early work of McWhiney and McDonald, in the late 1970s and 1980s, a trio of scholars at Southwest (now just) Missouri State University injected the study of the region's past with a major dose of the Scots-Irish thesis. Chief among these was historian Robert Flanders. Flanders, who began teaching courses on Ozarks history in the mid-1970s and founded the university's Center for Ozarks Studies in 1976, observed in a 1979 report that "the Scots-Irish persisted as a culturally similar population of sufficient density and local, even regional, predominance that they did not suffer rapid amalgamation into other ethnic-cultural streams." He went on to make a claim for their cultural uniqueness and its impact on an exceptional Ozarks region. "They had mixed but little with modernity, with ideas of 'progress.' They, alone of all the European immigrants to British America on both sides of the water, had remained outside the pale of the European Enlightenment, of rationalistic culture, and of the myriad influences of an emergent modern world. Their adaptation to a barbaric natural and social environment in Scotland and northern Ireland . . . was a prelude to a similar adaptation in the New World. . . . Their failure to modify significantly the environment along well-established progressive lines, thus bringing themselves into the mainstream of American frontier history, made them anomalous, little-known, little-understood, to be stereotyped along with other ethnic minorities."[9]

In other publications in the 1980s, Flanders's colleagues, cultural geographers Milton D. Rafferty and Russel Gerlach, similarly presented the Ozarks as a bastion of Scots-Irish cultural survival. In his influential *The Ozarks, Land and Life*, Rafferty claimed that the antebellum "Ozarks was inhabited by a hardy breed of Scots-Irish immigrants who . . . were poor but nearly self-sufficient and skilled at living under isolated conditions." Even though "the label Scots-Irish had largely been shed" by the time the region was settled by white Americans, argued Gerlach, Scots-Irish culture was alive and well in the nineteenth-century Ozarks in the form of the typical hill farmer's poor agricultural practices and reliance on open-range herding, his penchant for frequent relocation, and the impermanence of his buildings. Such claims reinforced popular, romantic notions of a place and a people largely forgotten by time, a population exceptional by choice. The Scots-Irish thesis also influenced other emerging scholarship on the

Ozarks. In a 1991 study of settlement in the rugged hills of Missouri's Current River watershed, historian Donald Stevens found that "Scots-Irish settlers . . . dominated the early development of the region" and "demonstrated a preference for a pre-modern or frontier existence rooted in the forests of the upland South." The persuasive and appealing notion of a stubborn Scots-Irish redoubt in the wilds of the trans-Mississippi has grown in popular culture in the twenty-first century. It survives in the scholarly record as well, including a 2003 study of pre–World War II life in the rural locale that is today Fort Leonard Wood, Missouri, and a 2010 study of nineteenth- and early twentieth-century farmsteading in the areas now contained within the Mark Twain National Forest.[10]

Gerlach's work especially highlighted the apparent differences between cultural survivals among the antebellum German immigrants on the Ozark Uplift's fringes in the Missouri River valley and their Anglo neighbors, whom he often categorized as Scots-Irish. And this provides additional insight into the growth of the Scots-Irish myth. In Gerlach's estimation, the Anglos or Scots-Irish constituted something of an exceptional population, exhibiting few of the progressive and admirable characteristics of the more community-centered and ethnically conscious Germans. This comparison of native-born with German stock along the edges of the Ozarks—a comparison in which the Germans always emerge victorious—can be traced back a century to the early scholarship of esteemed cultural geographer Carl O. Sauer. Sauer didn't use the term *Scots-Irish*, but the Missouri-born scholar of German lineage generally took a dim view of the inhabitants of the interior Ozarks, with characterizations that could be termed *hillbilly* or *Scots-Irish* depending on the context. In contrast to the diligent and successful German farmers of the region's fringes, Sauer believed that "many of those who came [to the Ozarks] were unable or unwilling to meet the competition of life in more progressive regions. The Ozark Center has held few prizes to stimulate the ambition of its people, most of whom have lived uneventful lives and therefore have made little local history." Sauer also adopted current theories regarding the cultural lag in the "retarded frontier" of the Ozarks. "This class [of rude hunters] was typical, of course, of almost any frontier. It existed in greater purity, however, in the Ozark hills, and remained longer there than in most sections because of the small and belated competition from agricultural immigrants."[11]

We know the Scots-Irish thesis has had a lasting impact on the study of the Ozarks. But is it defensible? Did the Scots-Irish—or at least their descendants—so dominate the peopling of the Ozarks that they placed an indelible cultural stamp on the region, one whose broad outlines can still be seen and felt in the twenty-first century? Let's approach this from a couple of angles. First, how important demographically were the offspring of the Ulster immigration? Given the fickle nature of surnames and the paucity of information contained in early US census records, there is no foolproof method of gathering accurate statistics on the ethnic origins of early Ozarks settlers. My own extensive research in Ozarks history suggests that it is likely that Ozarks settlers claimed Ulster ancestry just as often as they traced their bloodlines to any other single ethnic line, and in some areas it is likely that the descendants of the Scots-Irish even made up a majority of settlers. But any claim to an overwhelming dominance of this one ethnic strain in the Ozarks fails to account for the overlooked ethnic and even racial diversity of the region. Using a political analogy, it may be reasonable to suggest that the descendants of the Scots-Irish constituted a plurality among the various ethnic strains of the Ozarks and perhaps even a slim majority in some areas but certainly not a veto-proof one.

Old Lawrence County provides a good example. The French had been on the right bank of the Mississippi for more than half a century by the time Davidsonville was established, and by the early 1800s the Black River settlement was simply the farthest extension of a French settlement strand that had grown from Ste. Genevieve, Cape Girardeau, and New Madrid to Potosi and St. Michael. By the time Davidsonville really started hopping— as much as it ever hopped—the western part of Lawrence County had begun to be populated by Native Americans. In 1817 the US government signed a treaty with a portion of the Cherokee, granting an ill-defined segment of land between the Arkansas and White Rivers to the Cherokee and whomever else they saw fit to invite onto it. By the early 1820s, several thousand Shawnees, Delawares, Miamis, and other displaced natives lived along the White and its tributaries. Others resided up the Current River in Missouri, on the Meramec, and in the Springfield, Missouri, area.

The Indians would eventually be pressured out of the region—leaving a few stragglers and intermarriages with whites behind—and the French ultimately left but a faint footprint in this part of the region. But our Germans Shaver, Mock, and Plott were representatives of a more substantial and often hidden migration stream into the Ozarks. The antebellum German immigrants of the 1830s through 1850s—those who came directly from Europe—have received almost all the attention of historians and other scholars who have studied trans-Mississippi history and culture, but a significant number of settlers of German descent made their way to the region before Gottfried Duden and other German immigration boosters ever penned glowing words about Missouri. Jacob Shaver, Matthias Mock, and Daniel Plott were descended from eighteenth-century German immigrants to America—a group to which historians refer collectively as the Palatines. The story of the Palatines in many ways corresponds with that of the Scots-Irish. Motivated primarily by economic concerns but occasionally by political and religious ones, tens of thousands of German-speakers from the Rhine Valley region immigrated to America, usually Philadelphia or the greater Delaware Bay area, in the decades preceding the American Revolution. While many if not most of these immigrants remained in Pennsylvania, thousands also shared the path of the Scots-Irish, filtering into the Shenandoah Valley and into the Carolina Piedmont. When the Ozarks began to be settled by westward migration in the early 1800s, most of the Palatine descendants were first- or second-generation American-born. Some had likely lost German as their first language, and many had Anglicized their names.[12]

The Shavers of early Lawrence and Randolph provide an illustration. Jacob Shaver's paternal great grandparents and maternal grandparents were German immigrants—the Shaeffer family and the Schwarzwalder family. At some point in the eighteenth century, both families anglicized their surnames—to Shaver and Blackwelder. The Schaeffers/Shavers made their way from New York to Pennsylvania to eastern North Carolina to the Carolina Piedmont and to the Cumberland Plateau region of Tennessee before their move to the edge of the Ozarks in Lawrence County, Missouri Territory, basically a move per generation. And they certainly weren't the first nor the last Palatine Germans to settle in the region. The earliest families of the so-called Whitewater Dutch colony began arriving in southeastern Missouri in 1799, and the group's most prominent settler, George Frederick Bollinger, would bequeath his names to a mill, a ferry, a county, and to a town, Fredericktown. Most of the other Whitewater Dutch families sported Anglicized names, so that the Freimanns became Freemans, the Schnells became Snells, the Limbachs became Limbaughs and so on. Farther into the Ozarks interior, the Wolf family were early and influential settlers in the White River Valley, John C. Luttig of Poke Bayou was appointed one of Lawrence County's first justices of the peace, the Stahls became Steels and lent their anglicized name to the town of Steelville, and the Fulbrights (who left their European fatherland as the Volbrechts) were among the earliest and most influential settlers of

Springfield, Lebanon, and other southwestern Missouri communities. These early Germans and the thousands of others who came to the Ozarks remain to this day mostly unnoticed in our regional histories—at least when it comes to the issue of their ethnicity. In contrast to the post-1830 German immigrants, the Palatines who came to America before the Revolution seem to have blended more quickly and effortlessly into the fabric of the young nation. Their migrations predated the great age of European nationalism and ethnic pride churned by the Romantic Era, and their early days in the colonies and new nation coincided with a spirit of nationalism and inclusion generated by the Revolution.[13]

We could devote an entire book to all the Ozarks settlers who weren't Scots-Irish, but obviously there were many who were. The Hardins of old Lawrence County probably fit the bill, as do the McGarrahs, the Beans, the Daltons, the Murphys, and many other early settlers in the eastern Ozarks. But how much of their Scots-Irishness did they bring with them? If the Germans had undergone a process of assimilation and acculturation in the decades before arriving in the Ozarks, what of the Scots-Irish? James Leyburn, whose 1962 book on the group in America helped stir such intense interest in the Scots-Irish, suggested that ethnic distinctions largely melted away west of the Appalachian mountains. More recently, in his 2003 book on the upland South, cultural geographer Terry G. Jordan-Bychkov argues that "any notion of European ethnicity surviving into the . . . Middle Tennessee hearth of the Upland South is nonsense." Instead, he stresses, the common demands of life in the mountains and hills and the mix of ethnic and racial backgrounds molded "the constituent groups into a single, distinct new population and culture," an upland South culture.[14] Historian Patrick Griffin also dismisses the notion of ethnic survival, even beyond the Revolution. "In many ways, the revolutionary frontier brought an end to the 'Irish' story. . . . Ethnicity as a meaningful marker had little purchase. . . . Over the course of the nineteenth century, the descendants of those whose ethnicity was melted down in the revolutionary crucible would discover their Scots-Irishness. . . . Mythically, Scots-Irishness would be associated with the frontier. And as the frontier was associated with 'American' traits, Scots-Irishness could merge with American-ness. It became the anti-ethnic ethnic identity."[15] So ethnic distinctions and identities were at least severely curtailed by the time these upland southerners found their way to the Ozarks.

This was almost certainly the case with the vast majority of immigrants to the Ozarks from the upland South, especially those who crossed the Mississippi after 1815. By this time most of the "Scots-Irish" were American-born, many of them second generation so, and it would stand to reason that their descendants in the later, heavier migratory streams of the 1830s through the 1850s retained even weaker ethnic proclivities and consciousness. Yet the notion of an ethnically conscious community of Scots-Irish settlers in the early Ozarks may not be altogether nonsensical. The best and quite likely only documented example of a conscious Scots-Irish community in the Ozarks occurred in the very earliest days of Anglo-American settlement in southeastern Missouri, specifically in the Bellevue Valley south of Potosi. In the first two decades of the nineteenth century the rolling lands of the Bellevue attracted dozens of families from the Holston River valley of East Tennessee and the upper Catawba Valley of the North Carolina Piedmont, almost all of them of Protestant Irish descent. Though they could appear volatile and belligerent—as they did to a wealthy Frenchman threatening to lay claim to their lands—the community they crafted in their fertile basin scarcely resembled the marginal culture most often associated with the Scots-Irish. Instead, observes historian Robert Flanders, the Bellevue Valley became a "fount of nineteenth-century American culture." The settlers of Bellevue evinced "an admirable stirring, a quality of decency and taste, civility and discipline" absent from popular depictions of the Scots-Irish and the Ozarks. "Organized religion, education, village life, and other incipient middle class goals" occupied the attentions of the Bellevue farmers and artisans, producing the first organized Presbyterian church in the Missouri Territory and the first agriculture-based village in the Ozarks. Caledonia—its name, the Latin term for *Scotland*, an homage to a remembered if never seen homeland— was platted in 1818 on Goose Creek by merchant Alexander Craighead, an educated descendant of a long line of Presbyterian ministers. Featuring Fergus Sloan's blacksmith shop and Joshua Morrison's distillery, the prosperous little town eventually hosted a respected academy and Missouri's oldest surviving Masonic lodge.[16]

Nevertheless, Caledonia and the Bellevue Valley Scots-Irish constitute the exception that proves the rule. The ethnic proclivities of the vast majority of settlers in the pre–Civil War Ozarks—especially those of the largest waves of immigration between the 1830s and 1850s—were largely subsumed under the Americanizing forces of the frontier and the West. Conscious Scots-Irishness was indeed extremely rare in the Ozarks. But is it possible that a Scots-Irish culture persisted even as any ethnic identity waned? Does a group have to be ethnically conscious to maintain ethnic culture? Jordan-Bychkov for one dismisses the notion of the "'subconscious persistence'" of Scots-Irish identity. He doesn't, however, deny that the Scots-Irish played an important role in the shaping of the culture of the upland South. Gerlach, by contrast, suggests that in spite of the lack of a strong ethnic identification a recognizable Scots-Irish culture persisted among Ulster descendants. "Even when the overt behavioral manifestations attributable to the original ethnic group are lacking, however, an ethnic *culture* is often present." As one study of ethnicity posited forty years ago, cultural traits passed from generation to generation through families and in communities are "often so deeply imbedded in the subconscious fiber of individuals that they are unaware of their existence." "A submerged culture pattern is not lost," noted anthropologist Conrad M. Arensberg, "nor is it by reason of submergence any the less capable of further growth."[17]

Cultural transmission certainly played a role in the creation of the backwoods, southern culture of the people who dominated the first sixty-plus years of Anglo-American settlement in the Ozarks, and the Scots-Irish may have been the most significant ethnicity in that cultural cauldron. But, as we've seen, there were several other ethnicities contributing to the concoction, not to mention the matter of environmental adaptation. The Scots-Irish may have been culturally preadapted to thrive in the open-country neighborhoods of the southern frontier, but so too were the German Palatines, other peoples from Celtic Britain, and even Scandinavians. (Though of limited numerical consequence, the seventeenth-century colony of New Sweden contributed to the creation of the archetypal log house and likely bequeathed to the Ozarks the early-arriving Yocums, one of the region's most colorful backwoods families.) Distilling the white population of the early Ozarks into the folk category of the Scots-Irish is problematic and overly simplistic at best. Using the same ethnic term to encapsulate a supposed folk culture in the twenty-first century—as do popular books by James Webb and J. D. Vance—is simply irresponsible and misleading.[18]

One of the problems with the Scots-Irish thesis is the tendency of its purveyors to essentialize ethnic culture into a core list of sensational characteristics, most often in service to a broader thesis or political stance. For Webb, the Scots-Irish and their descendants are fiercely independent and inveterate fighters, bearers of a centuries-old warrior ethic. For Vance, the Scots-Irish are backwoods contrarians, scrappy, self-destructive, in-your-face hillbillies best exemplified by the author's cussing granny. But popularizers might be forgiven for pedaling one-dimensional portraits in the interest of driving home a point. Unfortunately, scholars have often indulged in the same sort of essentialistic description, creating the composite portrait of a consciously isolated dweller on the fringes of society—the moonshiner, the herder, the dangerous rebel. On occasion scholars have abandoned any semblance of objectivity in favor of blatant stereotyping. "A chronology of [Scots-Irish] economies in the Ozarks begins with market hunting," observed geographer Russel Gerlach, "followed in rough order by crop farming, ranching, mining, lumbering, market gardening, public assistance, moonshining, tourist bilking, and finally, marijuana growing." Even in instances in which scholars have recognized ambition and progress among the Scots-Irish or the Ozarkers, the group's and the region's overwhelming reputations to the contrary have molded interpretation. In his study of the Bellevue Valley settlement—with its churches and schools and market agriculture—Robert Flanders insisted that the Caledonians and their neighbors were exceptional within the world of their people as community-oriented, striving "high Scotch-Irish" achievers.[19]

Recent scholarship on the Ulster migration and its offspring indicates that the Bellevue Valley settlement was likely not that unusual. The town-builders and educators point instead to the diversity among the immigrants from Northern Ireland. As historian Warren Hofstra has recognized, "nowhere did the Scots-Irish live in cultural isolation, nurturing an essentialist and warlike culture based on individualism and an anti-elitist, working-class culture." They participated in the broader Atlantic world around them, and many even established orderly communities that stressed participation in the market economy and a desire for education. The Presbyterians were, after all, the great academy- and college-builders of the nineteenth century. "Never fixed and static," observes Hofstra, "the world of the Scots-Irish was ever open and responsive to the main tendencies of its times."[20] Their world was, in other words, part and parcel of the American experience, and no reductionist listing of characteristics could adequately encapsulate a broad range of responses to cultural diffusion and adaptation.

As we are prone to do, scholars of the past generation have made the study of the Scots-Irish something of a tangled mess. But we seem to be moving in the right direction, away from the romanticized notion of the independent, isolated, violent Scots-Irish and toward a more balanced portrait of a complex migration of tens of thousands of individuals and families. The Scots-Irish undoubtedly exercised an impact on the history and culture of the Ozarks, but they did so indirectly and primarily through their contributions to the development of an American upland South culture, not through the long-term maintenance of ethnic identity and solidarity or even through an overwhelming numerical dominance of settlement in the region. Anyone looking to explain an alleged exceptional history and culture in the Ozarks will have to do better than chalk it up to a mass of proto-hillbillies called the Scots-Irish.

CHAPTER EIGHT

Revisiting Race Relations in the Upland South

LaCROSSE, ARKANSAS

FORMER AUBURN UNIVERSITY professor Wayne Flynt has been my mentor for thirty years—and few scholars love a good story more than he does. Anyone who has known Wayne for very long can testify to that. Maybe it's the Baptist preacher in him. Maybe it's the southerner in him. Having read too many lifeless histories, I'm convinced it's not the historian in him. Whatever the reason, Wayne appreciates a good tale, be it fable, anecdote, parable, or just plain old yarn. His appreciation for the story has served him well over a long career, whether in the classroom, on the social crusader's trail, or at the tip of a busy pen. In a scholarly path that has been recognized most often for its social history, Wayne's dedication to telling stories—to keeping it personal, to keeping the humanity in history—has consistently infused his narratives with life and vitality.

I feel honored to have played a role in one of Wayne's stories for decades now. It's the story of how Wayne and I came to meet, of how a boy from the Ozarks found his way to Auburn, a place the boy only knew as Bo Jackson's university and a place that he had always thought was in Georgia, not Alabama. Wayne loves this story. He's told it each time he's had the opportunity to introduce me as a speaker or to slide me into a conversation with old friends. And in that true southern storytelling tradition—in which doctoring a few of the particulars is not so much changing the story as it is making it better—Wayne tells a slightly different version each time. Here's one version.

This essay was originally published in Gordon E. Harvey, Richard D. Starnes, and Glenn Feldman, eds., *History & Hope in the Heart of Dixie: Scholarship, Activism, and Wayne Flynt in the Modern South* (Tuscaloosa: University of Alabama Press, 2006). It appears here with minor revisions.

As a college junior in the spring of 1991, I had the good fortune to take a course on race and the civil rights movement under Elizabeth "Betsy" Jacoway, who was teaching on a one-year sabbatical replacement at Arkansas (now Lyon) College, a little Presbyterian, liberal arts school in the foothills of the Ozarks. As a requirement for the course, I completed a research paper, a project in which Betsy required her students to use both secondary and primary sources and one in which I had taken the interpretations of a few southern historians to task. One of these historians was J. Wayne Flynt, whose *Dixie's Forgotten People: The South's Poor Whites* just happened to be on the shelves in our small library.[1] Although I had a big time with the project, I thought little about the paper until late that summer when I got a package in the mail from Betsy—still Dr. Jacoway to me at the time. Unbeknownst to me, Betsy, undoubtedly amused by her student's temerity in hunting large prey, had given a copy of my paper to Wayne at a conference. (This is the point at which Wayne's story usually takes up.)

The paper itself dealt with race relations in a single Ozarks community, a community that I had used as a model for race relations in the highland South in general. The seemingly tranquil race relations found in this particular community had led me to take aim at Wayne, Numan V. Bartley, and any other historian I could fish out of the slim stacks at the Arkansas College library who seemed to view southern white people as a monolithic bunch, at least when it came to attitudes toward Black people. (Or perhaps my desire to find the antithesis to the common white-Black southern story had led me to this particular community—but I'll come back to this later.) Probably more amused than impressed, Wayne read the little paper and on the title page scrawled an encouraging note urging me to explore works on Appalachia for comparison, to continue working on the subject, and to consider applying to Auburn for graduate school.

I did a better job of following Wayne's last suggestion than his first two and, having been accepted to graduate school, made my first trip to see Auburn and to meet Wayne Flynt in the summer of 1992. He didn't remember my name, but upon mention of the belligerent paper and Betsy Jacoway the memories of the previous summer's preliminary tête-à-tête with the kid from Arkansas came flooding back. My unannounced drop-in during a busy finals week must have made Wayne's day. But he was polite and engaging to this youngster—ever the southern gentleman, as Betsy had promised.

Almost a decade and a half elapsed before I revisited that paper and its topic, when asked to contribute an essay for a Festschrift honoring the retiring Wayne Flynt. The question of whether or not Black-white interaction differed substantially—or if white oppression of Black people occurred at differing levels of thoroughness and harshness—in the southern highlands and lowlands had until recently gone almost completely unconsidered. Only in the final years of the twentieth century did a handful of prominent historians begin to shed considerable light on race relations in Appalachia. Yet in the Ozarks the subject remained unaddressed. Though this brief essay does not remedy that situation, I do hope to accomplish a couple of things: to reconsider my earlier conclusions on race relations in the highland South in general and in the rural Ozarks in particular by taking into consideration other works in southern history and subsequent scholarship focusing on the Ozarks and to analyze the process of historical interpretation by reconsidering my own motives underlying those earlier conclusions.

Highland Exceptionalism:
The Temptation of an Alternative Narrative

The motivation for writing the little essay that ultimately brought me to Auburn was a conviction that white residents of the upland South were too often lumped together with lowland whites when it came to the issues of race relations and attitudes toward race. (As a white native of the Ozarks, my predisposition to avoid *southern lumping* was perhaps a part of my cultural heritage.) Like many a young, white idealistic student from the upland South, I was reasonably positive that race relations in the hills and mountains had been more civil and involved less violence and severe oppression than had race relations in the lowland South. This notion is a product, I believe, both of the age-old sectional debate and struggle within the South and decades of coming to terms with a heritage that includes slavery, defeat, and racism, and the guilt—both self- and super-imposed—that comes with that heritage.

In the back of our minds, white upland southerners are proud that there were fewer slave owners and more anti-secessionists in the highlands, that parts of East Tennessee were overrun by Unionists, that residents of portions of Appalachia and the Ozarks were among the most divided in their Civil War–era loyalties. It was the plantation owners—those fat-cat slave owners in the lowlands—who dragged the South into the war. It was the denizens of the Deep South, we tell ourselves, who were to blame. Likewise, it stands to reason—through an admittedly twisted interpretation—that the upland New South, the place where one was most likely to find scalawag Republicans and less likely to find large numbers of freedmen, would somehow have been for Black people a less dangerous and oppressive place, an eminently more livable place, than would have the lowland New South. And if it were true, would this not be a soothing psychological balm for the white upland southerner? Not only were upland southerners not responsible for the war that still haunts the nation, but hill folks treated their Black neighbors better than white people did in the lowland South.

That last statement, which still carries weight within the popular if not scholarly imagination of the upland South, has roots that extend at least as far back as the middle of the nineteenth century. Traveling in the Southeast in the 1850s, Frederick Law Olmsted observed that in the mountains "the direct moral evils of slavery . . . are less—even less proportionately to the number of slaves." Highland slaves' "habits more resemble those of ordinary free laborers," he felt, "and both in soul and intellect they are more elevated."[2]

The most important literary foundations for the perception that race relations were more benign in the highlands focused not on the treatment of Black people by their white neighbors, however, but on the supposed absence of Black people in the region. In the late nineteenth and early twentieth centuries—the era of the "discovery" of Appalachia by missionaries, local color writers, and other newcomers—a number of writers "enshrined the stereotype of nearly all-white, antislavery Appalachia." Historians James C. Klotter and Nina Silber have both argued that it was the highland South's supposed lack of Black residents that appealed to northern philanthropists, missionaries, and social workers, which in turn helped foster the "pervasive mythology" of the highlanders' "unadulterated Unionism, pure and upstanding patriotism, and undiluted racial purity." In his influential *The Southern Highlander and His Homeland*, John C. Campbell informed his mostly northern audience that "large sections of the highland South were in sympathy with the North on the Negro question." Many observers of the era shared Campbell's view that the southern mountain people had little if anything to do with slavery, implying a racial innocence on the part of mountain whites. The jump from the mountaineer's supposed innocence on the slavery question to his modern views on race proved an easy one for many of these observers. According to historian Silber, this leap helped pave the way for the widely held assumption that highlanders "lacked the racial anxiety that supposedly preoccupied the poor white people of the lowlands."[3]

This ingrained notion has occasionally made its way into scholarship, but most often in the form of a blanket statement or offhand comment— again, reinforcing the idea that the Black experience in the upland South *should* have been different, so it probably was. Ironically, the first scholar to promulgate this popular notion was pioneering African American historian, and Appalachian native, Carter G. Woodson. In an essay published in the second issue of the *Journal of Negro History* in 1916, Woodson argued that southern mountaineers "have always differed from the dwellers in the district near the sea not only in their attitude toward slavery but in the policy they have followed in dealing with the Blacks since the Civil War." "In Appalachian America the races still maintain a sort of social contact," he continued. "White and Black men work side by side, visit each other in their homes, and often attend the same church to listen with delight to the Word spoken by either a colored or white preacher." Few scholars followed up on Woodson's observations until the latter part of the twentieth century. Appalachian scholar, and native, Loyal Jones observed that "Appalachians have not been saddled with the same prejudices about black people that people of the deep South have." Historian Willard B. Gatewood Jr., in a study of letters written by Black Arkansans to northern newspapers in the 1890s, agreed that there existed a clear sectional divide in terms of the Black experience in the South. "While the dispatches from Arkansas indicated an increase in Jim Crowism, they also suggest that the degree of discrimination varied from one locality to another in the state. Those from communities in northwestern Arkansas [the Ozarks], where the black population was relatively small, left little doubt that the color line there, especially in politics, was less rigidly drawn than in the black belt of the eastern counties." More recently, in an examination of Black and white Republicans in the post–Civil War highland South, historian Gordon B. McKinney noted a "relative lack of racial hostility between mountain whites and blacks," a condition explained in part by the region's small Black population.[4]

But the equation of a small Black population with a comparative degree of racial harmony has not always appeared so self-evident to scholars and observers of the South. W. J. Cash provides a rare example of "those who have posited that the lack of Black contact by many white mountaineers resulted in an even more intense hostility toward Blacks than that felt by whites in areas with more substantial Black populations." Employing an interpretation of Appalachian people that would have made Arnold J. Toynbee proud, Cash claimed that the mountaineer's depravity poisoned his outlook on race. The mountaineer, according to Cash, "had acquired a hatred and contempt for the Negro even more virulent than that of the common white of the lowlands; a dislike so rabid that it was worth a Black man's life to venture into many mountain sections."[5] More often scholars dealing with the South, whether during the Jim Crow era or the civil rights movement, have simply ignored potential intraregional differences or have glossed over the potential for differences, an understandable overgeneralization given the centrality of race in many scholars' definition of southern distinctiveness. As V. O. Key Jr. noted when discussing the prominence of the Black Belt in southern politics, "It is in this relatively small part of the South that attitudes thought to be universal in the South occur with highest intensity."[6]

A Case Study

Convinced that the "attitudes thought to be universal in the South" were not in fact universal and dissatisfied with the cursory way in which intraregional differences were either written off by some scholars or taken for granted by others, I decided those years ago to remedy the situation in the best way a naive student (and many a naive historian) knows how, a case study of a particular community—a case study that I would then proceed to use as a springboard to my own bloated overgeneralization. The community I chose for this case study was one with which I had a fair degree of familiarity. LaCrosse, pronounced *LAY-cross* in good southern fashion and located less than ten miles from my home in Izard County, Arkansas, was by the early 1990s a shell of a little community. Once a bustling crossroads farming village and home to a late nineteenth-century academy, LaCrosse had become a backwater community after being bypassed by the state-constructed highway in the 1920s. The old store and post office, which I drove by on my way to and from college, closed in the 1980s, and only a few scattered houses remained. By the time of my childhood, the most locally significant thing about LaCrosse was that it had been home to the last Black community in Izard County, and one of the last rural Black communities in the Ozarks. The final remaining member of LaCrosse's Black community, an older man who worked at the filling station in the little town of Franklin, died just a few weeks after I finished my project in 1991, but the community had been practically abandoned for thirty years.

Like many places in the eastern Ozarks, LaCrosse was a cotton-raising community from the post–Civil War years until the middle of the twentieth century. But this was not the reason for the small Black community there. There were plenty of other cotton-raising communities in the region that had no Black people at all. The core of the LaCrosse African American community traced its roots to the enslaved people brought into the area in the 1840s and 1850s by a handful of white families. At the center of the small slaveholding group in LaCrosse were three Watkins brothers from middle Tennessee who brought five bondspeople with them when they settled in the area in 1845. Over the next decade and a half, they would be joined by a number of relatives and acquaintances from middle Tennessee, some of whom also brought enslaved laborers to LaCrosse. By the outbreak of the Civil War, the eighty-five slave owners in Izard County owned just over three hundred humans, but the Watkinses and their kin and neighbors were among the county's largest slaveholders.[7]

After the war these freedmen and freedwomen—many of them bearing the names of their former owners—settled in an area a mile or so east of the village proper, likely on land owned, or once owned, by the Watkinses. Although the absence of county records for the two decades following the Civil War prevents a thorough examination of the developments between former masters and the formerly enslaved, community oral tradition has it that the Watkinses and other LaCrosse slave owners deeded parcels of land to their former enslaved families.[8] Whether accomplished by gift, purchase, or homestead, by the 1880 agricultural census at least three Black families at LaCrosse owned land (ranging from Joseph Watkins's 81 acres to Baalam Watkins's 214 acres) as did a few families in a smaller Black community a couple of miles away in neighboring Franklin township. By 1880 the African American community at LaCrosse contained a dozen households and 76 residents, and the nearby village of LaCrosse was home to an additional eleven Blacks or "mulattoes" who worked as servants or laborers for white families. Although tiny by the standards of most of the South at the time, in Izard County, which was home to only 220 African Americans in 1880, the LaCrosse settlement was significant and constituted the largest concentration of Black people in the entire hill country region above Batesville. When combined with the 30 African Americans in nearby Franklin township, this extended settlement accounted for more than half the Blacks living in Izard County. The existence of Black land ownership (which by 1909 had extended to at least nine LaCrosse-area farmers with a median holding of 120 acres), the concentration of a comparatively large number of Black people in one area, and the availability of seasonal labor on relatively prosperous, white-owned farms in the vicinity all likely contributed to the stability of the LaCrosse Black community well into the twentieth century, even as Black families gradually abandoned other parts of the county and region. By 1930, when the Black population of most Ozark counties had dwindled to minute levels, Izard County still contained 175 African Americans (including 8 farm owners), and the largest concentration (67) of these lived in LaCrosse.[9]

Another factor that helped account for the stability of the LaCrosse community was the apparent absence of racial violence or brutal intimidation in the community. Again, the scarcity of records prevents any thorough analysis of the county's late nineteenth-century history. Nevertheless, we can once again turn to the oral tradition and history of the community, and none of the former LaCrosse residents (Black and white) interviewed in 1991 or in subsequent years recalled having witnessed, experienced, or heard of any kind of race-related violence or intimidation in the LaCrosse area. Of course, the mere absence of violence did not in and of itself signal some sort of racial utopia in which Black folks and white folks lived happily side-by-side. But it was LaCrosse's and Izard County's ability to avoid the violence and brutality so common throughout the South that had first lead me to champion the idea of a more tolerant and less oppressive highland South.

The recollections and oral traditions of the Black former LaCrosse residents were consistent in painting a picture of relative racial harmony in their old community. Estelle Canada Rucker, who grew up in the community in the 1920s and '30s, recalled, "I don't ever remember any trouble. . . . We [Blacks and whites] got along together well." Lillie Mae Darty Watkins, another former LaCrosse resident and only a couple years older than Rucker, agreed. "We got along good in Izard County. They [whites] was real good to us." The situation seems to have altered little by the middle of the twentieth century, for according to Ray Kennard, who came of age in Izard County only after World War II, "Up there wasn't no problem. They [whites] were good up there. . . . As far as racial disturbances, we never had any up there."[10]

Although the majority of LaCrosse's Black residents lived in a rather secluded and tight-knit community, there appears to have been none of the suspicion, belligerence, and cultural and physical isolation that characterized the Kentucky highland community of Coe Ridge. Despite their similar populations and geographical settings and the fact that both

Lewis and Augusta Canada and ricked stave bolts, LaCrosse, Arkansas, date unknown. *Courtesy of Estelle Rucker Collection, Old Independence Regional Museum, Batesville, Arkansas.*

Black communities were practically abandoned by the end of the 1950s, Coe Ridge and LaCrosse shared little in common. In his groundbreaking study of the Kentucky foothills settlement, William Lynwood Montell found a community of Black outcasts and misfits who "lived in virtual isolation from the surrounding [white] communities." By comparison, LaCrosse was a community bustling with interracial activity. "We growed up together. We worked together, chopped cotton together. They came to our church. We went to their picnics. We lived together," recalled Estelle Canada Rucker. Thinking back on her life in LaCrosse, Lillie Mae Darty Watkins said, "See, they'd come to our church and sing, and we'd go to their church and sing. . . . We mixed. That's one thing that I can truly say . . . that the Blacks and the whites did mix up there."[11]

Assumptions

My undergraduate attempt to explain the rather benign nature of race relations in LaCrosse and Izard County during the Jim Crow era rested on two factors at work in the community and region, factors frequently identified with interracial settlements in the highland South. In my original essay, I suggested that the small number of African Americans at

LaCrosse and in other highland areas posed no physical or psychological threat to the majority white population and that, therefore, the white residents in these areas had little need for the violent social-control tactics found in places with larger concentrations of Black people. I also claimed that widespread poverty—among both Blacks and whites—and the Ozark region's rather egalitarian economic and social system instilled a sort of mutual appreciation for the hardships of survival in the hill country.

These reasons may, in fact, have played a part in the absence of racial strife in LaCrosse. Nevertheless, they comprise an insufficient foundation for a defense of southern highland race relations in general. The common interests and struggles of impoverished Black and white folks did on occasion trump southern society's racist and separatist mores. How often this happened in the upland South is still unclear. In his study of Black residents of the Arkansas Ozarks, sociologist Gordon D. Morgan noted that "poverty was common to both groups [Blacks and whites] and the requirements for making a living from the eroded hill soil [were] too strenuous for energy to be dissipated in useless squabbles over racial superiority." But the logic of this statement could easily be overturned by southern racial codes. It was more often the case, perhaps, that motives of economic competition and racist pathology soured relationships between Black and white people and even sparked eruptions of violence. In a 1923 article, NAACP field secretary and Arkansas native William Pickens leveled condemnation on the racism of his state's poor white residents, especially those of the hill country, who used what little power they possessed to "keep down the rising free Negro." Being unable to compete with the large, aristocratic landowners of the South, "nothing was left for" these poor whites, he observed, "but to hunt, fish, trap, engage in the illicit manufacture of spirits, and 'hate niggers.'" Scholars as well have found the roots of racism in white poverty. Wayne Flynt suggests that "because they possessed few of the tools necessary to improve their lives," poor whites "rested at the bottom of the white social structure and were most threatened by upward black mobility."[12]

White LaCrosse resident P. O. Wren Jr. observed that "there wasn't much difference in families [Black or white]. They was all so poor." But the social and economic system in LaCrosse and Izard County was not that simple. Within the white community, there were distinctions between and among farm families: sharecroppers and tenant farmers, small landowning farmers, and more prosperous, large landowning families. It was the latter group that Wren's family belonged to, after all. Even such a small

Black population as LaCrosse's also reflected subtle distinctions—between landowners and tenants and even among landowners. Most Black land-holding families owned something between 40 and 120 acres of land, but a few owned farms as big as or bigger than the majority of white-owned farms in the area. Estelle Canada Rucker, whose family owned more than 300 acres, found it amusing that children of a Black tenant farmer called her and her siblings "rich kids."[13]

LaCrosse was not a preindustrial highland community of subsistence farmers; it was not a community devoid of class and economic divisions. Since at least the early post–Civil War era, LaCrosse and most of Izard County had been a part of the South's cotton belt—on the northwestern periphery of that belt, to be sure, but in it nonetheless. The largest land-owners and most successful farmers relied on the sale of cotton as their primary source of income, and a few were prosperous enough to rent parcels of land to tenant farmers and to hire African American cooks or domestics. In this respect the community was not unlike the villages and rural hamlets of the lowland South. Given this comparison to the more typical South, it is likely that paternalism played a more important role than poverty in the stability and relative racial harmony of LaCrosse and surrounding Izard County. The Watkinses and allied families who had first given or sold land to freedmen and who developed the post–Civil War cotton economy remained as prominent residents of LaCrosse well into the twentieth century. These relatively prosperous white families, as well as others who joined them as significant landowners in the subsequent decades, relied on the Black community for tenant farming, for domestic help, and for a variety of day-labor services, most important of which was cotton-picking at harvest time. Black families, whether landowners or not, relied on the wages from domestic labor and seasonal activities such as the cotton harvest. Although the Black families of LaCrosse interacted with the area's poor white families on a daily basis, it was their economic rela-tionship with the community's most socially and economically prominent families that provided them the resources to scratch out a living in the hill country. This relationship may also have secured the paternalistic over-sight that could be a requisite for racial harmony in the Jim Crow South.

So, the idea that Black folks and white folks—bound together by a cul-ture of poverty and backbreaking toil—would somehow bridge the divide of race maintains its elusive and idealistic appeal but seems to promise little of substance when trying to explain the absence of racial strife in a place like LaCrosse, Arkansas. The second reason that I had originally posited

Gathering at LaCrosse, Arkansas, possibly at the Sweet Home Baptist Church,
date unknown. *Courtesy of Stella Kennard Collection, Old Independence
Regional Museum, Batesville, Arkansas.*

to explain LaCrosse's experience—the small concentration of Black residents relative to the white population—would seem at first glance to hold more promise, however. In the Arkansas Ozarks, according to sociologist Gordon D. Morgan, African Americans were "mainly ignored or forgotten by the larger society." Edward Cabbell noted a similar "black invisibility" in Appalachia. And, as observed earlier, historian Willard B. Gatewood Jr. ascribed the "less rigidly drawn" color line in northwestern Arkansas during the 1890s to the relatively small Black population.[14]

Despite a certain logic embedded in the theory that a relatively insignificant, and thus less threatening, Black population would somehow tend to alleviate racial violence, scholarship over the past three decades suggests that not only did small Black populations not lessen the likelihood of racial violence but that the very minuteness, and thus vulnerability, of Black communities in the upland South might actually have served as a provocation to more extreme episodes of violence. In his study of lynching in Georgia and Virginia, W. Fitzhugh Brundage found high rates of race-related violence in highland areas where "seemingly the preconditions for racial violence should have been absent." The small and vulnerable Black population of Appalachian Georgia posed little threat to whites, but "during the late 1880s and early 1890s, racial violence in northern Georgia reached levels that equaled those elsewhere in the state." And "nowhere in Virginia was the incidence of mob violence more concentrated, both in place and time, than in the southwestern corner of the state." According to Brundage, social and economic forces were as much to blame for this racial violence as was racial fear. These highland lynchings, he argued, "reflected the desperation of whites to define the status of blacks in a region where blacks were still uncommon and furious social and economic change was taking place."[15]

Recent scholarship on racial violence in the Ozarks tends to support Brundage's findings. The years surrounding the year 1900 appear to have been especially violent ones for some Black communities in the hills. Jacqueline Froelich and David Zimmermann documented two instances of white mob violence toward the small Black community in Harrison, Arkansas, in the first decade of the twentieth century. Brundage found social control to be the goal of most violent acts, but in Harrison the violence was "used to completely destroy a community." In her 2010 book *White Man's Heaven: The Lynching and Expulsion of Blacks in the Southern Ozarks, 1894–1909*, Kimberly Harper chronicles episodes of race-related violence in no fewer than four southwestern Missouri towns between 1894 and 1906. Beginning with the lynching of a Black laborer who had allegedly murdered a white railroad worker in Monett and concluding with a gruesome triple lynching in Springfield spurred by accusations of sexual assault on a white woman (accusations later declared lies by a grand jury), racial violence in the Missouri Ozarks resulted in the destruction and disappearance of the Black community in Pierce City and motivated many other African Americans to flee the Ozarks permanently. Sociologist James Loewen has also analyzed the flurry of racial violence in the Ozarks and has judged the exodus of Black people from the area significant enough to label the Ozarks a "sundown town" region—an area that was and is all white by design. More recently, scholars such as Guy Lancaster have continued to dig into the often-hidden pasts of small towns and rural communities in the Ozarks and elsewhere, finding evidence of long forgotten racial cleansings that left only the faintest imprint on the evidentiary record.[16]

All of this suggests that an "unthreatening" small Black community would not in and of itself allay the fears and passions that sparked episodes of racial violence, and that the upland South, despite its sparse Black population, was as prone to violence—and in some cases more so—than the lowland South. Does this recent scholarship render little LaCrosse an anomaly, instead of the model for peaceful coexistence that I had once labeled the community? If so, to what then do we attribute the relative harmony between Blacks and whites in LaCrosse and in Izard County, Arkansas?

From the perspective of the Ozarks—given the recent findings of Froelich and Zimmermann, Patrick Huber, Loewen, and Harper—it would appear at first glance that the experiences of the races in LaCrosse were notable for their lack of violent incidence. The research on the highland South in general is too spotty and incomplete to venture any blanket statements, but Brundage's findings suggest that one might have reasonably expected to uncover evidence of racial violence in LaCrosse and Izard County. It is obviously too much of a leap, however, to argue that the experience of Black folks and white folks in LaCrosse was unique for the highland South, or even that it was unusual. Even in the Ozarks, which experienced a relatively high rate of racial violence around the turn of the twentieth century, there are other examples of small Black communities living in peace amid larger white communities. The Exodusters and their descendants of the Hartville area in Wright County, Missouri, represent perhaps the region's most durable such community, while Red River and other African American settlements in Van Buren County, Arkansas, survived beyond the mid-twentieth century without apparent violence.[17] Undoubtedly, Appalachia has similar examples to offer. The scattered examples of racial violence in the highland South are more often chronicled than are the examples of peaceful coexistence—for obvious reasons. The race riots and lynchings provide real *stories*—chronologies of events complete with human drama and tragedy—that are most often absent in the histories of places like LaCrosse.

The South in the Southern Ozarks

Even if LaCrosse is not an anomaly of racial harmony, what factors accounted for the rather peaceful and fluid interaction of the Black and white people there and in other similarly uneventful places? Though the memories of former residents, Black and white, recall a significant amount of intermingling between the races—at Black church services, at picnics, in the fields, and at local stores, which African Americans entered through the front doors like their white neighbors—this day-to-day physical proximity was not uncommon in the South and did not in and of itself signify a racial utopia. In fact, the Black residents of LaCrosse and of other upland South communities were daily reminded of their separate and

Payne School and Colored Cumberland Presbyterian Church, Hartville,
Missouri, 1890. *Courtesy of the Lederer Collection, Missouri State
University Special Collections and Archives, Springfield.*

second-class status in a segregated and white-dominated society. Black
children in LaCrosse attended school in the Sweet Home Baptist Church
house, a segregated school that never went beyond the eighth grade, even
after the establishment of all-white high schools in neighboring communities in the 1920s and '30s. African American children wanting to attend
high school were forced to move to Batesville, thirty miles away, until
the establishment of a bus route in the early 1950s that transported all
Black students from LaCrosse to the segregated high school there. Only
in the 1960s did the children of the community's last Black family enroll
in the nearest white high school. LaCrosse's Black children learned that
"you didn't call [white men] by their name, . . . you called them Uncle or
Mister." They learned that "we weren't allowed to eat with [white people].
We had to sit back until [the whites] all ate and then we would come in and
eat last."[18] They learned that their ability to use the front doors at white-
owned establishments vanished at the edge of their community, that the
county seat was full of strange white folks and back doors for Black folks.
They learned that their light-skinned classmates were the offspring of a

local white landlord but that a victory on the baseball field was as serious a challenge to white manhood as was advisable.[19]

LaCrosse, then, was similar to lowland southern communities in that Blacks and whites understood the boundaries of segregated society and generally observed those boundaries. As one Black LaCrosse resident who moved away during the Depression recalled: "Blacks knew their place and whites knew theirs . . . didn't have no trouble." A white resident of LaCrosse attributed the community's segregation to "tradition." "We treated them good, but it was separate."[20] The LaCrosse area's reliance on cotton farming until the mid-twentieth century was also indicative of the lowland South, and the economic importance—to local white landowners anyway—of the small African American population likely figured into the peace and stability of the community. But two other factors might also have played key roles in sparing LaCrosse from the racial violence experienced in Harrison and other Ozark communities: the Black community's apparent observance of southern racial-sexual codes and the relative scarcity of Black newcomers to Izard County.

According to the oral history of LaCrosse, there were at least two instances in the early 1900s of Black women giving birth to and raising the children of local white fathers, and the census records for Izard County in the late nineteenth century suggest that these twentieth-century, mixed-race offspring were not isolated incidents in the community. But it appears that the racial-sexual double standard crafted by anxious white men—who, according to historian Joel Williamson, projected "upon black men extravagant sexual behavior" and "came to be obsessed by the possibility of sexual relations between black men and white women"—was upheld in LaCrosse. The oral traditions and available records contain no memories or mentions of the kinds of racial-sexual activities that could incite white riots and violence, such as sexual liaisons between Black men and white women or alleged sexual assault against white women by Black men—the one crime that most often justified racial violence in the minds of white people.[21] Again, the story here is primarily in the absence of a story.

Perhaps the key to the uneventful nature of race relations in LaCrosse and Izard County, however, was the community's relative isolation and its subsequent immunity to settlement by transient Black men. Historian Edward L. Ayers argues that lynching was most likely to occur in areas of the South with low rural population density and significant Black population growth in the late nineteenth century, a population growth that included many Black newcomers and transients by whom white folks felt threatened. "Lynchings tended to flourish where whites were surrounded by what they called 'strange niggers,' blacks with no white to vouch for them, blacks with no reputation in the neighborhood, blacks without even other blacks to aid them." Ayers continues: "Lynching seemed both more necessary and more feasible in places such as the Gulf Plain, the cotton uplands, and the mountains. In those places most blacks and whites did not know one another, much less share ties of several generations."[22]

Herein lies the primary difference between LaCrosse and the upland communities cited for racial violence in the works of Ayers, Brundage, Loewen, and Harper. The fact that LaCrosse was something of a backwater community—no railroad, no industry, nothing to generate lots of coming and going by young Black men—meant that few new African Americans ever came into the neighborhood, and most of the ones who did were from similar Black communities in north-central Arkansas and had married into a LaCrosse family. In other words, LaCrosse attracted few transients and strangers, such as the young, unemployed Black railroad workers who sparked the Harrison, Arkansas, riot of 1905 or the young, rail-hopping Black man lynched in Joplin, Missouri, for the alleged murder of a police officer.[23]

In the final estimation, it would appear that the decisive factors underlying LaCrosse's and Izard County's combination of racial harmony and relatively relaxed atmosphere in which Black and white residents comingled daily were the community's isolation-induced stability, the Black population's rigid adherence to racial-sexual mores, and the crucial economic interdependence of prominent white farmers and Black people in the area. In other words, it was the uncharacteristically lowland South flavor of social and economic life in LaCrosse and Izard County—combined with the upland South's characteristically tiny and unthreatening Black population—that seems to have created an environment in which local African Americans, while subject to the restrictions and second-class status found elsewhere in the South, felt safe and secure, at least within the confines of the broader LaCrosse community. This interpretation—that the relative harmony of LaCrosse, while not unique, is not the model for race relations in the upper South and that the community's avoidance of racial violence reflects not its difference from but rather its similarity to the lowland South—represents in some respects an ironic reversal of my original thesis, which rested on the assumption that in most ways life and historical development in the upland South had been fundamentally unlike that in the lowland South.

What implications does this turn of events have, and what, if anything, does the story of LaCrosse tell us about race relations in the highland South? For upland southerners and scholars alike who have assumed or argued that race relations were more fluid and race less of an issue in the South's highlands, the scholarship of the past three decades cannot be reassuring. In addition to the growing body of literature detailing the upland South's quite *southern* past of racial violence, historian John C. Inscoe has in recent years taken a more direct look at the issue of the historical treatment of African Americans in Appalachia and has discovered the "same prejudices and even violence that characterized the rest of the Jim Crow South." Despite "significant demographic variables in the biracial populace of the highland and lowland South," according to Inscoe, "blacks in the mountains . . . were subject to the same sorts of exploitation, abuse, and prejudice faced by blacks throughout the nineteenth-century South."[24]

It appears quite obvious that within the upland regions thus far scrutinized racial violence was as common, if not relatively more so, than in the lowland South. The topic of race relations—in some ways a separate issue from racial violence—is more slippery and as yet insufficiently addressed. The example of LaCrosse and Izard County does, however, offer one portrait of an upland South community in which Blacks and whites coexisted without any apparent violence or overt intimidation and suggests that, given the same set of circumstances, it is not unreasonable to expect other examples of relative racial harmony in the upland South. The fact that this one upland example resembled in many ways the communities of the lowland South reminds us that the upland South was in no way monolithic, that it was almost as diverse as the South itself. And that's not good news for those who would portray the southern highlands as an exceptional and fundamentally different domain, whether, in the terms of our argument, a region in which racial violence or "sundown towns" held sway or in which white folks were more humane—or at least more tolerant—of the small Black populations in their midst. It is clear that in LaCrosse the peace and harmony did not denote a community free of racism, oppression, and segregation. It is inconceivable that such a community existed anywhere in the South—or in the nation for that matter—during the era of the LaCrosse Black community's existence.

Out of LaCrosse and Back Again

Like many tiny upland Black communities, the LaCrosse African American neighborhood was abandoned in the second half of the twentieth century. The factors that effected this exodus were the same factors that revolutionized agriculture and rural life in the South. Federal cotton acreage allotments first instituted during the New Deal and streamlined after World War II gradually reduced Izard County's cash crop to insignificance by the early 1960s. The Black residents of LaCrosse and of most other places in Izard County had long been intimately tied to this small-scale cotton culture—both as farm owners and tenants and as seasonal laborers—and its demise forced them to look elsewhere for a livelihood, as it also did thousands of whites in the eastern Ozarks. Unlike the white families who supplemented their meager farming incomes with migrant agricultural labor in the 1940s and 1950s, most Black families owned no automobile and were thus forced to make the more permanent decision to stay or to leave their home for good. Almost all of them eventually left. By 1950 only forty-seven African Americans remained in Izard County, a 73 percent decline in the Black population since 1930. As usual, the landless and the day laborers were the first to leave. Between 1930 and 1950 the number of Black tenant farmers decreased from twenty-four to seven, and only one of the dozen Black sharecroppers living in the county in 1930 was still there twenty years later; the number of Black families who owned all or part of the land they farmed actually increased from eight to twelve.[25]

But the 1950s brought an unprecedented wave of outmigration by Izard County farm owners, Black and white alike, and by the end of the decade only two Black families remained in LaCrosse—an elderly couple who would live out their days as Izard County's last remaining Black family, and their son and his family who would soon move away to find a steady income and, likely, to escape the racial/cultural isolation. The last remaining member of the LaCrosse Black community, a bachelor son of this last remaining family, died more than thirty years ago.

Most of the Black LaCrosse out-migrants made their way to one of four destinations: Batesville, Arkansas (just thirty miles south of LaCrosse); Oklahoma City; Peoria, Illinois; and Beloit, Wisconsin. The scattered fragments of the community and their descendants continued holding biannual homecomings into the twenty-first century. Some descendants still own land in LaCrosse, and the oldest are returned to the community cemetery, just up the hill from the shell of a building that once was the

Sweet Home Baptist Church, for their final resting place. The memories of the former LaCrosse residents whom I interviewed are generally positive ones. Like their white contemporaries, they waxed nostalgic about life on the farm, about the innocence of childhood, about a simpler time. The mere fact that they shared these positive recollections suggests a certain degree of harmony between the races in LaCrosse and Izard County. But anecdotal recall can also block out the dull monotony of the more painful memory of segregation and second-class status. For a white college student from the hills whose grandparents once sharecropped on the same Izard County landlord's farm as a local Black family and who picked cotton alongside that Black family, the prominence of the positive memories could seem a welcomed vindication of the upland South's self-proclaimed superiority in the field of race relations. Nonetheless, if we are fortunate, the passion to vindicate becomes a passion to explain—and the apologist becomes historian.

Over the years, Wayne Flynt has helped lead more than a few apologists and others groping around the periphery of scholarship into the well-worn path of the historian. He has done so with patience and firmness and a commitment to truth and justice. And he has done so without losing his appreciation for the centrality of the *story* in history. Almost a quarter of a century ago at my dissertation defense, Wayne added to the story that began this essay when he told me that I had converted him, that he had come to accept the interpretation of my undergraduate paper that had brought the two of us together. I'm quite certain that Wayne was just being nice and that he could scarcely recall what my thesis had been those years before. My subsequent admission that I was the one who had been wrong probably rang just as hollow at the time. After reviewing the subject and taking into account subsequent scholarship, it seems more likely that I was right about being wrong. And once again, Wayne Flynt and other scholars who had for the most part avoided intraregional splitting when discussing southern race relations were, it seems, pretty close to the mark. It is too much of a stretch to present LaCrosse and Izard County, Arkansas, as a microcosm of race relations in the upland South. It is not too much to expect that a similar stifling peace was not uncommon in the hills and mountains. At the very least, it is a story of one community that escaped the violent oppression or forced removal of a small Black population, and, unfortunately, that may be as good as it got.

CHAPTER NINE

The Spruills

WHO AND WHY?

THE OLD TRUCK HAD "slick tires and a cracked windshield and rusted fenders and what looked like faded blue paint under a layer of rust. A tier had been constructed above the bed, and it was crammed with cardboard boxes and burlap bags filled with supplies. Under it, on the floor of the bed, a mattress was wedged next to the cab." Sounds a lot like the jalopy that transported John Steinbeck's Joads from Oklahoma to California in *The Grapes of Wrath*, doesn't it? Or the Clampettmobile from the popular sixties television sitcom *The Beverly Hillbillies*? On the fictional timeline, this old truck actually lands smack dab between these two—1952, in the world of John Grisham's novel *A Painted House*. Published in 2001 and turned into a Hallmark/CBS Television movie two years later, *A Painted House* is a fast-moving story exploring an Arkansas farm boy's experience with puppy love and culture clash against the backdrop of the Korean War and another Stan Musial batting title. Setting the story in his rural hometown of Black Oak, Grisham uses two different groups of outsiders to upset the equilibrium in this almost lily-white corner of the Delta—Mexican workers known as braceros and a family of poor Ozarkers named Spruill. The old truck belonged to the Spruills. "From a quarter of a mile away we could tell they were hill people," observes young narrator Luke Chandler upon first spotting the vehicle.

The braceros and the Spruills had come to the Delta for the same reason, to make money picking cotton by hand. At the beginning of the twenty-first century, readers likely took the existence of the braceros in stride, but more than a few must have been surprised by the post-Depression white migrant workers of the novel. They were no mere device for literary conflict. For generations, Ozarkers left their hills to harvest cotton and countless other crops. They came to the Delta in jalopies only slightly updated from those that carried the Okies and Arkies out west in the 1930s and early 1940s. They came in railroad cars with their meager belongings in trunks, satchels, or burlap sacks. They came in the beds of trucks driven by labor agents or by Delta farmers themselves. Like the Spruills of John Grisham's *A Painted House*, the majority of them came as families looking to make enough money to carry them through the winter back home in the hills.

The story of the hill people who helped harvest a generation of eastern Arkansas's cotton crops has almost completely disappeared from the record of twentieth-century agricultural and social transformation in the mid-South. Grisham's peripheral treatment of this phenomenon in *A Painted House* brought the fictional Spruills—and their nonfictional Ozarks models—into a light brighter than could ever have been expected from a scholar's treatment of the subject. As the ranks of the real-life Spruills grows ever thinner, let's look back to see what created the last of America's white migrants. Who were they, why were they here, and where did they go?

Making Migrants

Like many Ozarkers of Generation X, I grew up hearing parents' and grandparents' stories of migrant labor journeys beyond the hills. The names of faraway destinations like Wenatchee and Yakima seemed as familiar to me as the nearest county seat, though I would not visit them until after I had children of my own. On occasion my families' laboring peregrinations proved confusing as well. As a small child (and a budding historian) I always insisted on knowing when and where the people around me had been born, no doubt to the consternation of a few teachers and fellow churchgoers. My mom's birthplace—Harrisburg, Arkansas— was long a source of puzzlement. Harrisburg was located almost one hundred miles from our home in Izard County, we had no relatives there, and we never once visited it during my childhood. It seemed such a far-off place, and Mom told me nothing more specific about the town than that it was somewhere in the "bottoms," our term for the flat country beyond the eastern rim of the Ozarks. Her lack of specificity reflected Mom's own unfamiliarity with the little town on the edge of Crowley's Ridge, for she had probably never revisited Harrisburg after her birth. It was only happenstance—and something near destitution—that placed my grandparents (both natives of the Ozarks) there in the late 1940s. Two teenagers married not quite a year, Junior and Ollie Trivitt had trekked to the "bottoms" to find work in the cotton harvest. Desperate for every penny and no stranger to unceasing toil, my grandma picked cotton until shortly before my mom's birth. Dorothea Lange and her fellow Farm Security Administration photographers had long abandoned the search for desperation, but Ollie and many more young women of her generation greeted motherhood as a migrant.

Migratory labor—and cotton-picking specifically—had been a widespread activity among Ozarkers for well over half a century by the time real-life hill folks like my grandparents and fictional ones like the Spruills ventured into the bottoms in the post–World War II years. It was a phenomenon of necessity. The declining rate of infant and childhood deaths combined with a high birth rate in the Ozarks and heavy post–Civil War in-migration to place a population strain on a rugged and frequently infertile landscape. Though the Ozark Uplift was still sparsely settled by the standards of the eastern United States, the marginal nature of agriculture and limited industrial development created a population surplus by the late nineteenth century. The result was a region with a cheap, necessarily mobile labor force for several generations.

As early as the late nineteenth century, rural families from the southern Ozarks ventured southward to pick cotton on the large farms of the Arkansas River valley. Traveling in wagons loaded with bedding and cooking utensils, the harvest hands camped out or found shelter in abandoned houses. In the rugged Boston Mountains of southern Newton County, the remote community of Fallsville came alive each autumn as men on foot and families in wagons passed through this "gateway" to the valley, hopeful of returning home before Christmas with "much needed change and some folding money." Even more common in this era were the thousands of young men who left the Ozarks each year destined for the sprawling wheat fields on the Great Plains. In his journal of the late 1800s and early 1900s, Laclede County, Missouri, farmer Anderson McFall noted the goings and comings of these traveling harvest hands. Hopping freight trains for the western journey, industrious young men could earn up to $5 a day plus room and board by the second decade of the twentieth century, a windfall unheard of back home in the hills.[1]

Widespread migratory labor among Ozarks families blossomed after World War I, in large part due to the mobility provided by the automobile. Young men and full families from around the Ozarks began to take to the roads and highways in the 1920s and '30s. The destinations were almost as numerous as the flivvers lurching down the byways. Many headed for the golden dreams of California, some settling in urban Southern California and many others destined for the Central Valley. Others trekked to the Pacific Northwest and found seasonal employment in the apple orchards and hops farms, or, like the family of future Arkansas governor Orval Faubus, in the timber industry. Ozarkers also found their way to the orchards and truck fields of Michigan, the cornfields of Illinois, tomato patches in Indiana, the cotton fields of Arizona, and citrus groves in Florida.[2]

In the five years following the Treaty of Versailles, Marvin Lawson of Lawrence County, Arkansas, supplemented his meager earnings from teaching a one-room school by shocking wheat on the Oklahoma plains and by traipsing the migrant trails within his home state—picking apples at Harrison, stacking lumber at a Marked Tree sawmill, and shocking rice at Stuttgart. The spring strawberry harvest in Arkansas and Missouri required thousands of day laborers, and the apple orchards of southwestern Michigan and central Washington became major destinations for eager Ozarks workers. In fact, all sorts of fruit harvests beckoned in the burgeoning West. In 1919 Pres and Mary Mahnkey made their way from southern Missouri to the Pacific coast, where Mary found work in an apple cannery outside of Puyallup, Washington, while Pres picked raspberries, hops, and blackberries. By 1923 California's Central Valley had become such a magnet for Ozarkers that a summer picnic near Visalia attracted two-hundred Missourians from little Dade County alone.[3]

Some of these early Ozarks travelers stayed out west. They provided contacts and sometimes temporary homes for the growing throngs following the trail of Steinbeck's Joads during the Depression. One Cedar County, Missouri, native recalled truckloads of neighbors making the trip to the Central Valley in the 1930s, where they found work thinning grapes, hoeing lettuce, picking cotton, and irrigating crops until the fruit harvest provided the big payoff. In Hickory County, Missouri, the migrant journey to "Californy" became almost a rite of passage for young men, who by the late 1930s generally banded together to make the cross-country trip via automobile. Women and girls made the migrant's journey only with kinfolk, and the family migration grew increasingly common in the decade's desperate times. "At least once a week there was an auction sale," wrote Don West in his fictionalized autobiographical account of life in rural northwestern Arkansas toward the end of the Depression. "Another farmer was selling out and leaving for California, Oregon, Washington to make ten, twelve, fifteen dollars a day. And the man who had the nerve

Family of Arkansas migrant fruit pickers in Berrien County, Michigan, 1940.
Courtesy of Library of Congress.

to sell out and leave was, for a week, an important man." On the migrant trail, however, he and his family were anything but important, often struggling to secure the next meal. A trip to Hood River, Oregon, in 1937 found Izard Countians Dovie and Edna Lee earning $3 or more a day in apple orchards, canneries, and other odd jobs, but it was still too little to afford even the smallest of Christmas presents for their children.[4]

The Bottoms

It is unclear when the first hill folks hit the trail that John Grisham's Spruills would follow, but by the early twentieth century many Ozarkers were old hands at cotton-picking. You'll find nairy a stalk of the stuff in the region today, but between Reconstruction and World War II cotton was the most reliable cash crop for farmers in the southeastern Ozarks. In 1929 farmers in the southern Ozarks planted more than 160,000 acres in cotton, and the range of the fiber extended even into the southernmost tier of Missouri counties. Just as had the landless poor in the Delta, Ozarks sharecroppers and tenant farmers—as well as poor landowners—had long made a practice of supplementing their meager incomes by picking cotton on the larger farms of neighbors and kinfolk in the hill country. So, Ozarkers were no strangers to the cotton field.[5]

There were a number of processes and connections that brought white hill people to the Delta cotton fields in the period from the 1920s to the 1950s. Kinship linked more than a few Ozarkers with eastern Arkansas. The clearing of swamps and cutting of forests in northeastern Arkansas in the early twentieth century attracted newcomers from many locations, including the Arkansas Ozarks. Ozarkers with the means to invest—and the willingness to trade ticks and chiggers for mosquitoes—sold their farms in the hills and bought or rented new places in the Delta. My paternal grandfather bought his Izard County farm in 1943 from a Tom Jones, who had left the hills in the 1930s to settle on a plot of Mississippi County soil that, as Grandpa always noted, "could grow a bale to the acre without airy fertilize." My other grandfather recalled a great uncle who had fled the hill country for a little farm in eastern Craighead County. Ozarks expatriates like these provided key contacts for migratory cotton-picking.

Though it is likely that hill country cotton pickers had ventured into the prairies and Delta of northeastern Arkansas at least a generation before, one of the earliest detailed accounts of such a journey relates the experiences of the Humphreys family. In September 1922, Clara Humphreys and her children traveled by train from Mammoth Spring, Arkansas, to an area of the northern Delta known as Buffalo Island, a "sunken land" created by the New Madrid earthquakes of 1811–12. Only recently cleared of timber and drained, the "island" between the St. Francis and Little Rivers boasted some of the richest soil found anywhere on the planet. The Vaughns, former neighbors of the Humphreyses, had abandoned the rocky hillsides of Fulton County for the fertile flatlands of eastern Craighead County, renting a forty-acre farm in the community of Mangrum, a few miles south of the Black Oak setting of John Grisham's *A Painted House*. Here Clara Humphreys and her children set up temporary living quarters in a one-room shack behind the Vaughn home and awaited the arrival of Clara's husband, Albert, who made the journey in a wagon loaded down with bedding, utensils, food, and other necessities. The Vaughns paid the Humphreys family on Friday evenings for the week's work, one dollar for every one hundred pounds of cotton picked. Albert Humphreys assigned each child a quota for the week and promised the children they could pocket any excess earnings. So impressed with the quantity and quality of cotton on Buffalo Island were Albert and Clara that they rented their own Delta farm near Caraway. A bumper crop in 1923 generated more money than they'd ever seen—and with less labor—but incessant bouts of malaria and other illnesses drove the Humphreyses back to the hills a year later. They were content to pick cotton in the bottoms, not grow it.[6]

The Depression knocked the floor out of both cotton prices and picking wages. When Evening Shade, Arkansas, native Tom Edwards made his first harvest trek to the Delta in 1933, he received only forty cents per one hundred pounds, less than half the rate earned by the Humphreys family eleven years earlier. Forty cents was the first wage Zela Stuart Rhoads remembered from her childhood in the heart of the Depression. For Zela the journey by train to northeastern Arkansas became an annual autumn exercise. Raised by her mother and grandmother on the grandmother's eighty-acre Fulton County farm, she first accompanied her family to Lake City (just across the St. Francis River from Buffalo Island) in the early 1930s, where they picked cotton on a small farm owned by a relative. After the relative died a couple of years later, the family found cotton-picking jobs as far from home as the Missouri bootheel before they struck an annual deal with a farmer near the little Buffalo Island town of Monette. Each August thereafter, and until her marriage in 1943, Zela's family rode the train to Monette, where their employer, a farmer named Ben Ball, provided them a one-room house and all the cotton they could pick. The three generations of Ozarks women would stay on at Ball's farm until late October, cooking their meals over an open fire in the small yard and carefully saving their earnings, which rebounded to a dollar per hundred pounds during the war years. Zela's family was not alone in their dependency on the cotton harvest. It was "the only way any of us had of making any cash," she recalled. "Some of 'em would plant a cotton crop here, and they'd go down there and pick a while and come back and pick their cotton."[7]

In Stone County, Arkansas, the Gayler community effectively emptied out each fall in the latter years of the Depression as young families hit the pickers' trail. Each October the ten members of the Thomas family piled into the back of a livestock truck for the slow ride out of the hills and across the bottoms to the Mississippi River town of Osceola. Hauling as much produce and canned goods as they could, the Thomases also returned to the same farm multiple times, sleeping on quilt-covered piles of straw in an old shotgun house. After five-and-a-half days of pulling cotton sacks up and down endless rows, the family made their way to town on Saturday

Cotton pickers near Strawberry, Arkansas, 1939.
*Courtesy of Hail Bryant Collection, Old Independence
Regional Museum, Batesville, Arkansas.*

evenings, where they mingled with other hill people and gawked at the
unusual sight (for them) of African Americans. Much of the family's
earnings went for winter clothes and material for dress-making, with a
pittance for a frozen treat on the last night in Osceola. "The lights were
beautiful, the ice cream was wonderful, the new clothes were cherished
and there was a little money left," noted Jack Thomas of the sojourn each
fall in the Delta.[8]

Thomas recalled that the war years reignited the Stone County timber
industry, putting the men of Gayler (at least those not in military service)
back to work and bringing a halt to the cotton-picking excursions to the
Delta. But it proved a mere temporary stoppage. With family and community connections in place and transportation less of a challenge, the
stage was set for the flood of migrant laborers that burst forth after New
Deal agricultural legislation and World War II–era mechanization began
to chip away at the dam of tradition. The Agricultural Adjustment Act and
subsequent federal legislation set in motion a process that would gradually
bring an end to the sharecropper system and stimulate the mechanization
of cotton farming. The massive exodus of the landless, rural poor—many
of whom were finally pulled from the South by employment opportunities up north or out west—left many Delta farmers looking for seasonal
labor during the bottleneck portion of the cotton season. Tractors, along

with planting and cultivation implements, were available long before the development of an efficient, workable mechanical picker for upland cotton, which meant that Delta farmers could abandon the southern system of a resident peasantry but that they could not do without an army of cheap labor at harvest time. Along with an increasing number of Mexican braceros after World War II, white hill people from the Ozarks rushed into this labor vacuum and provided many Delta farmers with their most reliable and consistent workforce into the mid-1950s.

Ozark cotton-picking in eastern Arkansas peaked during the decade following World War II. Shrinking acreage allotments on hill farms, struggles against the boll weevil, and the increasing hopelessness of competition with larger, more mechanized and more fertile farms in the flatlands all worked to create an atmosphere of dislocation in the Ozarks, a situation compounded by the lure of distant jobs created by the mid-century economic boom. More and more farm families—owners as well as the landless—found migratory labor essential for survival, or at the very least a dependable way to supplement sparse incomes. And the mass exodus of sharecroppers and tenant farmers from the Delta continued to create a labor vacuum that many flatland farmers were happy to fill with Ozarks choppers and pickers.

In the immediate postwar years, the cooperative extension service developed into a recruiting agency in the poorest Ozarks counties by coordinating local efforts of the federal Farm Labor Program. In Stone County, Arkansas, for example, a local field assistant oversaw a sixteen-member labor committee that headed up recruiting efforts. In 1947 the committee signed up more than 1,200 migrant workers destined for five different harvests, including strawberries in White County, Arkansas, tomatoes in Indiana, wheat in Kansas and the Dakotas, and peaches in the Arkansas Valley. Over half the workers were destined for the cotton fields of the Arkansas Delta. Though single young men accounted for some of the "out of county" laborers, the largest contingent consisted of small farmers whose marginal lands and meager resources made "outside work . . . the chief source of income." Typical of these struggling farmers was Ellis Martin of the Onia community. In five weeks of cotton-picking in the Delta, Martin, his wife, and child cleared $400, almost three times the return they got on their own two-acre cotton patch and an acre of strawberries.[9]

Like Grisham's Spruills, more than a few hill clans who came to the Delta to pick cotton resembled Steinbeck's Joads. But in many respects, the Spruills are as stereotypical as their jalopy. This one truck holds an extended clan of seven, including such stock characters as a crippled boy (perhaps the result of in-breeding?), a comely and hypersexual teenage girl, a deferring and largely silent wife, and a mean, overgrown, hillbilly boy—a sort of evil Li'l Abner. The Spruills set up a messy camp in the yard of the Chandlers, their host family in Black Oak, and the patriarch of the hill family invariably appears with a Lester Jeteresque messy mouth— whether it's stray food on the lips or a ring of dried tobacco juice under- neath his maw. Despite such stereotypes, however, most former migratory cotton pickers and eastern Arkansawyers whose memories extend back to the mid-twentieth century will find much of Grisham's account to be pretty true to form.

The small-town weekly newspapers of the Ozark region in the 1940s and '50s were full of news and notes of real-life Spruills leaving for or returning from the cotton fields. The most mobile among them (and especially those from the eastern edge of the hill country) often made weekend trips back home during the harvest season. That was the case with the King family from Sharp County. When farmer Ellis King purchased his first truck in the late 1940s, he began taking his wife and three daughters into north- eastern Arkansas or the Missouri bootheel each fall for a week, sometimes two, at a time. Like many of their neighbors in the hills, the Kings had their own small cotton allotment but waited to pick their crop after the harvest in the bottoms came to an end. Requiring even the youngest of the children to put in an adult's day of work, Ellis pushed the family to "pick a bale a day"—about 1,300 pounds of unginned cotton. So common was migrant work among rural people in the Kings' eastern Ozarks of Arkansas that school districts arranged their calendars accordingly. Ellis King's daughter, Geneva, recalled that the one-room elementaries and the high school she attended in the 1940s and early 1950s maintained split sessions—classes in winter and summer with recesses for spring planting and fall harvest.[10]

For many Ozarkers, a season or two in the Delta cotton fields served as initiation into the peripatetic existence of the migrant laborer, a life that carried them far beyond the confines of a single state or region. Geneva King and Steve Emerson were already seasoned migrant laborers by the time they married in the early 1950s—she a veteran of the cotton fields and central Arkansas strawberry patches and he of the Wisconsin English pea and corn harvests. In California's San Joaquin Valley for most of their first decade of marriage, the Emersons toiled in berry fields and packing sheds, in nut groves and apricot orchards, and in various other jobs before returning to Arkansas. Stone County, Arkansas, native Stonewall Treat "could pick that cotton," but his incessant quest "to make enough to do us from one year to the next" took Treat and his family not only to the Delta but on more than a dozen trips to Colorado, California, and Washington. Fellow Stone Countian Walter Severs earned his first Delta cotton-picking stripes shortly before enlisting in the Navy during World War II. After the war Severs made three migrant trips to California—finding work in peaches, potatoes, and dates—and in the late forties and early fifties he and wife Dorothy returned to the Delta cotton fields whenever life on the farm was "kindly slack in the fall."[11]

More and more hill people went to the cotton fields after World War II by private automobile, but Delta farmers continued the practice of supplying rides for pickers and families who needed transportation. "They needed us as much as we needed them," recalled Ripley County, Missouri, native Ray Joe Hastings. The rapid decline of sharecropping and a national economy booming with jobs made the task of finding willing migrant workers more crucial than ever before. In the late forties and early fifties, according to Hastings, cotton farmers from Missouri's bootheel region drove into the hills in search of families of pickers. When desperate enough the farmers simply stopped at random houses until they found their labor supply. The Hastingses found work on the Gobler, Missouri, farm of a man named Berry. Bunking in a tent on Berry's farm and picking every day except Sunday, the family could earn $125 in a week—more than Ray Joe's father made hacking railroad ties or working at a sawmill in a month. "It wasn't an adventure you looked forward to," reminisced Ray Joe, whose unusually tall frame poorly suited him for stoop labor, "because you knew what it was gonna be—sore fingers from them cotton bolls sticking in and bent over all day picking cotton. That wasn't my idea of an adventure."[12]

Mississippi County, Arkansas, farmer L. V. Waddell drove his truck into the hills—as far west as Sallisaw, Oklahoma—to recruit cotton pickers to carry back to his Manila cotton fields. R. W. Lyerly, who grew up on a Mississippi County farm in the 1940s and '50s, remembered his father driving a flatbed truck to Cushman, Arkansas, year after year to pick up the Shaws, a mother and her two children who would then spend part of the fall living on the Lyerly farm before his father took them back home at the end of the harvest season. But most postwar migratory families were like the Gilmores of Heber Springs, who came to the Lyerly farm each year in their own vehicle. The personal and professional relationships between the Lyerlys on the one hand and the Shaws and Gilmores on the other were quite common. Small Delta farmers, especially, sought to build long-lasting relationships with hardworking hill families in order to assure a stable workforce each year. Most farmers provided housing for their annual guests and workers. The Lyerlys provided the large Gilmore family the use of a vacant sharecropper shack, while the smaller Shaw family found lodging in the smokehouse in the Lyerlys' backyard.[13]

The premium on labor during and after World War II meant that rates for pickers improved considerably. Working in the fields near Lepanto, Arkansas, in 1942, Walter Severs earned $3 for every one hundred pounds of picked cotton—three times as much as Missouri migrant Ernest Webber received in Oklahoma just four years earlier. Ray Joe Hastings recalled that $3 was still the going rate in the Missouri flatlands in 1949 and 1950. According to Geneva King Emerson, pickers' wages on her family's journeys to the Missouri Bootheel and northeastern Arkansas rose from $2 to $3 from the late forties to the early fifties. R. W. Lyerly recalled that the local pay scale in western Mississippi County, Arkansas, increased from $2.25 per one hundred pounds in the early 1950s to $3.50 by the latter half of the decade.[14]

The Last of the White Migrants

It is obvious that race played a role in the phenomenon of Ozark migratory cotton-picking. Although hill people did venture into the old plantation sections of the Delta to pick cotton, the most popular destinations were the farms of the whitest section of the Arkansas Delta, the belt of land between Crowley's Ridge and the Little River extending from the Missouri line down into parts of Poinsett County. Due to the recent draining and clearing of much of this land, the farm culture and demographic situation that developed here in the 1920s and '30s was quite different from that farther east and south. Large swaths of this "white Delta" had been devoid of even Black sharecroppers. While the small farmers of Craighead County and western Mississippi County frequently imported busloads of African Americans from Blytheville and Memphis or Mexican braceros to chop cotton in the early summer—an equally onerous task that brought less pay than picking—they preferred white workers from the hills when harvest time rolled around. According to R. W. Lyerly, it was the opinion of most farmers in the white Delta that white pickers "did a much better job [than

Black pickers] and took better care of what you had. That's the reason they recruited and went up and got them and was glad to get them."[15] Family connections between Delta farmers and hill folks in the eastern Ozarks likely played a part as well.

The 1952 setting of Grisham's book would have been very near the peak of Ozarker cotton-picking in the Delta. The bottoms were crawling with real-life Spruills at the time. But two developments brought an end to the era of the last white migrants in the Arkansas cotton fields. One was the Mexican bracero program. Beginning in the labor-shortage days of World War II, Delta planters and farmers searched for a cheap, dependable labor supply at harvest time, arguing for access to such disparate groups as German prisoners of war, imported Bahamian nationals, and Tejanos. The search continued in the postwar era. Despite the fact that whites had been employed as pickers in the region for years, one Delta cotton grower justified his request for Mexican laborers by referring to cotton as a "slave crop." He assured researchers from the President's Commission on Migratory Labor that "nobody is going to pick it that doesn't have to. . . . The [Mexican] national is about the only reservoir of labor that we know of that really wants to pick cotton, because he gets more money than he ever saw in his life."[16]

In 1948 Arkansas farmers began participating in the bracero program, which provided seasonal agricultural workers from Mexico. Though worker activism and a busy Mexican consulate pushed Delta planters and their towns to treat Mexicans as first-class citizens in the age of Jim Crow, cotton growers were less forward acting when it came to economics. Pressure from the Mexican government resulted in the South's first minimum wage for agricultural workers in 1952 (for braceros only), but stagnating rates for Mexican-picked cotton ensured equally low pay for white and Black workers. Ozarker migrant labor in the Delta fell off sharply in the latter half of the 1950s as the number of braceros in Arkansas peaked at almost forty thousand in 1959. That year marked my grandparents' last migrant-labor journey to the bottoms. Spending nights in an old sharecropper shack with no electricity or plumbing, they occupied the daylight hours harvesting cotton in the flat expanses near Walnut Ridge, Arkansas. My hard-driving grandpa pushed himself to pick at least five hundred pounds per day and assigned quotas to the other members of the family— three hundred for my grandma and one hundred each for my mom (then ten years old) and her eight-year-old brother. But the Trivitts were among

Hill-country cotton pickers near Lake City, Arkansas, 1960s.
Courtesy of Craig Ogilvie.

the last of the hill-country cotton pickers in the flat lands. Their rural
school back home had even adopted a modern calendar by 1959, forcing
the children to make up weeks' worth of missed work upon their return.[17]

More crucial than the bracero program to the demise of the hill-country
cotton hand—and cotton harvesters of all origins—was the mechanical
cotton picker. As historian Donald Holley observes, the introduction of
mechanical pickers and a dwindling supply of migratory and day labor
worked in tandem to bring an end to the hand-harvesting of cotton.
Between 1950 and 1955, the percentage of Arkansas cotton harvested by
mechanical picker increased from 5 to 25 percent. R. W. Lyerly recalled
that his father was the first farmer in the Leachville area to make the
technological transition when he purchased a mechanical picker in 1954.
By the early 1960s the shortage of harvest labor—caused in part by the
steady introduction of mechanical pickers—had influenced even the most
recalcitrant Delta farmers to abandon hopes of avoiding modernization.
Mechanical pickers harvested more than 90 percent of Arkansas cotton in
1967, three years after the state ceased its bracero program.[18]

The era of the Spruills had mostly come to an end when the decade of
the sixties dawned, but the era of the Ozarker as migrant laborer had not

yet run its course. Hill folks continued to follow the fruit harvests for a few more years. Both sets of my grandparents (along with my parents) made their final migrant trips in the early 1960s, working in the Columbia Valley apple harvest in central Washington. In an odd twist of fate, both my parents—though they did not know each other at the time—lived on the same orchard near the small town of Monitor in different years, possibly even in the same migrant shack. A dwindling stream of Ozarkers continued to leave the region for seasonal agricultural labor throughout the 1960s, but in places like the Washington apple orchards Mexicans and other Hispanic migrant workers had largely supplanted whites and Native Americans by the end of the decade. My great aunt and uncle, Totsie and Wayne Wood, were anomalies by the time they made their last annual trip to the orchards and packing sheds in 1980, capping off four decades of migrant labor.[19]

The cash from picking cotton and apples helped many hill people stave off hunger and permanent out-migration. It lured others away from their home region for good. The fictional Spruills represent thousands of real-life hill people whose shared story is one of perseverance and struggle. In the eastern Arkansas Delta they found an appreciative group of farmers, many of whom became annual employers and some of whom even became friends. The whiteness that supposedly made them unfit to harvest what the old Delta farmer referred to as a "slave crop" played no small role in opening these doors of opportunity to them. When placed in the larger context of the social transformation and dislocation of the mid-twentieth century, the Ozark cotton pickers were just one piece of the migratory-worker puzzle. And like most of the other pieces of that puzzle, the Ozarkers' wanderings and workings went unnoticed by mainstream American society at the time and are now largely forgotten, except by those who traveled the trails, and by those of us, like me, who have benefited from their unceasing efforts to not only get by but to make a better life for their children and children's children.

For some Ozarkers, experiences on the migrant laborers' trail conditioned a deeper appreciation of modern demographic changes and the economic forces behind them. In the early 2000s, at a time when unprecedented numbers of Hispanic families were finding work in the poultry-processing plants around the region, I attended a local historical society meeting in which three white, middle-aged Ozarks residents recounted their experiences as children in migrant labor families. All three expressed an understanding of the hardships and challenges facing their new

Latina/o neighbors and an appreciation for their determination and hard work. They were sentiments that many other white residents did not share. A bridge of common lived experiences was a starting point. At the very least, the story of Ozarks migrant workers made it into print—and in pretty accurate fashion—in a best-selling novel by a good storyteller, and that's something to build on.

CHAPTER TEN

Collectors of the Ozarks

FOLKLORE AND REGIONAL IMAGE

ULITZER PRIZE–WINNING POET John Gould Fletcher still ranks near the top of the pantheon of Arkansas writers. He was also one of the leaders in a revival of interest in Arkansas and Ozarks folkways in the middle of the twentieth century. But he was at best an unlikely ambassador to or for the *folk*. Raised in a wealthy, prominent Little Rock family, educated in private schools and at Harvard, Fletcher spent most of his adult life in Europe, circulating in a network of avant-garde writers and artists. Even after returning to his home state during the Depression, Fletcher retained the formal speech and stilted manners of the patrician, likely never fully comprehending just how "foreign" he was to the musically inclined scratch farmers and woodcutters whose homes he visited with an assistant who also served as a sort of cultural arbitrator and dialect interpreter. But the music and stories contained in the drafty hovels of the Ozarks fascinated him. In 1949, while in residence at the University of Arkansas in Fayetteville, Fletcher grew so enamored with a local banjo picker that he convinced the man and his friends to put on a concert for a group of university faculty and students. Stage fright overtook the amateur musicians, who had only played in private while kicking back and drinking. The day was saved when the men agreed to hold forth from inside a smokehouse. "From time to time they could be heard whispering among themselves," recalled one of the university students in attendance. "Then they would burst into song."[1]

I have pictured this scene in my mind many times, in all its irony and incongruity—a severe case of the gawking of the elite, the observer effect fundamentally altering the dynamics of an otherwise ordinary activity, sapping a moment of its "authenticity." Such is the challenge of bringing the intimate and private into the public realm, consuming unselfconscious expression in the marketplace of self-consciousness. It was the challenge awaiting any organizer of folk festivals, any champion of the vernacular artist. Yet the temporary predicament that threatened to scuttle Fletcher's grand display of a humble, downhome jam session emanated from a place of passion and sincerity. Fletcher felt the romantic pull of the collector—the desire to discover the past living in the present—and the concomitant urge to display his discovery.

Even more intoxicating for the collector was the intimacy of the hearth, experiencing living history in its natural habitat. That same year, 1949, University of Arkansas English professor Mary Celestia Parler took her new tape recorder into Fayetteville's hinterland, to the little town of Goshen, where she and an assistant recorded banjo picker Jim Means. I have thought about that moment often as well. Though Parler wasn't quite as strange a duck as Fletcher, she was nevertheless solidly middle class, highly educated, and a native of the Deep South, not the twangy southern margins of the Ozarks. It must have been both jarring and enlightening for a medievalist who had had no inkling that such an experience awaited when she arrived in Arkansas little more than a year earlier. For Parler it was the beginning of a transformative, sixteen-year journey into the front-porch world of Arkansas folkways. More immediately, it was a moment in which she understood the joy of discovery, the thrill of collecting—that moment when history comes to life in the present in a way that can never happen in a book, when the spirits and echoes of the past manifest themselves in weathered pine planks or aged voices and you feel the weight of time in your marrow.[2]

Perhaps nothing has so captured the essence of romantic primitivism—the human desire to make contact with the ancient, to drink of the waters of the origin pool—as has the gathering of folklore, and specifically the collection of ballads. The digitization of Mary Parler's Ozark Folksong Collection—the third large collection of Ozarks recordings to be made available on the internet—offers the perfect opportunity for a brief recap of ballad collecting in the Ozarks and its connections with the American ballad-hunting tradition in general.[3] Parler's career as a collector provides valuable windows into the world of ballad hunting, both in an academic context—in relation to trends in American folklore—and a geographical context—as it regards her chosen ground, the Ozarks. Ultimately, the passions and labors of Parler and fellow collectors would exercise a significant impact on one of the most fundamental facets of Ozarks history and culture—the region's image.

Mary Celestia Parler recording musicians in a barber shop, ca. 1950s. Small Manuscript Collections, Box 6, Mary Celestia Parler Photographs, Folder 1, Item 8. *Special Collections, University of Arkansas Libraries, Fayetteville.*

Child and His Children

Probably all ballad and traditional music collecting in the Ozarks, and almost all of it in America in general, traces its roots to the monumental five-volume work *The English and Scottish Popular Ballads*, written by Harvard English professor Francis James Child and published between 1882 and 1898. (The phrase "Child ballad" derives from this collection and has nothing to do with children's songs.) Child was not a collector in the way that you and I think of ballad collectors. His discovering took place not on back roads and front porches but in libraries and archives, especially in Britain. His interest was textual, in song lyrics, and he eventually collected more than three hundred songs and their variants, all of which he suspected had disappeared from the oral tradition. Through the efforts of his students and disciples—most notably his Harvard successor George Lyman Kittredge—Child's ballads were quickly canonized as the most important and essential songs of their kind in the Anglo-Saxon heritage.[4]

But it was Child's suggestion that the songs no longer survived in oral tradition that sparked the ballad-collecting frenzy in the United States. As early as the 1890s, periodicals began to carry articles detailing the discovery of Child ballads on this side of the Atlantic, especially in relatively poor and isolated regions such as Appalachia. These discoveries prompted English folklorist Cecil Sharp to venture into the Appalachian Mountains with his assistant, Maud Karpeles, during World War I. Cultural forces at work in this era, ones that affected the efforts of Sharp and many other ballad collectors indirectly if not directly, included the eugenics movement and Anglo-Saxonism. They were elements of a cross-Atlantic racist celebration of northern European heritage prompted by an explosion of imperialism on the world stage and on our national stage by the flood of so-called "new immigrants," whose odd traditions and religions and in some cases Mediterranean swarthiness must surely have masked any number of societal dangers, from socialism to anarchism. Working together, Sharp and Karpeles documented more than five hundred songs of British origin in one of the most ambitious ballad-collecting projects of the first half of the twentieth century. Shepherded into publication by Karpeles in 1932, eight years after Sharp's death, the two-volume *English Folk-Songs from the Southern Appalachians* reinforced popular perceptions of Appalachia (and by extension the Ozarks) as a homogenous land of white people of British descent—a place only slightly touched by modernity—and established the notion that ballad collectors would have to seek out the people of the hills and hollers to find the greatest number and variety of Child ballads and other English songs.[5]

By the time Sharp's work was published in the heart of the Depression, a notable change was underway in American ballad collecting. Whereas Sharp and Karpeles, and most of their contemporaries, had largely ignored the plethora of songs they encountered that were not of old-world origin, the 1920s and especially the 1930s introduced a broader appreciation of traditional music in general, as many American collectors began to focus on songs that were clearly of native origin, a movement popularized on a national scale by the publication of Carl Sandburg's *The American Songbag* in 1927, which included at least half a dozen numbers collected in the Ozarks.[6]

At this point comparatively little collecting had been done in the Ozarks, though the region certainly played a role in Missouri's leadership in the burgeoning folklore society movement. Given the influence of English professors in early ballad collecting, it should come as no surprise that the primary figure in the early story of Ozark collecting was University of Missouri English professor Henry M. Belden, a New Englander who landed in the Midwest after completing a doctorate at the Johns Hopkins University. In 1903 the establishment of the State Historical Society of

Missouri on the Mizzou campus in Columbia spurred interest in the folklife of the state, which in turn resulted in the founding of a club in the English department that would eventually develop into the Missouri Folk-lore Society. It was at one of the initial meetings of the club that Belden heard a student sing a traditional ballad, one that he recognized as a Child ballad. This student became the club's first designated "collector" in the summer of 1903 and sent Belden the first songs in a collection that would finally make it into print thirty-seven years later as *Ballads and Songs Collected by the Missouri Folk-lore Society*. Like many other early ballad collectors, Belden conducted no fieldwork himself, relying instead on the labors of students. Also like many other early collectors, Belden was motivated, at least initially, by a desire to find Child ballads and their variants surviving in contemporary oral tradition. In fact, a sort of cottage-industry competition arose among collectors who tried to find more Child ballads than did their peers in competing states, a competition that played no small role in the early proliferation and growth of state folklore societies. Although the collecting of Belden and his students was statewide, two of his most generous informants sent ballads and songs from the Ozarks. West Plains high school teacher Goldy Hamilton supplied more songs than any other contributor, and thirteen of the songs came from across the state line in Carroll County, Arkansas, courtesy of Mizzou student Emma Simmons.[7]

Though Belden's published folksong scholarship in the early twentieth century focused almost exclusively on the survival of British ballads, in speeches and correspondence he evinced an independent streak and broad-minded approach that challenged the "Child first" method of the day and set a precedent that subsequent Ozarks collectors would follow. By 1910, when Belden was elected to the first of two terms as president of the American Folklore Society, the Missouri Folk-lore Society had already begun to collect and publish nursery rhymes, play-party tunes, "Negro songs," and humorous ditties. In his presidential address to the American Folklore Society in Providence, Rhode Island, in 1910, Belden urged members to collect "native American balladry," referring not to the songs of American Indians but to ballads of American origin in general.

Sounds of the Ozark Folk

Arriving in the Ozarks after World War I, Vance Randolph would not only take Belden's advice but would do so with his own tablet and pencil (and later recorder) in the field. You would have been hard-pressed to find two people more different in disposition and career path, yet Belden and

Goldy Hamilton, from the 1910 issue of
The Zizzer, the yearbook of West Plains
(Missouri) High School.

Randolph carried on a cordial correspondence for years, with Randolph likely viewing the older professor as a sort of mentor. But Belden's name is largely forgotten today outside of the small world of folk music scholars and enthusiasts, while Randolph's, now more than four decades after his death, remains miraculously entwined with everything Ozarks. It's too easy to declare that few writers have ever been so inextricably linked with an American region. And it may not be hyperbole to claim that the public perception of no other region has ever owed so much to one person's labors.

Maybe it's because I've spent my whole adult life stepping in and out of the furrows Randolph left behind, but it seems that the story of "Mr. Ozarks" is too well-known for me to belabor it here. So I'll just focus on the song collecting of this Kansan whose work so shaped the Ozarks image. At the urging of Carl Sandburg, among others, Randolph began collecting ballads—as well as just about every other kind of folklore imaginable—in southwestern Missouri in the 1920s and for a time later in that decade edited a regular folksong column called "The Songs Grandfather Sang," first in the weekly paper at Pineville and later in Otto Ernest Rayburn's magazine *Ozark Life*. In 1934, he helped identify singers and musicians for a series of local regional folk festivals in southern Missouri and northern Arkansas that preceded Sarah Gertrude Knott's first National Folk Festival in St. Louis; that festival featured an entire day devoted to Ozarks music makers and ballad singers. From 1941 to 1943, Randolph recorded songs on a portable, acetate disc recorder for the Library of Congress's Archive of American Folk Song. Three years later the State Historical Society of Missouri published the first of four volumes of Randolph's most monumental work, *Ozark Folksongs*. Though criticized by a few old-school folklorists for its populistic, come-one-come-all inclusion of everything from Child ballads to "Brush-Arbor Music," *Ozark Folksongs*—with over 1,600 texts to almost 900 songs—remains among the most valuable and revered works of its kind. The collection's publication granted the now middle-aged Randolph the academic respect that had heretofore eluded him and cemented his reputation as "Mr. Ozarks."[8]

The ballad-collecting craze, which swept much of the nation in the interwar years, would be unleashed in full frenzy on the Ozarks only after World War II. Nevertheless, Randolph wasn't the only ballad hunter roaming these hills in the 1930s and early '40s. Among the now-forgotten collectors were University of Arkansas history professor Clement L. Benson, whose collection apparently disappeared after his untimely death in 1934; University of Arkansas graduate student Theodore Garrison, whose 1944 thesis analyzed forty-five songs gathered in Searcy County; College (now University) of the Ozarks instructor John Stilley, who collected more than one hundred ballads and fiddle tunes in the Clarksville, Arkansas, area; Carroll County native Fred High, who later self-published a collection of ballads after World War II; Springfield, Missouri, newspaper columnists May Kennedy McCord (the "Queen of the Hillbillies") and Lucile Morris and Aurora, Missouri, newspaper columnist C. V. Wheat, all of whom published a variety of traditional song texts; Monett, Missouri, music teacher Lynn Hummel, whose University of Missouri master's thesis focused more on tunes than texts; and Springfield businessmen Paul Holland and Ben Rice, both of whom collected to augment their own local performances. And then there were the government workers. Sidney Robertson Cowell, an employee of the Farm Security Administration's Special Skills Division, made recordings in Van Buren County, Arkansas, and Springfield, Missouri, among other locations. In Searcy County, Arkansas, home demonstration agent Alba Askew reportedly gathered more than two hundred songs and helped organize the county's first folk festival in 1941. The

Vance Randolph.
Courtesy of Missouri Writers Portraits (P1195),
State Historical Society of Missouri, Columbia.

WPA Writers' Project collected ballads (among many other things) in both Arkansas and Missouri. Especially fruitful was Missouri's project, which under the direction of Geraldine Parker collected hundreds of songs in the Springfield area alone. The fate of these Writers' Project songs remains shrouded in mystery.[9]

By the time Mary Parler arrived in Fayetteville in the fall of 1948, ballad and folklore collecting had been spotty and unsystematic, but Vance Randolph's *Ozark Folksongs* had recently placed the Ozarks on the map as a rich source of folk materials. She later admitted that Vance Randolph was one of only three Arkansas names she recognized at the time of her arrival, but Mary Parler did not come to the university with designs on building the largest collection of traditional Ozarks music. It seems to have been a happy accident.

A South Carolina native with a master's degree in English from the

University of Wisconsin, Parler taught at a succession of small colleges around the South before, at age forty-three, accepting her position as associate professor of English at the University of Arkansas. She shared with folklore pioneers Francis James Child and George Lyman Kittredge a love of early English writings from the Middle Ages and quickly earned the sobriquet "Miss Chaucer" from her students. But Parler also taught courses in folklore (developing the university's first official class in the field in 1949) and thus was asked to take part in the formation of the Ozark Folklore Society (also founded in 1949 but soon renamed the Arkansas Folklore Society), which she would serve as secretary-treasurer for its first decade of existence. This sudden baptism into the folklore scene also witnessed the creation of Parler's University of Arkansas Folklore Research Project, which she directed in association with her folklore courses and students until 1965.[10]

Whether due to the influence of Vance Randolph (whom Parler wed in 1962 after a courtship of many years), or to Parler's own egalitarian sensibilities, or to a tradition of broad Ozarks folklore collecting first espoused by H. M. Belden and practiced by the Missouri Folk-lore Society, or to a blossoming inclusion movement among folklorists in general, the University of Arkansas Folklore Project grew into an unusually diverse and wide-ranging collection. There were examples of American Indian and African American folklore and music, regional versions of popular, recorded songs, ballads derived from eastern and southern European traditions, and thousands of note cards containing handwritten observations by Parler or student interviewers on superstitions and folk beliefs, riddles, proverbs, and dialect. Perhaps most crucially, the University of Arkansas Folklore Project was not made up of texts alone. Upon launching the project, Parler purchased one of the new, affordable, reel-to-reel tape recorders that had just hit the market the previous year, the portable device that revolutionized ballad collecting. So, a full decade before esteemed ethnomusicologist D. K. Wilgus implored collectors and archivists to step up their audio recording to balance out text-heavy music libraries, Mary Parler and her field assistant, Merlin Mitchell, headed into the heart of the Ozarks with the new tape recorder and came back with the songs that started the region's most extensive collection. Eventually, Parler sent students into the field as well, and much of the collection represents recordings that were made as student projects. Ultimately, sixteen years' worth of collecting generated some 442 reels containing over 4,500 recordings, 80 percent of which are ballads and other lyric songs. Parler was more collector than writer, though she did self-publish a cross-section of the project's ballads in 1963 under the title *An Arkansas Ballet Book*.[11] (That's not a typo. *Ballet*, pronounced with a hard *t*, was the most popular pronunciation of *ballad* by old-timers in the Ozarks.)

The quarter century following the founding of the University of Arkansas Folklore Project marked the pinnacle of ballad and music collecting and recording in the Ozarks. It's likely that thousands of people used cheap tape recorders to make informal recordings of grandparents, aunts, uncles, or neighbors singing the old songs during this era, especially in the wake of the folk revival of the late 1950s and early 1960s. But there were also a number of ambitious collectors who amassed valuable collections of ballads and instrumental tunes. Most were untrained enthusiasts who spent weekends and vacations at hoedowns and in back-roads parlors and whose collections lack the scholarly detail found in Parler's. But they remain valuable artifacts nonetheless.

Most similar to Parler was John Quincy Wolf Jr., a Batesville, Arkansas, native with a Johns Hopkins PhD who served as head of the English department at Southwestern at Memphis (now Rhodes College.) A Wordsworth scholar who had imbibed his father's colorful tales of growing up in the rural Ozarks in the 1870s, Wolf had been interested in traditional ballads long before buying a portable tape recorder in 1952. He located his first subjects through a tried-and-true method of ballad hunting—an ad placed in weekly newspapers. Wolf, along with his intrepid wife, Bess, spent summer breaks in Batesville at the old family home, which they used as a base for their ballad-hunting trips into the eastern Ozarks. Wolf's early forays into Cleburne and Stone Counties introduced him to Jimmy Driftwood (who would enjoy fame for his folk-inspired compositions in the late 1950s) and to a number of singers and musicians who would achieve a modicum of celebrity on the national folk circuit in the 1960s and '70s, most notably Ollie Gilbert and Almeda Riddle, the latter of whom became arguably Arkansas's and the Ozarks's most revered singer of traditional, white southern music. Like Parler, Wolf eventually developed folklore courses and integrated student projects into his collection, but the location of his institution, in Memphis, meant that most of his student recordings focused on such genres as the blues and Sacred Harp congregational singing, both of which occupied much of Wolf's own recordings late in life. After Quincy's death, Bess Wolf donated the collection to Lyon College. Today, almost all of Wolf's recordings in the Ozarks are available digitally online.[12]

John Quincy Wolf Jr.
Courtesy of the Bess Wolf Estate Collection,
Old Independence Regional Museum,
Batesville, Arkansas.

At least three major Missouri-based collectors scoured the Ozarks in the same era. The earliest was Loman D. Cansler, a farm boy from Dallas County who earned bachelor's and master's degrees from the University of Missouri on the G.I. Bill. Cansler spent his career as a high school counselor in North Kansas City but began recording ballads, jokes, home remedies, proverbs, and other folklore in 1954, mostly in Missouri but occasionally in Kansas and in his wife's native Illinois as well. A guitar player and singer himself, Cansler released two albums of his own renditions of traditional songs: *Folksongs of Missouri* in 1959 and *Folksongs of the Midwest* in 1973, both on the Smithsonian's Folkways Records label. His collection is housed at the State Historical Society of Missouri in Columbia. Just two years after Cansler bought his first tape recorder, a traveling salesman from Springfield followed suit and began a twenty-year odyssey of collecting that would result in the recording of almost 1,600 songs and variants, as well as jokes and sayings of various kinds. The salesman was Max Hunter, and his collection reflects the broadest geographical scope of any of the Ozarks collections, as his job took him from corner to corner in the region. Hunter did much of his collecting in northern Arkansas, corresponding with Parler, Randolph, and Wolf for advice and for leads on singers. Like Cansler, Hunter was a singer in his own right, releasing a single album, *Ozark Folksongs and Ballads*, in 1963. The Max Hunter Collection, housed at the Springfield-Greene County Library, was digitized and transcribed by Michael Murray and others affiliated with the Missouri State University music department between 1998 and 2001.[13]

While Cansler and Hunter focused primarily on lyrical songs, Missourian R. P. Christeson concentrated on fiddle music. A native of the railroad town of Dixon in Pulaski County, Christeson learned to play the fiddle as a child and during a long career with the US Department of Agriculture (which took him as far away from home as New Mexico and Washington, DC) began recording fiddlers and studying their tunes. Making his initial recordings on a wire recorder while home on vacation in 1948, Christeson often accompanied his fiddlers on the melodeon. Moving back to Missouri upon his retirement in 1970, he published his life's work, *The Old-Time Fiddler's Repertory*, in two volumes in 1973 and 1984. The State Historical Society of Missouri houses his collection. Succeeding Christeson as the region's acknowledged authority on fiddle music was Gordon McCann. A printshop owner in Springfield, McCann was introduced to traditional music only in the early 1970s, but his passion for Ozarks heritage and fiddle-playing led to a working relationship with an elderly Vance Randolph and years of recording and promoting the work of a number of old-time fiddlers in southern Missouri, such as Lonnie Robertson and Art Galbraith. In recent years, McCann cowrote the book *Ozarks Fiddle Music* (2011) and donated his massive collection of recordings and notes to the special collections at Missouri State University.[14]

There have been a number of other collectors of the Ozarks in the past forty years: Leo Rainey of Batesville, founder of the Arkansas Traveller Folk Theatre in Hardy, Arkansas, and author of the 1976 book, *Songs of the Ozark Folk*; Missouri-based folk duo Cathy Barton and Dave Para; Bob Cochran of the Center for Arkansas and Regional Studies at the University of Arkansas. Perhaps first mention of the modern-era collectors should go to the late W. K. McNeil, an Indiana University–trained folklorist, prolific writer, and tireless researcher and collector who spent almost thirty years at the Ozark Folk Center State Park in Mountain View, Arkansas.

These Were the Last, Right?

We may have gotten a late start in the Ozarks, but thanks to the efforts of Mary Parler and other collectors, today the region boasts some of the richest and most accessible collections of ballads, tunes, and folklore in the country. One could make the argument that no other region is so closely identified with its traditional music and folklore as is the Ozarks. The region remains so prominent in the field of traditional music in America that the Ozarks was the only specific region of the nation to warrant its own chapter in the book *The Ballad Hunters of North America*, edited by Scott B. Spencer. Music and folklore are so central to our understanding of what the Ozarks stands for and what it means to be *Ozark* that Arkansas maintains a state park dedicated to the "perpetuation and interpretation of the heritage of the Ozark region," as the Ozark Folk Center's website puts it.[15]

Was/is there something special about the Ozarks that rendered the region an extraordinary depository of traditional Anglo-American music and folklore? Was/is the region truly exceptional? Those are, of course, separate questions. The Ozarks certainly possessed the requisites for the incubation of anachronism. The region, or at least vast, rural stretches of it, was and is poorer and more isolated than most other places in the United States. And poverty and isolation are two of the characteristics most associated with the survival of traditional folkways. While the homogeneity of the population has been exaggerated, there is no denying that the strong upland southern, white heritage of the Ozarks played a major role in cultural transmission. By the post–World War II era—by the time Mary Parler launched her collecting project—the Ozarks was, along with parts of rural Appalachia, the most fertile field for collecting remnants of Anglo-American folkways and music. What the Ozarks possessed in its great age of ballad hunting was a sort of temporal exceptionalism. It's not that the Ozarks existed in a timeless vacuum where all women gardened in bonnets and Mother Hubbard dresses and all men moonshined until brush arbor time. The Ozarks was changing—had always been changing— but at its own rate, often at a pace that lagged a generation behind other American places. The same forces of modernization that had expunged the Child ballad from the rural Midwest a generation earlier—remember, many of Belden's students did their ballad hunting in the non-Ozarks portions of Missouri in the early 1900s—were at work in the hills and hollers. The collectors recognized this and rushed to the harvest.

Gordon McCann.
Courtesy of Gordon McCann.

As ethnomusicologist Norm Cohen puts it, wryly, "For decades, virtually every collector was confident that he or she was gathering in the last leaves of traditional folksong, only to be handily survived by the tradition itself." Parler, Wolf, Hunter, and the other Ozarks collectors were guilty of such presentism. And it is somewhat ironic that the collectors and folklorists—with able assistance from travel writers, novelists, and Hollywood—helped mold an image of an unchanging people and place in the Ozarks, for it was the recognition of rapid societal change that spurred their efforts.

Folklorists, professional and amateur—Vance Randolph chief among them—impacted the public's perception of the Ozarks as they did few other regions. Sixty years after the last ballad was added to Parler's University of Arkansas Folklore Project, three quarters of a century since the release of the final volume of Randolph's *Ozark Folksongs*, the folklorists' and collectors' influence lives on in the perpetuation of a public perception of a static, homogenous Ozarks past, a romantic, exceptional story that leeches into the art, literature, even the scholarship within and about the Ozarks in the twenty-first century. For good or bad, the collectors responded to and contributed to the essentializing of the idea of the Ozarks, to the evolution of the social construct of a region. But their doing so wasn't motivated by deviousness or subterfuge. Collectors do what they do, and those of an academic bent generally acknowledge the fluidity of folk culture and oral tradition and the folly of drawing stark lines between eras or focusing on pre-this or post-that. Mary Parler and John Quincy Wolf Jr. both recognized the ever-changing nature of traditional music, the performer's freedom to alter the presentation of a ballad, and the impact of the observer effect on the whole enterprise of collecting. But in a way the practice of folklore contains within it the seeds for distorting history, especially when that folklore is produced by the untrained and consumed by an inattentive, grazing public. Even those folklorists who share with the anthropologist a modern appreciation for an ever-evolving body of folklore passed on by an ever-evolving folk in various forms and stages of contact with other ever-evolving folks—even those honest and level-headed collectors like Parler—are ultimately in search of anachronism, the thrilling survival of the primitive (whether accidental or deliberate) in the modernized and modernizing world. And is there not something within us—all of us—that yearns for authenticity, for genesis, for contact with the beginning of it all, the purity of that which has no precedent?

For whatever reason—poverty? relative isolation? because they looked really hard?—the collectors found in the rural Ozarks (especially the Ozarks of the halcyon days of Mary Parler's era) the survival of a good deal that was primitive, generally alongside a good deal that wasn't. The collectors knew that the Ozarks, like other American locales, was in the throes of change—that the region had possibly never been free of the throes of change—but they were here to salvage the scraps of a world we willingly abandoned, even in the Ozarks. They could see it happening, thus the rush to collect. We are richer for their efforts. But we're also subject to the implications of their efforts. For many around the nation, reading features in travel magazines or enticing descriptions in *Mother Earth News*, the Ozarks of the ballad hunter—the Ozarks of double shovels and milk stools and "Lord Bateman" and "The House Carpenter," the Ozarks of primitive survival—was the Ozarks writ large. Thus, the industriousness of the collector in the Ozarks and the intrinsically essentializing nature of his and her enterprise reinforced the idea that the Ozarks was out of step with a nation of Levittowns and television and moon rockets. Whether in a good way or bad way depended on one's own interpretive prism. In reality, the contrast that outside observers noted between the old ways of the Ozarks and the new ways of the nation was a contrast internal to the region, a process playing itself out over time.

Perhaps, with the perspective of more than fifty years, we can now recognize that the Ozarks wasn't the antithesis to the American story of progress, nor was it the Shangri-la that would shelter the weary who rejected whatever it was that America had become. The Ozarks was yin to its own yang. Collections like the Ozark Folksong Collection make that clear through a populistic, inclusive collecting strategy that doesn't favor the Child ballad over some plumber's rendition of a Stamps-Baxter gospel tune, that illuminates the variety and diversity and organic quality of the oral tradition, even in the remote Ozarks. Despite folklore's intrinsic tendency to tell us how much remains the same, the wealth of cultural artifacts gathered by Mary Parler, her assistants, and her students also remind us that the only thing immutable about culture and folkways is the element of change. We, with our snapshot comprehension of time, our finite, imperfect grasp of the human saga, will continue to yearn for the primitive. So it goes, the human urge to reclaim lost innocence. We will continue to collect and recover and document the fading past (in defiance of our fading future), for our gut tells us, as their guts told them, that this must surely be the remnant of something purer and better than that which we now have. The old ballads survived, however, not because of their connection to a forgotten past; they survived because of the universality of their themes. They still have the power to tell us who we were, who we are, and who we may become. The collectors recognized it. Those who passed them down through oral tradition recognized it. We recognize it. We proclaim that we have not forgotten. And we go on collecting.

CHAPTER ELEVEN

The Ordinary Days of Extraordinary Minnie

DIARIES OF A LIFE ON THE MARGINS

T IS NOT MY FINEST MOMENT. It's my wife's birthday. In a couple of hours she will get off work and carry the kids home from school. I've planned nothing to celebrate the occasion. In fact, I'm far from home and won't be heading back anytime soon. I'm obsessed with another woman, and I've journeyed seventy miles across the White River watershed to find her house. She's the kind I always fall for. An outsider, intelligent, neurotic, determined, defiant—and deceased. I first met Minnie four months ago, in the rambling diaries she scribbled on notebook paper, at least the ones that survived long enough to be rescued from her old house by a conscientious neighbor. I've thought about her every day since, and now, almost forty years after her death, I've come to the place where she spent most of her life.

I find traces of her in old courthouse records in the little town of Marshall, Arkansas. In the library I find a clipping of a local newspaper article about Minnie's eccentric, hoarding junkman son, Lawrence. I stop by the hardware store on the square. It looks like the kind of place that holds the ghosts of everyone who trod these crumbling sidewalks. They're here sure enough—in the memories of seventy-something proprietor George Daniel. It turns out George's nephew was a college classmate of mine. In the rural South we still like to know someone's people—compare family trees and acquaintances until we find a connection—a social ritual that almost always quickens the flow of information. It works. George has

This is the revised version of an essay originally published as "Life on the Margins: The Diaries of Minnie Atteberry," *Arkansas Historical Quarterly* 75 (Winter 2016): 1–30.

*been here all his life. He remembers Minnie, recalls making deliveries to
her little house out in the country when he was a teenager working for his
dad, Elmer—the E. in E. Daniel Hardware on the window. He even knows
who owns Minnie's old place now. George gets on the phone, and a few
minutes later in comes Robert "Ace" Hensley, my guide for the afternoon.*

*I follow Ace north out of town, onto a winding dirt road to a secluded
little place called Zack. A tiny stop on the Missouri and North Arkansas
Railroad in the first half of the twentieth century, it's nothing more than
a scattering of houses now. Its only claim to fame was a sickly native son
named James Baker who learned to play the guitar and yodel, hightailed
it to California in the Depression, changed his name to Elton Britt, and in
1942 recorded the first country song to reach gold-record status—"There's
a Star Spangled Banner Waving Somewhere." A mile beyond Zack and up
a steep hill overlooking Bear Creek, we reach our destination. Minnie and
Lawrence had settled here only a year before Baker left. From the looks of
the drooping, unpainted three-room house that sits on this hillside—the
only surviving sign of their years here—fate had a different trajectory in
mind for Minnie and Lawrence.*

*It is one of those early fall days when it seems as if the sun is trying to
burn off all its stored energy in one brilliant afternoon. Its gaze is merci-
less on the treeless hillside where I stand shielding my eyes, squinting at
a rocky field grown up in ragweed and sedge grass, trying to picture the
jumble of rusting implements and discarded appliances that once littered
this ground. Ace spent years erasing the signs of their existence, hauling
loads of scrap metal to the recycler, toting piles and piles of worthless trash
to who knows where. I wish he hadn't. I want to see what she saw. I want
to feel the suffocation and disorder of living in a house surrounded by
acre upon acre of rusting machinery, broken glass, and tin cans. I want to
touch Minnie's world.*

———

THAT WORLD STILL EXISTS only through Minnie's relentless chronicling.
It survives only because she refused to be ignored and overlooked in death
as she usually was in life. Minnie's world—however uninviting it may seem
to us—lives in her diaries. With pencil and tablet she found order, forced
its resurrection from her blighted, eroded Ozark bald. By most measurements, hers was a life that should have been forgettable. Minnie's diaries (and a few surviving letters) are not extraordinary in the usual sense.

They recount no hardships of a wartorn home front. They reveal no hidden life of crime or sexual intrigue. They unveil no political machinations, no social movements, no breakthroughs of scientific import. They offer not a single description of anyone deemed important by the arbiters of the American story.

Her life was a seemingly endless procession of ordinary days punctuated with occasional tears in the fabric of domestic monotony, days when the human drama trespassed on her cluttered hill, when sunlight illumined the storefront windows through which she gazed, when unseen airwaves carried the big world into her little house. Yet, all these days Minnie rendered meaningful with a stubborn insistence on documenting even the minutest details of the instinct to survive—and with a voice that was often singular. Diaries most often represent an educated and privileged layer of society whose literacy and leisure provide them the time and motivation to record for posterity their thoughts and actions. It is rare to find a bequest like Minnie's, an extensive collection of diaries and papers chronicling in minute detail the lives of common people, especially the poor.

The window into the lives of folks living on the economic and social margins of the peripheral South is just one facet that makes Minnie's diaries valuable. They illustrate the gradual process of modernization in the rural Ozarks between the New Deal and the Great Society. They also reveal the challenges faced by a strong-willed, unmarried woman in the male-dominated world of the Arkansas backcountry. Ultimately, though, it's Minnie's unique voice and style that set the diaries apart.

MINNIE'S DIARIES may be packed with the prosaic details of a life that was far from extraordinary, but her path to the Arkansas backcountry was anything but typical. Born on a Wayne County, Illinois, farm in 1888, the first-born child of John Henry Lincoln and Wilhelmine Elizabeth Mathes, she was christened Wilhelmina Eusebie Mathes. The family called her Minnie after her German-born maternal grandmother, Wilhelmina Breining. She grew up on the family farm, taught school briefly, and married John Gardner in 1909. The young couple had two children (Lawrence in 1910 and Della in 1912) before divorcing in 1916. Two years later, Minnie married twenty-five-year-old farm worker Joseph Sylvester "Ves" Atteberry.[1] On July 4, 1922, Minnie gave birth to her only child with Ves Atteberry. In one of her occasional "flashback" diary entries, Minnie recalled the event.

July 4, 1957: This is Minnie's son, Robert Atteberry's birthday. He was born July 4, 1922 which is 35 yrs ago. If he were alive he would be celebrating his 35th birthday anniversary today. At his birth Minnie hemorrhaged until she was drained of nearly all her blood and 'blacked out' for awhile. The Dr. attending her did what he could to save her, and then left, instructing those caring for her to not let her go to sleep. . . . Minnie's sister Lavinna, who was with her later told her she was 'blacked out' for probably 30 minutes. . . . As Minnie began to come out of that 'black out' she thot 'Where am I? Who am I?' and then she was conscious of who she was and that she had given birth to a son, and opened her eyes . . . so that sister knew she was conscious again. So Lavinna asked her if she thot it would be alright for Della, Minnie's 10 yr old daughter to sit there and keep her awake? Minnie told her it would . . . [and] that she would fight the sleep herself as she knew what was at stake, having gone thru this experience when Della was born. . . . So Della sat there and called her name every time she even started to close her eyes. It seemed like she sat there one hour at least or even more keeping Minnie awake. It was an experience Minnie never wanted to go thru with again. And did not ever. Every Fourth of July, in memory, Minnie relives that day again.[2]

Minnie's last child, a boy for whom she almost gave her life, died in childhood. She and Ves Atteberry divorced before little Robert's death. Minnie never remarried but kept the name Atteberry for the rest of her days.[3]

Not long after her Independence Day ordeal, Minnie radically changed her life—or at least her circumstances. Over the previous dozen years Minnie had endured three near-fatal births, two failed marriages, and the death of both her parents and subsequent scattering of her siblings. The diaspora spurred by the death of her parents found her in unfamiliar surroundings in northern Illinois, 180 miles from her native Wayne County. It was at this low point that she made the decision to follow a sibling who had recently moved to Arkansas.

Her five-hundred-mile journey from northern Illinois to the Ozarks was a chapter in one of the Ozarks's most peculiar historical episodes, the Incoming Kingdom Missionary Unit of John Battenfield. A Disciples of Christ minister in Illinois, Battenfield believed he had cracked the millennial prophecies encoded in the books of Daniel and Revelation. Spreading his teachings through his own personal magnetism and his weekly publication, *The Kingdom Harbinger*, Battenfield convinced hundreds

Della, Minnie, and Lawrence.
Courtesy of Leon Cooley.

of followers that Armageddon—his version a worldwide war between
Protestants and Catholics—would devastate the planet before the 1920s
came to an end and that survival depended upon the establishment of
separatist, self-sufficient colonies in remote mountainous areas. His primary focus was a retreat in the Ozarks near Gilbert, Arkansas. It was to
this Searcy County hamlet on the banks of the Buffalo River that John
Battenfield and his brother, Ben, led more than two hundred disciples in
1920 and 1921.[4] One of those disciples was a former ministerial student
named Francis Mathes, the oldest of Minnie Atteberry's six brothers. At
some point following the birth of her youngest child, Minnie moved south
with her three children to join Francis in Arkansas.[5]

We know little about Minnie's first decade in Arkansas, for her sur-viving diaries pick up her story only in 1934. By then John Battenfield's millennialist vision was a fading memory. Nine years earlier, hubris had gotten the best of the prophet. He promised to raise a recently deceased follower from the grave. The deed undone, the preacher slipped away in the dark of the night. His confused and angered flock dwindled in the days that followed, though several dozen remained and carried on the new lives they had made for themselves.[6] Francis Mathes stayed and farmed, as did Minnie and her children. She would spend the rest of her life in the rugged and remote hills of Searcy County. What little we know about those early years is that tragedy followed Minnie to Arkansas. Son Robert was only three and a half when he died in 1926; of what, we do not know. Half a dozen years later Minnie's daughter Della, who married local farm boy Arther Rea at the tender age of fifteen, died less than six months after giving birth to her second child. She was barely twenty years old. Minnie was the only momma Della's children would ever know.[7]

Marginal Lives

I've always been drawn to figures on the margins. It's probably the birth-right of someone raised in the rural, hardscrabble Ozarks. In all my years of research I have encountered few people more marginal than Minnie Atteberry and Lawrence Gardner. In a prosperous county their steep, rocky forty acres just east of Bear Creek—purchased in 1929 for $75— would have been tillable only in desperation.[8] But the Buffalo River hills provided little more than bare survival in a good year. Like most of their neighbors, Minnie, her two grandchildren, and Lawrence existed on a near-subsistence level of farming in the 1930s and '40s. Lawrence sup-plemented the family's meager coffers by cutting and selling firewood and with seasonal labor at a nearby canning factory. In addition, Minnie received occasional packages of money and gifts from her grandchil-dren's father, who spent the latter Depression years tramping the country for work.

By the late 1930s, Minnie and her family had slipped into destitute cir-cumstances. Though several neighbors signed their names to government relief rolls, Minnie and Lawrence maintained an impoverished independ-ence. They epitomized the almost hopeless poverty of a growing number of residents of the rural South who survived with inadequate or nonexis-tent public-health services and who suffered in anonymity and isolation,

Minnie at home, 1938.
Courtesy of Leon Cooley.

forced to depend on neighbors only slightly better off or on government relief programs whose stigma many of the proud impoverished avoided for as long as they could.

In the winter of 1941, their living conditions deteriorated to an unprecedented low. Minnie recalled the family's dire straits in a letter to her sister. "We had no fruit nor vegetables canned, had no meat nor eggs. What we had canned we'd eaten up most of it by Xmas and ate the last can of anything on March 9. All we had to eat was lard, sugar, cornbread."[9] Like many women in similar conditions, Minnie frequently went without food or ate inadequate amounts in order to provide for her grandchildren. It was a recipe for malnourishment. Minnie found herself bedfast for days at a time. She had come face to face with pellagra, the niacin deficiency illness that once plagued the South's pockets of one-crop agriculture and other places dependent on a corn-heavy diet.[10] Minnie later recounted her bout with the disease that her Arkansas neighbors referred to as "Plagury."

> Then last year I got down in bed and in such a shape that I . . . knew myself I was going to die and soon if something were not done soon to help me. . . . When my food supply would run out it would seem that every beat of my heart would be the last and then when I would eat a meal and get a new food supply then my heart would beat so fast and hard that it felt like it would jump right thru my chest. . . . On the afternoon of the 10 of March I went to bed. Lawrence was gone from home working for a man to get some money to get things we needed, such as food etc. The little grandchildren were here. I had them to do up the evening work and start supper. . . . I told them I might die. I told them not to be afraid. I told them what to do till Lawrence came if I did die. . . . I was in such a condition . . . that I didn't know whether I would live a minute or an hour longer or even if I would live thru the night.
>
> I knew Dr. Bing could cure me, and next day . . . Lawrence . . . went to Marshall to get Dr. Bing to come out to see me. . . . The sun was going down while he stood by my bed and examined me and we lit the lamp before he left. That was the only trip he made out to see me. . . . Dr. Bing gave me some medicine that in about an hour after I took it would tingle with life clear out to the very tip ends of my fingers and toes. . . . You know I wish I could feel like I did then. That's what you would call robust health, just brimful and running over with life and well-being. One would feel like moving the world. That medicine would last 12 hrs. He gave that the first few days and then put me on that Fleischman's Yeast and a red coated tablet.[11]

Minnie's brush with death swayed her to compromise her independence and allow Lawrence to sign up for government commodities from the county welfare office. Like other Americans existing on the margins, over time Minnie and Lawrence came to rely more heavily on a variety of government welfare programs. In addition to commodities, Minnie received a federal Aid to Dependent Children benefit check during the war years, and the return of hard times in the 1960s would cause them to again turn to various public assistance programs.[12]

Despite her efforts to convince the local draft board to defer her son as the sole means of support for her and the grandchildren, Lawrence Gardner was drafted in December of 1942. Minnie recorded the somber farewell on the day after Christmas.

> Lawrence ... got dressed & ready to leave. Then he chopped out some tin for me to put around the stoves. I got breakfast ready & called him to eat. We sat down to the last meal together for awhile. After he finished eating he got ready to start. Then the parting & he walked out of the yard & away. It made us sad & it was lonesome. It was rainy all day. We worked between showers & finally got the wood in the dry.[13]

Financially, Lawrence's three years in the Army proved more valuable to the family than did his presence at home. But Lawrence's departure cost the family in other ways. Minnie's diaries reflect an almost constant preoccupation with cutting and hauling wood for the heating stove and the cook stove, a job that had always belonged to Lawrence, and she and the grandchildren kept the farm going as best they could. These new chores took a mental and physical toll on middle-aged Minnie and prevented the children from attending school regularly.

A New Voice for a New Age

Following Lawrence's return from the army, Minnie's increasingly detailed diaries provide a glimpse into the modernizing forces affecting rural and small-town America in the years following World War II. For many in the Ozarks this meant rapid change, as a tornado of technology and market forces threatened to strip hill folks of their nineteenth-century vestiges and hurl them into the atomic age. Even people on the margins of society found themselves swept up, usually willingly, in the winds transforming American life. Minnie's writings capture the life-changing developments and optimism of the postwar years. Lawrence and Minnie purchased what appears to have been their first radio soon after his discharge. On March 5, 1946, Minnie listened to Winston Churchill's "Iron Curtain" speech broadcast from Westminster College in Fulton, Missouri.[14]

Farming in rugged areas of the Ozarks was a paying proposition for almost no one, including Minnie and Lawrence. Ultimately it mattered little, for Lawrence, a shade tree mechanic and inveterate tinkerer, was no farmer at heart. After two years he "decided he'd not crop but work at a public job" and made the transition from marginal producer to laborer at a Marshall cheese plant.[15] For years afterward, Lawrence worked long hours six days a week at the cheese plant during the warmer months, when the supply of milk from area farms was greatest, and labored winters at one of the many small sawmills in the area. Locals remember Lawrence as something of an eccentric mechanical genius and often credit him with inventions that he never patented. A nephew recalls Lawrence's fondness for engineering journals and technical manuals and his unrealized dream of crafting a perpetual motion machine out of the discarded implements he piled in long rows on their rocky hillside.[16]

But his alleged mechanical wizardry never elevated Lawrence above the level of common laborer. Mother and son's fiscal solvency ebbed and flowed on the waves of Lawrence's seasonal paychecks and his periodic brushes with unemployment. Minnie and Lawrence also gradually drifted toward almost complete dependence on store-bought consumer goods. Before this gradual decline set in, however, things didn't always look so grim for Minnie and Lawrence. The early and mid-1950s proved a comparatively comfortable time. It was during this era that Minnie's distinctive, detached third-person voice emerged in lengthy, compulsive passages. The reason for this transformation is unclear. Given Minnie's history of struggles and tragedies, it is certainly within the realm of possibility that her third-person journaling was protective "self-distancing"—a mechanism that can be triggered by psychological trauma—but there is nothing to indicate a reason for the timing of the change.[17]

Whatever it was that activated her new perspective and voice, they arrived in time to record the coming of electricity, which exercised a greater impact on Minnie's day-to-day life than any other development in her diaries. Though more than three-quarters of the homes in the state of Arkansas had electricity by 1950, it was only in early 1954 that the Petit Jean Electric Cooperative put Minnie and Lawrence's house on the grid.[18] Minnie's hopeful words exude a verve and wonder befitting a woman still reveling in a minor miracle. Times were comparatively good for Minnie and Lawrence—as good as they would ever be. His steady job at the cheese plant and a check for driving one of the plant's milk routes provided the means to purchase a refrigerator, electric range, and electric iron. They also owned a gasoline-powered washing machine, and for a time Lawrence could even afford to hire a local woman to help Minnie do the weekly wash. Minnie's accounts of daily chores and experiences in the spring of 1954 offer some of the richest vignettes of a woman's ordinary days in an extraordinary time of modernization in the rural Ozarks.

May 12, 1954: [Minnie] read the Instruction Book for the Electric Range. Listened to the radio for Thirty minutes . . . cleaned the Electric Range and got it ready to bake a cake. . . . Started to get cake ready to bake but didn't have all the measurements analyzed, so 'worked' the analysis out and by that time it was dark and she did not want to bake the cake after dark. As she has not used the oven, as yet, and this is the first time she has used it. She wanted to have daylight to see what she was doing this first time.[19]

May 13, 1954: [A] Mrs. Mack from Little Rock, Ark. called. She was selling Armstrong _____ plastic rugs, size 12 × 18 ft. At first she asked $15.00 for one rug and get the second one free. Seeing that Minnie had three rooms, she then offered three rugs for $20.00 and Minnie still refusing to buy she (Mrs. Mack) offered the three rugs for $18.00 and again, offered two for $12.00. Minnie did not buy any rugs, for two very main reasons. She had no money at hand to buy anything with, much less these rugs. Second, Lawrence was not present to sanction the 'deal' and she would not buy without his consent.[20]

May 16, 1954: Then she fixed to bake the Wacky Cake she has been planning to make for the last several days. She was going to use the new Electric oven for the first time. Without anyone to help her and be entirely responsible. She was rather nervous about it as she had not ever used an electric oven before and realized her responsibility in using it. She got the dough and everything ready, then preheated the oven according to instructions Mrs. Daniel gave and which the Instruction Book with the range gives. Then she baked the cake and made the icing and had very satisfactory results. She will not feel so nervous from now on when using the oven.[21]

May 21, 1954: They let her out in front of Lay's store. She went into the store and noticed on their clock that it was only 7:40 A.M. She stood around in the store, bought groceries, and then noticed it was 9:00 A.M. . . . She came back to Eoff's store and stopped to look at their electric stoves, refrigerators and irons. Then stopped at the Post Office and got the mail which had not been got for about 12 days. There was a stack of it. She went back to Lay's store and found a seat and sat down to look over the mail. There was . . . three letters to Lawrence and the Pet Milk recipe booklet and the Larido Ball Point Pen from Folger's Coffee which she had sent for. . . .

On her way back to Lay's store she stopped at Jack Treece's store intending to have them show her an electric Maytag washer if they had one. When she went into the store no one came to wait on her. She noticed the television set they had going and sat down to look and listen. The 11:30 program was just beginning. It was an economist giving recipes. It was very interesting to her as she's always collecting recipes. The next program, 'At Home with Julie' 11:45 to 12:00 was an interesting program. Julie had a special guest as she does each week day. This guest was an artist and had several pictures to show. The next program 12:00 to 12:30 'Little Rock Today' gave the news and the weather and showed a 1902 model car as a special entertainment along with the giving of news and weather. . . .

It was now 12:30 and she had sat there a whole hour! She had to tear herself away. She could have sat there all afternoon, but she knew she'd better come on home. She wanted to look at Mays' electric irons so went on over to their store and looked at them, then stopped in at Daniel's store to look at his irons and to have a word with him about the electric range and refrigerator. She went back to Lay's store. They were about ready to bring her home, but she had time to eat her lunch she had taken along and then she went to Russel's to weigh herself. She weighed 202 pounds. Seems she's going to have to eat smaller helpings of the foods she eats so that she can lose some weight. She should only weigh 165 to 170 lbs. That means she should lose about 35 pounds.[22]

Those optimistic entries from the spring of 1954 represent something of a pinnacle of happiness for Minnie, still robust and active in her mid-sixties. Throughout the years of her diary-keeping, Minnie only occasionally ventured beyond her little piece of land. Her brother Francis had moved to California in 1942, and by the early 1950s both grandchildren had left Arkansas for good, Leroy settling in Peoria, Illinois, and Christie in west Texas. Minnie and Lawrence now had no blood family in Arkansas.[23] As she neared her seventies, Minnie's world constricted. After the 1950s she recorded no visits from siblings, and she seems never to have enjoyed a single close friendship in all her days on the ridge overlooking Bear Creek. Given such an isolated life, it is no wonder that Minnie could not conceal her giddiness over an unexpected visit from grandson Leroy Rea in 1959.

> They had just said, We'll try to sleep some more until the alarm rings. Then heard a car coming, and Minnie said, Now who can that be, this early, about then the horn began to blow and Lawrence said, that's Leroy, Minnie said, Surely not. Lawrence said, Listen at the horn blow, no one does that but Leroy. By that time the car stopped. Lawrence was getting out of bed to go out to see who it was, and what was wanted. When he got to the door, he saw that it *was* Leroy. Minnie said, Is it Leroy? Lawrence said, yes, she said, sure enough, Lawrence said, yes, it is Leroy. . . . In the afternoon Lawrence remarked, We were so sure we weren't going to let any one or anything hinder us *today* almost looked like God planned it different for us.[24]

Whether due to her advancing age or Lawrence's seasonally precarious wage-earning, Minnie's modernizing efforts were mostly spent by the mid-1950s. In the summer of 1956, Minnie and Lawrence made their last significant domestic purchase, an eight-piece set of Miracle Maid Waterless Cookware from E. Daniel's in Marshall. It was an unusually steep outlay for them, almost three weeks' wages at the cheese plant, but it was an expense that Minnie likely felt was justified by Miracle Maid's claims that its cookware would enhance the healthfulness of food.[25] Though she remained in her house into the early 1970s, Minnie and Lawrence never had indoor plumbing. A granddaughter recalls the electric range sitting unused in the 1960s as Minnie continued to bake bread and cook beans with the old wood-burning cook stove. And, despite Minnie's infatuation with television on her day trip to Marshall and diary references to a television inside their home, Minnie and Lawrence and their rural neighbors were unable to receive television signals via antenna.[26]

But increasing isolation and the apparent end of her efforts to modernize did not spell the end of Minnie's curiosity with the world around her. Other than Lawrence, her most loyal companion was the radio, at least when it was working. Her only regular visitors were on-air personalities—radio homemakers, Springfield folklorist May Kennedy McCord (the "Queen of the Hillbillies"), and radio evangelists.[27] Minnie, like many elderly shut-ins, grew enamored with the various radio preachers whose programs ran on Springfield and Little Rock stations. Most of them were nationally syndicated evangelists, such as Billy Graham and right-wing exhorters Billy James Hargis and Bill Beeny. Given Minnie's connection

Minnie at home, 1960.
Courtesy of Leon Cooley.

with the Battenfield ministry of the 1920s, perhaps it is not surprising that she was especially drawn to ministers espousing millennialist messages. The two radio evangelists to whom she sent small cash donations both fit that bill: Herbert W. Armstrong, founder of the Worldwide Church of God, and Springfield, Missouri, minister Floyd Hitchcock, who drew many of his sermons from the prophecy-heavy books of Daniel and Revelation.[28]

Even more important to Minnie's life, and more stimulating for her curious mind, was reading. "Minnie calls this reading her play, as play is recreation and reading is recreation to her," she confided to her diary.[29] Reading seems to have been Minnie's only form of recreation, and it was important enough to her that she devoted what little disposable (and sometimes indispensable) income she had to buying subscriptions and books. Her diaries mention no fewer than eight periodicals to which she or Lawrence subscribed over the years.[30] Descendants recall that Minnie never threw away her magazines and newspapers, keeping string-tied bundles of them neatly organized in the tiny attic.[31] For a time in the late 1950s, Minnie also maintained a membership in the Doubleday Book Club, and her diaries note more than a dozen books she read during that time. Minnie's favorite interactions with Lawrence may have been the occasions when she read to him. On a summer day in 1959, when Lawrence was home with a back injury, Minnie received a new mail-order book, Art Linkletter's *Kids Say the Darndest Things!*

> After she had taken it out of the wrapping, of course she had to look at it and write the date, rec'd, and her name in the book. Lawrence was interested so she aimed to read the foreword and Introduction and table of contents and then put it up and get to her other work. But Lawrence wanted her to read some of it so he could hear it. She started looking at the book at 10:38 and started reading the first chapter about 10:45 A.M. and kept reading on and on until it was 1:30 P.M. when she stopped to eat lunch, and Lawrence ate lunch, too.[32]

Financial straits likely rendered Minnie's Doubleday dalliance a brief one. In the early 1960s, the cheese plant closed, costing Lawrence his best job and his milk route. For the remainder of Minnie's life, he held a succession of low-paying, manual-labor jobs at sawmills and stave mills, with longer periods of unemployment than before. Lawrence and Minnie stayed in perpetual debt to the various Marshall merchants with whom they traded. They lived from week to week and month to month and apparently had no bank account, cashing paychecks, unemployment checks, and social security payments at court-square mercantiles. Minnie was no stranger to want and adjusted her activities accordingly during hard times. She picked and prepared "poke Salett," cut up cardboard boxes to use as insoles in her shoes, and spent hours sewing up the binding on a slipper, "a long and tedious job . . . but it will make the shoe wear longer."[33]

The struggles of Minnie and Lawrence after the closing of the cheese plant illustrated the slippery financial slope on which many of their neighbors found themselves. In 1959, the first year that the US Census Bureau released poverty statistics, three in five families in Searcy County lived below the poverty line, more than three times the national average. At times the federal government was the sole support for such families. Minnie's "old age welfare checks" provided her and Lawrence their only steady stream of income. Through most of the 1960s, Minnie and Lawrence received government commodities from the local welfare office. On February 21, 1967, Minnie noted in her diary that she had received a "Surplus Food" allotment consisting of two cans of chopped meat, ten pounds of flour, five pounds of yellow corn meal, two pounds of margarine, two pounds of pinto beans, three pounds of rolled wheat, two pounds of rice, and peanut butter.[34] The diary indicates that Minnie and Lawrence shared their "Surplus Food" with friends and neighbors, giving twenty pounds of flour to Lawrence's best friend, Riley Rea, and other commodities to a family whose husband/father had recently died.

This display of generosity bore the mark of Lawrence, a caring and giving neighbor who performed innumerable small kindnesses for the people of their rural community. Lawrence shared with Minnie an odd, often unappreciated intelligence. In later life he even began to scribble dense, minutiae-laden accounts of his daily activities. But where Lawrence was easygoing and pliable, her diaries suggest Minnie was resolute and unbending. Where he was generous to a fault, she could be miserly. Where Lawrence was unreliable and whimsical, Minnie was steady and predictable. Where he acted in blind faith and rarely anticipated repercussions, she was perceptive and even paranoid when it came to dealings with others.

Putting Minnie on the Couch

My visit to Minnie's old house only stokes my interest in her unusual diaries. I read through page after page. I transcribe day after day, almost fifty thousand words, and it's only a drop in the bucket. It is clear that Minnie was not your average diarist. The third-person voice? Something I've never encountered before in all my research. There are other oddities as well, enough of them that I decide to seek professional help—for me and, belatedly, for Minnie. I contact the head of the psychology department at my university, explain my quest in a way that I hope won't make me seem as creepy as I feel, and ask if he can recommend one of his professors. On a blustery January day, I trudge across campus to the office of psychologist Brooke Whisenhunt. Turns out her big sister and my wife were college basketball teammates. There is no need for us to connect—we're both professionals, after all—but as natives of the rural South it is a comfortable happenstance. I am taken aback when she is familiar with Searcy County. Her father grew up there, she tells me, and they are descendants of one of the county's most notable families. It's a good omen. I introduce Dr. Whisenhunt to Minnie—or at least to the bundle of eccentricities leaping from her papers—and Dr. Whisenhunt puts her on the couch.

I walk Dr. Whisenhunt through Minnie's profile. In addition to her third-person journaling, Minnie seems to have been a chronic chronicler, keeping minute track of everything from the number of eggs she gathered each morning to the exact price of each item she and Lawrence purchased. She studiously maintained a narrative daily "weather record." Minnie spent inordinate amounts of time writing. Her surviving papers contain lengthy rough drafts of letters (sometimes as long as twelve handwritten pages) that she presumably rewrote before mailing. They also reveal stacks of "memos," copious notes on chores and activities that informed her daily diaries. As she grew older, her diary entries grew longer and more minutely detailed. By the 1960s, the diaries were densely packed with what seemed to be every thread of her life—what time she got up, when she ate meals and got dressed, when she emptied slop jars and brought in water from the cistern. Even more unusual was that she chronicled Lawrence's life with equal gusto, a practice that occasionally caused friction between them. Scarcely a day went by when Lawrence did not leave the forty-acre junk farm. His days were full of interactions with other people. At night, or at the breakfast table the following morning, Minnie quizzed Lawrence on the things he did and the people with whom he dealt. She wanted to know and record every detail.

The diaries and memories of descendants also reveal other traits: perfectionism, orderliness, judgmentalism, paranoia, and a proclivity for hoarding, though a much more organized brand of hoarding than that of son Lawrence. For Dr. Whisenhunt, the psychological profile cobbled from family memories and Minnie's writings leads to a possible diagnosis: Obsessive-Compulsive Personality Disorder (OCPD), with perhaps a touch of Obsessive Compulsive Disorder (OCD)—a different but often overlapping diagnosis. Modern psychiatry defines OCPD as "a pervasive pattern of preoccupation with orderliness, perfectionism, and mental and interpersonal control, at the expense of flexibility, openness, and efficiency." Minnie, like people with OCPD, exhibited an abnormal "preoccupation with details, rules, lists, order, organization, or schedules," an intense perfectionism that often prevented her from completing tasks, an inflexibility "about matters of morality, ethics, or values," an inability to "discard worn-out or worthless objects," and a penchant for miserliness in financial matters.[35] I thank Dr. Whisenhunt and head back out into the cold, admiring Minnie's perseverance and indomitable spirit.

PERHAPS MINNIE FACED her psychological disorder throughout her life. Perhaps her OCPD was conditioned by her increasingly vulnerable position as she aged, an older woman living in rural Arkansas and navigating a man's world. Whatever the case, she knew well the precarious and too often secondary position of women in the transactional world of the Ozarks. She was firm and direct in her dealings with women and men, demanding respect with an intelligent and proud bearing. "She could hold her own with any person in town," recalled a descendant.[36]

But there were gender and age barriers that she could not overcome. Once he reached adulthood, Lawrence assumed the mantle of head of household, as society mandated. As she grew older, Minnie came to rely more heavily on Lawrence—to earn a living off the farm, to take care of business at the courthouse, to buy groceries. But Minnie knew better than anyone her son's limitations. Easygoing Lawrence exhibited little discernment when it came to finances or interpersonal relationships, and he was frequently taken advantage of as a result. He once loaned an acquaintance money to help save his house, only to have the man sell the house and move away without repaying Lawrence. For years Lawrence allowed his employer at the cheese plant to dump truckloads of whey on Minnie's hillside—and never received a penny in compensation. In short, Minnie's son, her conduit to the world and her only support, was not up to the task— and she realized it.[37]

Yet, there was little that an aging Minnie could do to shelter her son. As a poor, eccentric man best known for piling other people's refuse on his little farm, Lawrence Gardner circulated within a network of fellow marginal men. To a person, they were characters who failed to meet Minnie's approval. In the hundreds of daily diary entries Minnie wrote, she never expressed a kind thought toward any of her son's friends and acquaintances. She tolerated his best friend, Riley Rea, though she considered him a directionless hanger-on, an anchor weighing down her son.

> [Minnie] would *not* tolerate if it were she dealing with Riley. She'd soon let him know she had not had any intention of having him to help her and therefore would not pay him, and would let him know that she didn't care for him to ride to town, but that once there she expected him to mind his business . . . and not follow her around, 'sticking his nose' into her business. . . . But Lawrence lets him pull this stunt time after time, and Minnie is sure greived [*sic*] that he does.[38]

Minnie universally disapproved of Lawrence's other "cronies," the unambitious types who went "to town and sat around on the streets seeing and being seen," and chided him for bringing home a "Coxy's [sic] Army" of young men who loitered away the hours making trades and talking over piles of rusting metal.[39]

She was especially critical of a trio of brothers, new arrivals in the area, who befriended Lawrence in the spring of 1959. The transient Bradberrys offended Minnie's sensibilities by making themselves at home, eating up her food, and making pushy requests with which Lawrence generally complied, such as asking to hear Uncle Josh cylinders on the novel old machine in their cluttered parlor. Sizing up the situation after a few weeks' acquaintance with the Bradberrys, Minnie decided that they were not the type to pick up on subtle cues that their company was not appreciated; she reached her limit one spring morning when one of the brothers insisted on trading a used school bus to Lawrence. "Minnie up and told him . . . that we did not want nor need the old school bus," she confided to her diary, "so why couldn't he shut up about it and not keep trying to sell it to us? So he shut up and . . . got gone. (He is nothing but a nuisance.)" Minnie expressed relief a couple of days later when she heard that the Bradberrys' brief stay in Searcy County was coming to an end. "They are one family of people that Minnie is glad to have go elsewhere. She would not have missed much . . . if she'd never met them."[40]

In the twilight of her life, Minnie seemed to write under an ever greater urgency to record even the minutest details. The more prosaic the activity, the more intense and unrelenting its chronicling. As the years wore on, Minnie found her desire for order challenged by Lawrence's ever-expanding junkyard, a blight over which she exercised no control. Perhaps it was this challenge that most motivated her to bring order to her life's narrative through increasingly detailed diary accounts of each day's activities. Most of the time this resulted in sheer tedium.

Sometimes it offered an unintentionally humorous window into the humdrum interactions of daily life.

Minnie had sorted all of the clothes and done other things and worked all she could on her dress and about four o'clock P.M. she made a fire in the cook stove and burned up some refuse paper that had accumulated. Washed up dishes and fixed supper and had it ready to put on the table when Lawrence got home. They ate and Lawrence went right to bed at 8:30 P.M. Minnie washed up what dishes were dirty, mixed powdered milk and got everything done and turned the light on in the bedroom to fix her bed so when she did some writing she would have it ready to go to bed. The light waked Lawrence, whereupon he started a big 'howl' about her waking him and stomping around and making noise so he can't sleep. Short, he just wanted to show how 'stinking' he can be. . . . It was 10:00 o'clock P.M. when she waked him by turning on the light in the bed room. It was about 20 min till 11:00 when she went to bed. About 12:30 she waked up coughing and coughed until she coughed some phlegm up. She got up to spit and went to the kitchen to get some salt to eat to stop the cough, used the night bucket, and at this time Lawrence got up and went out on the porch, and 'bawled' out, why don't you do something to stop that cough? Minnie answered that that was what she was trying to do. She took a dose of Wait's Green Mountain cough syrup, and went back to bed. Then Lawrence began a tirade about what he was going to do, and she had to go to bed and bla, bla, bla like he does to be hateful to her. They talked about the weather at this time.[41]

Occasionally it exploded into gripping narrative, complete with flash-backs or stories within stories. One such example was her harrowing recollection of an encounter with an unwanted intruder in the summer of Minnie's seventy-eighth year.

Was putting the breast in the sauce pan was going to cook it in, turned to get something out of the safe, and when she turned back toward the door, to her startled surprise here was a snake crawling into the kitchen. She was so startled, now what was she to do, no ax to kill it with. At first she thot it was a copperhead snake, but then she noticed it was making a noise, and looked closer and saw it was colored different from a copperhead, and realized the noise it was making was rattling like a rattlesnake makes. This made her more startled than when she thot it was a copperhead snake. It was the size of a copperhead snake. When she first noticed it, it was half way in. She made a movement and it knew she had seen it. It crawled faster and crawled along back of the cook-stove into the corner where there was things it could hide in and around. It stopped so that its head was visible. Minnie punched at it with the new ax handle and it crawled behind the iron pot in the corner and she couldn't see it any more, but she knew it was there, because it kept those rattles going almost constantly. It was 1:15 P.M. by our clock when she noticed it crawling into the kitchen. The question now was how to get it killed and out of the kitchen as Minnie didn't relish its company.

So she remembered that Ollie McCracken, Jerd Farmer's sister, who lived out in Oklahoma, had had a 'bout' with a rattlesnake, years ago. Minnie does not remember for sure but thinks it was a diamond-back rattler, tho it may not have been. It had got into the house and behind the bed and her daughter had got bitten by it. Mr. McCracken was gone to work for the day. Mrs. McCracken knew the best thing she could do was to send for an Indian neighbor. She knew he would know how to get the snake out of the house, so sent one or two of her younger children to get the Indian to come help her. He came, and when he got there, he wouldn't come into the house, because Mr. McCracken was not at home. Mrs. McCracken had a time convincing this Indian that it would be alright for him to come into the house, even if Mr. McCracken was not at home. She got him convinced. He came in, saw the snake, said to let it alone, to put her tea-kettle on and heat water boiling hot. He fixed medicine to doctor the wound on the girl that had been bitten. When the water was boiling hot he took the teakettle and poured the boiling hot water on the snake and it crawled out of the house and the Indian said to let it crawl away, because if it crawled away, there would not ever be anymore rattle-snakes about.

Therefore, Minnie recalling this incident, decided to heat water and scald this snake. She had the teakettle half full of hot water, so she filled it full and put it on the high heat on the electric stove, and while it heated she got ready to pour the hot water on it. She had to decide how it would come out, so she moved things she thot would be in the way. By that time the water was boiling. She put water in another vessel to set on the red hot unit, turned the switch off, moved a bucket off of the iron pot, and proceeded to pour the hot water on the snake. It came out of the corner and up over some wood and card-board boxes back of the cookstove and fell down in front of the cook-stove at Minnie's feet. She kept pouring hot water on it, especially on its head. Then used the ax handle to lift it out of the house. Placed it so she thot Lawrence would see it when he got home. He did not see it because the outside light was not turned on. Minnie asked him if he saw the snake? He said he didn't and then looked at it. It was a kind of lead color and there were diamonds, it had five rattles and the but-ton. Minnie is keeping the rattles. Lawrence carried it off Saturday morning. Lawrence kept saying he was so glad that Minnie succeeded

Lawrence Gardner's Fantastic World of Plain and Fancy Junk

From an article in the *Mountain Wave*
(Marshall, Arkansas), February 14, 1974.

in killing the snake. It was 2:15 P.M. when Minnie got thru with the snake. She had spent one whole hour getting thru with it. She was so taut that she didn't feel.[42]

Minnie's dramatic account of her battle with a serpent was anomalous by the 1960s, however. As Minnie advanced into old age, her dense, third-person accounts of mostly unchanging days took on an absurdist quality, refracting her utterly plain existence into bizarre purposefulness. It was as if she willed meaning into a life that by some measures should have claimed none. One of her last surviving entries noted that Lawrence, now sixty years old himself, had to help her into bed. Minnie eventually moved into a Marshall nursing home, where she had access to indoor plumbing for the first time in her half century of life in the rural Ozarks. Though often strained by an intense dependence on one another over six decades filled with struggles and financial hardship, the bond between Minnie and Lawrence remained a strong one until the end. Officials at the home had to ask Lawrence to stop dropping by in the middle of the night to wake Minnie and "sit and talk, just like they always did." She died there in 1974. Lawrence Gardner stayed on the farm-turned-junkyard, in the weathered, unpainted house with no indoor plumbing until moving into Marshall shortly before his death in 1992.[43]

<hr />

I'M READING THROUGH Minnie's diary entries from the fall of 1952. "For whoever who may read this," she begins one of them. The words catch me off guard. What follows is typical Minnie—a too long and overly detailed account of her accidentally ingesting shards of broken glass in a dish of fruit cocktail and the subsequent health problems that she blamed on the episode. It was a matter of great importance to her at the time, but now it seems inconsequential, even silly. In her compulsion to record the movements of her life, to seemingly prove her existence in the face of a skeptical and inattentive world, Minnie subjected each day's experiences—no matter how trivial they may have seemed then or seem now—to a rigorous recounting, a daily, blow-by-blow narrative. You and I—the "whoever who may read this"—are left to decipher her accounts, to make sense of the world as she saw it. I hope that doing so grants meaning to her efforts. Minnie is not forgotten.

CHAPTER TWELVE

A Time Zone Away and a Generation Behind

APPALACHIA AND THE OZARKS

I F YOU ARE A YOUNGER SIBLING, you know how we feel in the Ozarks. You remember what it's like to be the little sister or little brother. You never got to do anything first, and life was all about hand-me-downs. Everything you did—from first steps to potty training to T-ball to the first day of school to piano lessons to the tooth fairy, school plays, church camps, and senior prom—had all been done before, amid much greater fanfare and in front of a camera. You wore hand-me-down clothes. You got the ball glove that your older brother broke in wrong, the rusted *Waltons* lunch box, the inside of which he covered in Dallas Cowboys stickers even though you were more of a Terry Bradshaw guy. You were never first, never original, never completely yourself. Even at school, your teachers knew you as your big brother's little brother. If that's your story, you know how the Ozarks feels.

To appease my resentment, I offer a couple of informational nuggets favorable to the Ozarks. The core of the Ozarks, a small range known as the St. Francois Mountains in southeastern Missouri, dates back approximately 1.4 billion years, making my mountains roughly three times older than the Appalachians. And European exploration and settlement in the Ozarks began in the first half of the eighteenth century, in the same era that such settlement commenced on the eastern fringes of what we today know as Appalachia. Yet, due to its location in the middle of North America in the historical era—the era of European-dominated, westward-moving colonization—the old Ozarks has found itself always a generation or so behind Appalachia in the American story. (It didn't help our case that those earliest Europeans in the Ozarks spoke and wrote French.) Just about everything Appalachians did, Ozarkers have done, too—only later. And the Ozarks has often borrowed from or emulated the Appalachian experience. We have similar varieties of terrain. The American settlers who began trickling into the Ozarks in the 1790s and pouring into the region following the War of 1812 came largely from Appalachia, or at least spent time seasoning in that cauldron of upland South culture. Even the Native Americans of Appalachia, the Cherokee, repeated the experience, for the land granted them in the northeastern corner of the Indian Territory is largely the Oklahoma Ozarks. In other words, the Ozarks has for hundreds of years received Appalachia's hand-me-downs. If there's a tag somewhere on the landscape of southern Missouri, it probably has on it the word "Appalachia" written in Sharpie.

So how does a region get to be a younger sibling? We'll get to that directly, but first of all let's look at the evidence in the historical record— the hand-me-downs from Appalachia. I'll concentrate on the post–Civil War era—the era during which the social constructions of Appalachia and the Ozarks evolved. There are any number of examples I could use, but let's focus on a few developments that contributed to the construction of these regions in the national consciousness, namely regionalist literature, the mountain-mission school phenomenon, the publication of documentary studies before World War II, and the creation of federal regional commissions in the 1960s.

Regionalist Literature

We know that the depiction of Appalachian mountain folk by the local colorists was a seminal development in the formation of regional identity. The mountain people of the southeast began to attract literary attention as early as 1873, with the publication of Will Wallace Harney's "A Strange Land and Peculiar People" in *Lippincott's Magazine*.[1] Appalachian local-color fiction hit its stride in the following two decades as a number of writers specializing in mountaineer fiction—most notably Mary Noailles Murphree (who wrote under the nom de plume Charles Egbert Craddock) and John Fox Jr.—painted romantic, backward, generally exceptional portraits of their subjects. These stories not only influenced American perceptions of the mountaineers in their midst; they also influenced more than a few missionaries and entrepreneurs to head south.[2]

Local colorists also found the Appalachians' kinfolk across the Mississippi, but only a generation later. The earliest known example of Ozarks local color is an 1887 story in *Outing* magazine, "A Camp in the Mountains of Arkansas," by Minna Caroline Smith.[3] Smith seems not to have returned to the Ozarks for her subject matter, though ten years later another obscure author, Mary Stewart, set her novel in the Missouri Ozarks and found in the natives the same *otherness*, deviance, and time-lessness that pervaded descriptions of the people of Appalachia:

> The natives of the Ozarks are a people peculiar unto themselves. They represent the advancing wave that moves on before the tide of civiliza-tion. As civilization approaches, they recede until the fastnesses of the mountains become their stronghold, where they persistently refuse to tolerate any innovation, and progress is an unknown quantity among them. They are content to cultivate the corn on the hillsides with the hoe, just as their fathers did, which is sufficient to furnish them with bread and fatten a few hogs for meat. The women wear cotton dresses made with the same spinster waists their grandmothers wore a cen-tury ago. Their houses, which are all alike, consist of one room built of logs, with a "lean-to" or "shed-room" on one side—their ancestors built just such houses in the Carolina forests before the States were born. They regard education as pernicious, and woe be unto the reformer that seeks to press upon them the adoption of his modern ideas of progress and civilization. They are, indeed, "Original in word and thought, Because unlearned and untaught." They belong to the happy-go-lucky, come-day-go-day-God-send-Sunday class, who are content if they know where the next meal is coming from, and have enough tobacco to last through the day. Seldom do the smoldering fires of ambition break out among them to consume even a single individual of a household. The year comes in and finds them satisfied, and goes out leaving them even more content.[4]

But only on rare occasions did the region attract local colorists before the dawn of the twentieth century. The foundational work in Ozarks local-color literature appeared in 1907. In no small part derivative of the formu-laic novels of John Fox Jr. and other Appalachian and regionalist writers, Harold Bell Wright's novel *The Shepherd of the Hills* follows the story of a burnt-out city man, Dan "The Shepherd" Howitt, who flees Chicago for the bucolic countryside of southwestern Missouri—the same countryside into which his artist son had disappeared years earlier. Howitt befriends a couple of local families, brings a little culture and learning into the iso-lated Ozarks backcountry, and ultimately finds redemption for his weath-ered soul in this almost holy land. Like all local color worth its salt, *The Shepherd of the Hills* peddles Ozarks stereotypes, despite (or because) of

Wright's romantic appreciation for the backcountry. The wild popularity of Wright's novel sparked a tourism boom in the Branson area and inspired a flurry of knockoffs that carried the local-color genre into the World War I era and beyond. The book also inspired a number of film adaptations and an outdoor drama. The most famous film version, directed by Henry Hathaway and released in Technicolor in 1941, came out, true to form, five years after the same director's adaptation of John Fox Jr.'s most successful novel, *The Trail of the Lonesome Pine*, hit theaters (in Technicolor) with two stars (Fred MacMurray and Henry Fonda) instead of *Shepherd*'s one (John Wayne.) And the time-lag parallels didn't stop there. The two novels were later adapted into outdoor dramas, both of which are still in business. In this category, at least, the Ozarks can claim older-sibling status, Branson's *The Shepherd of the Hills* having preceded Big Stone Gap, Virginia's *The Trail of the Lonesome Pine* by four years.[5]

Mountain Mission Schools

Turning to a topic a lot less fun but no less crucial to the story of the upland South, the mountain mission-school movement also illustrates the generational lag in the Ozarks. Motivated by a variety of factors—Progressive Era maternalism, denominational competition, eugenics, Protestant evangelism—teachers and missionaries established schools in the rural upland South, usually in areas unserved or underserved by public education. Mountain mission schools generally provided mountaineers in remote settlements their first opportunity at anything beyond a basic, elementary education. Many also followed the era's industrial education model by offering vocational classes justified by condescending if well meaning assumptions that the remote poor of the highlands—similar to Native American and African American children of the era—were developmentally unfit for a more rigorous academic course of study.

Appalachia's first institution dedicated to "mountain whites" was Asheville's Home Industrial School for Girls, established in 1877. The first boys' mountain mission school sprang up in western North Carolina two years later, and the next two decades witnessed dozens of such schools come to life across the mountains.[6] It was only in 1905, however, that the founding of the Helen Dunlap School for Mountain Girls in northwestern Arkansas marked a clear beginning of the movement in the Ozarks.[7] (By that date, the Presbyterians alone had founded some sixty-five mission schools in Appalachia.) Eventually a variety of religious denominations established almost twenty mission schools in the Ozarks. None was a settlement school—the most culturally intrusive institution that has received more than its share of scholarly attention—but many of the Ozarks schools dabbled in the same "politics of culture" that motivated their Appalachian forerunners.[8]

In the world of mountain missionaries, not only did the Ozarks come much later to the game but the region's scale of activity differed significantly as well. The Russell Sage Foundation's 1929 booklet *Southern Mountain Schools* listed 149 institutions remaining in Appalachia but only ten in the Ozarks. Even taking into account the more expansive area covered by the eastern mountains and Appalachia's larger population, the fifteen-to-one ratio was extreme and suggested a greater emphasis on mission-school work in Appalachia. In fact, so incidental was the Ozarks to the movement that Olive Dame Campbell's 1921 directory of southern mountain schools made no mention of the smaller highland region whatsoever.[9]

Regional Books

Olive Dame Campbell's husband, John C. Campbell, made a major contribution to our next area of comparison—what might be termed the regional documentary book. Unlike the local colorists, Campbell and his fellow documentarians eschewed fiction in favor of an anthropological-sociological approach to chronicling Appalachia. Like the local colorists, according to historian John Alexander Williams, the documentarians "tended to reinforce images of Appalachian otherness." *The Spirit of the Mountains*, a 1905 book by Emma Bell Miles, is generally identified as the first of this genre. Whereas Miles's book often viewed life in Appalachia through the domestic lives of women, Horace Kephart's *Our Southern Highlanders* in 1913 focused to a greater extent on the region's masculine pursuits such as hunting and logging, with side trails into such topics as feuding and mountain dialect. Eight years later, the posthumous publication of Campbell's *The Southern Highlander and His Homeland* offered readers the most textured look at the massive and diverse region.[10] James Watt Raine's *The Land of Saddle-Bags: A Study of the Mountain People of Appalachia*, published in 1924, offered yet another romantic look at an exceptional region and people—with emphasis on such tropes of highland South uniqueness as Elizabethan language, the survival of ancient folk ballads, moonshining, and feuding.[11]

By contrast, it was only in the latter part of the 1920s that a firm social construct of the Ozarks started to emerge in national magazine articles, and it was 1931 before the publication of the region's first documentary, nonfiction book. *The Ozarks: An American Survival of Primitive Society*, by folklorist Vance Randolph, was in many respects derivative of earlier Appalachian models—so much so, in fact, that Randolph lifted lines, almost verbatim, from the preface of the 1922 edition of Kephart's *Our Southern Highlanders*. Kephart favored "the real mountaineers . . . living up the branches and on the steep hillsides, away from the main-traveled roads"; he was "not concerned with the relatively few townsmen, and prosperous valley farmers, who owe to outside influences all that distinguishes them from their back-country kinsmen."[12] Likewise, Randolph's book was "not concerned with the progressive element in the Ozark towns, nor with the prosperous valley farmers, who have been more or less modernized by recent contacts with civilization"; *The Ozarks*, instead, dealt "with the 'hill-billy' or 'ridge-runner' of the more isolated sections."[13] Randolph also borrowed Kephart's claim of veracity. Kephart assured readers that "the narrative is to be taken literally. There is not a line of fiction or exaggeration in it." Randolph closed his preface in the same spirit, with almost the same words: "Every statement in the book is intended to be taken quite seriously and literally; there is not a line of fiction or of intentional exaggeration in it."[14] As the subtitle suggests, *The Ozarks: An American Survival of Primitive Society* was grounded in the romantic, exceptionalist regionalism of the era. Chapters devoted to "The Ozark Dialect," "Signs and Superstitions," folk songs and play parties, and moonshining highlighted the "diverting and picturesque" elements of the Ozarks, as such topics had earlier served the *othering* of Appalachia.

Randolph's *The Ozarks* was followed by other documentary texts on the region. Some, such as Charles Morrow Wilson's *Backwoods America* (1935), Otto Ernest Rayburn's *Ozark Country* (1941), and Marguerite Lyon's *Take to the Hills: A Chronicle of the Ozarks* (1941) were even more unapologetically romantic than was Randolph's work.[15] Rayburn's *Ozark Country*— whose first two chapter titles, "A World Apart" and "Anglo-Saxon Seed Bed," underscored the author's fascination with *otherness*—was in many respects a less erudite version of James Watt Raine's *The Land of Saddle-Bags*. Wilson's *Backwoods America*, published by the University of North Carolina Press and a rare work that included examples and anecdotes from both Appalachia and the Ozarks (though 90 percent of the book was devoted to the latter, smaller region), was an unabashed celebration of all things backwoodsy and old-timey. It was also unique in the annals of our documentary books as one written by a native Ozarker, albeit a native who was the product of an upbringing in one of those progressive towns that Vance Randolph wanted nothing to do with. Another Ozarks documentary book published in the decade preceding World War II, Catherine Barker's *Yesterday Today: Life in the Ozarks* (1941), traded romantic celebration for sober judgment, sometimes condemnation.[16] Presaging Jack Weller's *Yesterday's People*, Barker found a different side of the Ozarks as a case worker for the Federal Emergency Relief Administration. The isolation and lack of opportunity that cocooned Randolph's and Rayburn's and Wilson's Ozarkers in primitivism rendered Barker's subjects impoverished, uneducated, and backwards. Like *Cabins in the Laurel* author Muriel Early Shepard, Barker was the wife of an outsider professional living in the upland South, but the two women came away from their mountain sojourns with very different stories to tell.

Regional Commissions

The image-building of local colorists, mountain missionaries, and pre–World War II documentarians played their roles in the establishment of regional identities. The existence of regional identities, combined with renewed interest in American poverty during the Kennedy years, ultimately resulted in the formation of federal regional commissions. Appalachia, the granddaddy of regional otherness in *The Other America* (both a new state of consciousness in the early 1960s and the title of Michael Harrington's influential book), was, not surprisingly, the first region to be granted its own federal agency designed to funnel taxpayers' dollars into the depressed region.[17] (It certainly didn't hurt matters that at least ten governors could lay claim to Appalachian lands—and, thus, ten governors were motivated to use their political power to push for the initiative.) Initially created by executive order in 1963, the Appalachian Regional Commission (ARC) was officially founded by congressional act in 1965.[18]

This time it did not take the Ozarks a generation to catch up, though ultimately the region's quick catch-up proved of no long-term benefit. The Ozarks Regional Commission (ORC) was launched in March 1966, just one year after the official birth of the ARC. Consisting of 125 counties in Missouri, Arkansas, Oklahoma, and Kansas, the ORC promised to bring valuable federal funds to an area suffering from a poverty rate about 45 percent greater than that of the counties in the ARC. As historian J. Blake Perkins has illustrated, however, the "story of federal regional development efforts in the Ozarks was one of initial high hopes that turned rather quickly to disappointment."[19] Mirroring the strategy of the ARC, the ORC's grants tended to widen intraregional gaps between the haves and have-nots, between a few urban oases and vast stretches of depressed, rural hills and hollers. The result was an uneven distribution of limited funds. "Although the federal government's regional program had been initially justified by underscoring the severe poverty of rural communities," Perkins observes, "the growth-center strategy ensured that most projects ignored those areas that needed assistance the most."[20]

Indicative of this federal pattern was the failed attempt of little Melbourne, Arkansas, to secure grant money to help establish a trade school. Though the ORC ultimately awarded more than ninety grants earmarked for vocational education, Melbourne's applications to that agency and to the Economic Development Administration (EDA) were rejected on the basis that the county-seat town of only fifteen hundred people was too rural and isolated. Despite the absence of federal funding, however, community doggedness and the influence of a prominent local politician landed Melbourne on the Arkansas Department of Education's list of sites for new vocational-technical schools. Citing the "combined problems of difficulty of transport, lack of needed job skills and the resulting out-migration that characterizes the . . . North Central Arkansas region," Governor Dale Bumpers had faith that technical training would "halt the decay of our rural areas and improve the quality of life for the residents of Ozark hill country." Still, the opening of Ozarka Vocational-Technical School in 1975 represented a rare triumph for places beyond the growth centers. Some of the region's poorest counties—counties like Arkansas's Newton, Searcy, and Stone that were most severely plagued by out-migration and underemployment—received not a single grant from the ORC.[21]

As time went on, pork-barrel politics expanded the range of the ORC to encompass all counties in the four-state region, as well as the entire state of Louisiana, prompting Gov. Bumpers to dismiss the agency as a "cruel hoax."[22] So unpopular had the ORC become inside the region by 1981 that almost no one protested when Ronald Reagan killed the agency as part of his social-spending cuts. The ARC exists to this day. As usual, the Ozarks's emulation of Appalachia had reproduced to a certain degree Appalachia's results, on a much smaller scale. Only this time, the emulation was temporary. The survival of the ARC and the demise of the ORC had something to do, at least in part, with a stronger regional identity in the larger region. The boundaries of the ARC did not expand appreciably beyond those initially established in 1965, while people in the Ozarks, a region with a less developed sense of identity, watched the ORC's territory expand until it lost any cohesiveness or relation to a physical place. It is this sense of regional identity among those who live in the Ozarks that lags behind once again.

———

THIS RETURNS US to the "why" question that I back-burnered earlier. Why the lag, especially when dealing with historical developments that affected and entwined with issues of regional image and regional identity? Perhaps the most obvious explanation is a geographical one. The Ozarks is almost a full time zone's trek west of Appalachia. That's why the Ozarks attracted westerly migrating upland southerners from the 1790s until the early twentieth century, why most old family Ozarkers have ancestral roots in Appalachia. Even though European settlement on the Ozark fringes began in the mid-1700s, most of the region was in fact settled a generation or so later than corresponding subregions of Appalachia. So, it would certainly seem logical that later settlement patterns could translate into later cultural recognition.

But the answer to any "why" question is never that easy. Another explanation relates especially to the rise of regionalist literature in the post–Civil War era. A generation or two ago, it was a widely held notion within historians' circles that regional, local-color literature became the country's dominant genre at the very moment when big overtook little, when national (or international) market and social forces superceded local autonomy and isolation.[23] Using this model, one could argue that these outside, integrating forces arrived in the Ozarks perhaps a generation later than they did in Appalachia—via the railroad, industrialism, extractive industry, etc. However, most scholarship of the past generation has dismissed this model of modernization as overly simplistic and too dependent on the longheld misconception of the existence of isolated, static, premodern societies in places like Appalachia and the Ozarks.[24]

Assuming that the current consensus on the process of modernization in the mountains is at least closer to being accurate than were earlier interpretations, let's return to the mountain mission movement for a possible explanation. In the 1920s, Southern Methodist denominational leader Elmer T. Clark posited an explanation for the comparative scarcity of Ozark mission schools—an explanation that could also perhaps account for the generational lag in establishing them. "The Ozark Mountains, lacking the flavor of romance which attaches to the Appalachians," wrote Clark, "have not attracted the interest of the denominational mission boards in so marked a degree."[25] Though I would question the "lack of romance" surrounding Ozarks imagery—especially by the 1920s, almost two decades after publication of *The Shepherd of the Hills*—if in fact there was a lack of romance it appears to have been a product of the delayed "discovery" of the Ozarks by the local colorists and missionaries whose accounts defined Appalachians as an exceptional population in the last quarter of the nineteenth century. This delayed discovery, and the tangential status it bequeathed the Ozarks, undoubtedly had something to do with the Ozark region's remoteness from the nation's cultural and publishing locus in the Northeast. The Northeast was home to most of the nation's book publishers and to most of the country's nationally distributed magazines. The East in general claimed the headquarters of all the religious denominations that played key roles in the mountain mission movement; no denomination that built schools in the Appalachians or Ozarks had a seat of power farther west than Nashville. Thus it is perhaps not surprising that it was only in the early twentieth century that Ozarkers found themselves portrayed in popular literature, and that only in the 1920s did the region begin to attract significant attention from travel writers and social commentators. The delayed attention by mountain missionaries reflected this latent discovery of the Ozarks and may have been affected by it.[26]

Most of our generational lag examples predate World War II. It appears that the Ozarks had mostly caught up with Appalachia by that time, at least in terms of broadly held regional, cultural images. The quick establishment of the ORC on the heels of the ARC suggests that much of the gap had been bridged. The persistence of the ARC and the demise of the ORC likely owed a debt to image. The image makers, with the able assistance of the concentrated squalor and injustice of big coal and the crusading of Harry Caudill and other activists, managed to partially reshape the Appalachian image for post-Eisenhower America. This image of poverty and neglect demanded the existence of the ARC and maintained a certain geographical integrity for the enterprise. The Ozark region, whose poverty lacked vocal crusaders and coal-town clarity, did not undergo a transformation of image or a politicization that honed its identity.

One by-product of the diverging regional images of the past half century has been a new generational lag. This modern-day lag has come in the field of academic study and scholarship. More than four decades after the founding of the Appalachian Studies Association, the Ozarks finally got its equivalent body of academics and activists in 2019. Likewise, scholarship on the region has lagged about a generation behind. But there is promise that we in the Ozarks will again uphold our end of the lag. In 2010, Missouri State University established the region's first Ozarks studies minor for undergraduates. Five years later, the University of Arkansas Press launched a monograph series in Ozarks studies. We may never be first in the Ozarks, but we get around to it eventually. Such is the life of a regional little sibling.

THIRTEEN

Back to the Land

ACADEME, THE AGRARIAN IDEAL,

AND A SENSE OF PLACE

WASN'T EVEN CERTAIN if it was there or not. But in my mind I could see it—a scraggly cedar standing defiantly on the hillside across the creek from the barn. The greenbriers and prickly pears and ragweed conspired to choke it out, but still it stood, sometimes swaying in the wind, sometimes motionless, always perched atop the crest of a terrace on this rocky hillside. I knew that beyond the cedar, on top of the hill, was a little glade—unfit for anything save more cedars and greenbriers and maybe a collared lizard or two—and below it stood an old white oak, where the whitetail would gather before sunup on frosty autumn mornings. But I never could see the glade or the white oak, only that lone cedar, not big enough for a fence post and too ugly for a Christmas tree.

If a sense of place could be expressed with a single image, then I reckon this vision does it for me. I'm not sure when the picture of this little cedar on a hill first jumped into my head. I do know that my little cedar had a habit of appearing in dreams, of flashing across the screen in my mind in times of stress and loneliness. Eventually it became so ever-present a part of my waking existence—a sort of subconscious memento that could be summoned into the conscious realm at will, a spiritual-neurological salve—that the vision's representation of reality—the question of whether there really was a scrawny cedar on a terraced hillside and, if so, did it look anything like the picture in my head?—became a moot point.

Had I been much older and living on the other side of the planet from the place I called home, I suppose my dalliances with this vision could have

This essay was originally published in Zachary Jack, ed., *Black Earth and Ivory Tower* (Columbia: University of South Carolina Press, 2005). It appears here with minor revisions.

been labeled nostalgia. But I was a twenty-something graduate student, some five hundred miles from home, from this hillside—just a good day's drive in modern America. Some would probably still label it nostalgia, or at least some variation of nostalgia, but I prefer to call my experience with this vision a manifestation of an acute sense of place.

Lots of folks have written about this thing we call *a sense of place*, and we southerners have been particularly fond of exploring the idea. It seems to me, though, that there are different degrees of sense of place, multiple levels of a sense of belonging in and of a region or locality, just as there are multiple levels of consciousness. After traveling abroad, a person from Montana or Mississippi might experience a sort of "I'm home" feeling upon landing in New York or San Francisco. A southerner living in New England or on the West Coast might tune in to a country music station just because it reminds her of the South. More often, of course, we have smaller areas in mind when we talk about a sense of place—a particular region (Appalachia, the Delta) or state or county or town or community. I recall navigating the senses of place on the many trips from graduate school in Alabama to my home in Arkansas. Crossing the Mississippi at Memphis sparked one sense of place (being in my home state), which was soon trumped when I arched over the Black River and into the Ozarks. In another hour, I was crossing the line into my home county, and within minutes I would start to pass the homes and farms of people I knew, people my grandparents had known, people whose ancestors had known my ancestors a century earlier. By the time I turned off the state highway and climbed the hill by the Gilbreaths' milk barn, I was home, but it was three more miles to *the* place, the little farm on which I had been raised, on which sat the glade and stood the white oak. The place with the terraced hillside and the lone cedar of my dreams.

For me, as for many people raised on the farm, the ultimate sense of place was more tangible and more specific than a region or a county or even a hometown. It was 320 acres of hilly, rocky land traversed by a wet-weather branch and a creek that used to keep water all year but no longer does and delineated from the neighbors' hilly, rocky plots by barbed-wire and hog-wire fences of varying ages and in varying states of disrepair. It was the place with no fewer than four glades, a remote back forty with a stand of white oaks that have been trying to die off for years, three narrow creek-bottom fields that my grandpa knew were as good as any in the county for growing corn and cane and later fescue and brome, a place with a creekside line of sycamores, one as large as any I had ever seen. It was the farm where my dad as a little boy had followed my grandpa with his team and plow, looking for the flinty glimmer of arrowheads hiding among the rocks in the sandy-clay soil, where my brother and I had hogged for blue-gill loitering in pockets beneath the creek banks and fought cottonmouths who liked to loiter there too. It was the place where I had learned to haul hay and split wood and dig potatoes and set a minnow trap.

———————

AN ACUTE SENSE OF PLACE most often works at odds with a career in academe, especially for the child of the farm. Colleges and universities are invariably located in towns or cities, often many miles from someone's homeplace. To make matters worse, for academics in humanities fields like mine jobs are so few and hard to come by that the odds of landing one within a day's drive of the childhood farm are slim, much less the odds of finding a position within commuting distance to the farm. In some ways entering the academic world is like joining the military. You're relinquishing control of your own geographical fate. How often have you heard a youngster on the farm say, "I think I'll go earn a PhD in the humanities, come back to the farm, and find a job nearby?" That would be like the high school graduate who grows up across the road from an Air Force base and joins the Air Force so that he can come back home and work there. Ninety-nine to one says it's not going to happen. So, most academics simply try to find that good, tenure-track job, wherever it may be, and adapt to the surroundings as best they can. After all, don't we make a living with our minds? What difference does it make *where* you teach world civilization or comp I? Isn't the physical world ultimately superfluous to the life and career of the intellectual?

But to some of us our physical surroundings, our place, is integral to our lives as academics and as thinkers. Of course, this idea of the interconnectedness of the physical, the mental, and the spiritual is not a new one. The ancient Romans talked about this stuff, and Americans from Thoreau and Emerson to Wendell Berry have championed such a holistic approach to living and thinking. It was just such an approach to life and career that I had when I trundled off to graduate school in 1992.

I had already decided I wanted to be a historian, or at least to study history. In fact, I couldn't remember the time when I hadn't loved history. Growing up across the farm from my grandparents, who had come of age during the Great Depression, and surrounded by their siblings on neighboring farms, it had always seemed as if history was all around, as if crucial bonds with the past were very much intact, continuities mingling with change to create a modern environment speckled and streaked with tradition. My grandpa's great-grandparents had helped found the Baptist church we attended every Sunday, and their graves lay just a stone's throw from the church's outhouse. On the way to church or school, we passed the farm where my grandpa had been born, and on the way back we took notice of the trail leading to my grandma's homeplace and the massive post oak that stood sentinel the day the team of mules came up pulling the wagon with her father's large, lifeless body slumped in the seat. The stories of family and community lingered in the air, a haze of history and legend. We never once fixed fence or drove a cedar post without my grandpa recounting the day the maul flew off the handle and knocked old Aunt Maude colder than a wedge. I never knew who Aunt Maude was, and I'm not convinced he did, either. We children never dared get near a pot of boiling water for fear of listening to my grandma recount the day that her little brother—tow-headed Milam, smart as a whip—escaped his mother's gaze long enough to tip over a kettle of scalding water, burning the little fellow to death. And that one, unfortunately, I knew to be true.

It was only in my senior year of college, when a young professor raised in suburban New York City convinced me that even my home region was worthy of attention, that I realized what kind of history I wanted to spend the next several years studying. And in the summer after graduation, I read through those two dusty volumes of Wendell Berry essays I found beneath the bottom shelf in the college bookstore. It was all coming together, I thought, and it all made sense. I would leave the farm, go off to graduate school, and while there study the people of the region I had left behind. Afterward, I would come back home, to the farm, and teach history somewhere. In all my idealistic dreaming, I had somehow overlooked the fact that the nearest college campus to my family's farm was some forty miles away and that this small liberal arts school, my alma mater, employed only one professor of American history, the field I had chosen as my own. Such is the power of the acute sense of place, and such is the romantic future of the youthful.

It was sometime during those years away from home in graduate school that I first started catching mental glimpses of that cedar on a hill. I came home frequently during those four years. By the time I got back to the farm that first Christmas break, my grandpa had already lined up a succession of jobs, and my grandma stared at my hands as we talked. "They don't look like Brooks's hands," she said finally. Indeed, three months in the classroom and the library had done little to preserve the callouses and swollen fingers that mark a life close to the land. Grandpa aimed to work me back into shape with fence-fixing and rock-hauling, but old age and illness had softened his edges as well. It would be the last time we went to the field together. Spring break took place right at fertilizing time, and my dad continued to plan the hay harvest to coincide with my arrival for summer break. Nothing says "welcome home" quite like a couple of weeks of dirty, backbreaking labor. I wrote most of my master's thesis one summer at home. My dad and I would go to the woods before daylight and cut firewood and split posts till mid-morning. After noon, I would write about the agricultural history of the Ozarks—very Wendell Berryesque, I thought—while Dad played golf. Like I said, the modern world streaked with the traditional.

It doesn't take long for a graduate student to figure out how the life of the academician plays out. In the humanities, especially, jobs are as rare as hen's teeth, and younger students watch their older peers fling themselves on the market for a shot at one of the handful of those teeth. By the time most of us reach the stage of job-hunting, the consideration of a job's geographical location has ceased being a factor in the overall equation, and instead has been reduced to a luxury enjoyed only by the idealistic or the naive. I came to this realization long before I finished the course work for my PhD and, as a result, decided that I would move back home to write my dissertation.

I told my friends and professors that I was moving home to be closer to my research sources. And that was certainly true. I was also going home to spend what would likely be my final years on the farm. My grandparents having died while I was away at graduate school, my wife and I moved into their old farmhouse. I was struck first by how small the house was— it seemed so much bigger in memories of childhood—and next by how unfamiliar the atmosphere was in the absence of my grandparents and their possessions, almost all of which had been parceled out to descendants after my grandmother's death. It had been about four years since my grandpa's declining health had severely limited his activity around the farm and three years since he and Grandma had raised a garden. These years also brought increasing levels of off-the-farm responsibility for my parents, both public school teachers. Consequently, the place was already showing the signs of neglect, even for a little Ozarks farm whose final days as the family's primary source of income lay some three decades in the past.

———

THE LITTLE SPOT OF LAND that I call home had been a working farm, sustaining an Ozarks family for a hundred years or more up until about the time of my birth in 1969. My grandpa began renting the place, located a mile northeast of his father's farm and just over a glady ridge from his mother-in-law's home, just before the outbreak of World War II. The strongest man in the community (and proud of it), Grandpa was nevertheless declared physically unfit for military service. Flat feet and bleeding ulcers were two of Uncle Sam's reddest flags. Grandpa continued to farm what was then known as the Tom Jones place because Mr. Jones had left the hills behind for a farm in the fertile flatness of the eastern Arkansas Delta—"where a feller could grow a bale to the acre without airy fertilize." In 1943, with crop and livestock prices better than Grandpa had ever seen, my grandparents bought the Jones place, 280 acres for $4,000. Young and ambitious, they wasted no time paying off the place and making it their own, building a small rock bungalow, a large wooden, all-purpose barn, and a little chicken house. By the time Harry S. Truman exited the White House, there was nothing left of the old Jones place except the land itself.

In the years after 1943, this farm, almost evenly divided between woodland and cleared fields, grew corn, cotton, and sorghum, hay and pasture grass and vegetable gardens large enough to feed four families. My grandparents raised four children, milked cows, gathered eggs, plowed with horses and then tractors, killed hogs, picked cotton, put up silage, hulled peas, and cut firewood. As time went on, the Grade C dairy operation supplanted cotton-raising as the primary source of income until my grandpa took his first off-farm, full-time job in the mid-1960s. Working as the foreman on a mobile-home anchoring crew in a nearby retirement community, he continued to help Grandma milk cows every morning and evening for a few more years before selling all but one of the dairy cows and switching to beef cattle. I came along during one of the many periods of transition on the farm, perhaps the most monumental period of transition—from working, livelihood farm to part-time farm. The key to the maintenance of the Blevins farm and some semblance of the agrarian lifestyle was off-farm income and adaptation. And for the Blevinses, as for thousands of agricultural families in the upland South, the least obtrusive and least expensive way to maintain a link with the agrarian past was through the raising of beef cattle, an enterprise tailor-made for the small, part-time farmer.

The reason that I grew up on the family farm during an era when less than 5 percent of Americans lived on the land was my dad's acute sense of place. Perhaps it's a genetic trait. I have often thought of my dad as one of the last of a generation of American farm kids raised on the back side of a sweeping technological divide, the Amish and Old Order Mennonites not-withstanding. His generation were the ones who knew what it was like to hitch up a team and go to the field, the ones who knew what it was like to milk a cow by hand, the ones who knew what it was like to spend long autumn days picking cotton or gathering corn, the ones who knew what it was like to rise with their parents before dawn because there were real chores to be done. Though a baby boomer, my dad did all these things in the 1950s and 1960s, the last days of the general family farm in the upland South. The farm ceased to provide a living only after my dad went away to college. Most farm boys of his generation (like any generation, for that matter) who managed to get away never returned to the land. But my dad came back home with a wife, a rural girl from a neighboring county, was fortunate enough to find a job teaching at the local high school (as did my mom), built a house on the southeastern corner of the farm, and took responsibility for more and more of the work around the place until finally buying the farm when I was in junior high. So, like almost all the other farm kids I knew in school, I grew up on the farm only because my parents had off-farm jobs that provided them the luxury of losing money year after year in the cattle business.

My dad was the only one of four siblings who came back home—at least in those early years—and the only one to settle down within a two-hour drive of the farm. Never one for public contemplation of life's deeper currents, he nonetheless expressed his sense of place, his love for the farm his dad had bought off old Tom Jones before his birth. My dad had made the conscious decision to return and turned down more lucrative job offers throughout his career in order to stay where he felt he belonged. Occasionally he related his reasons for coming home and staying home by recalling his own vision, his own manifestation of the acute sense of place. Like tens of thousands of rural folk during the decades sandwiching World War II, my grandparents had on occasion found it necessary to migrate in search of seasonal labor, most often to the orchards or hops farms of the Pacific Northwest. My dad recalled how, as a boy in Washington state, he would sit on a fence rail or on an irrigation pipe and daydream about home in Arkansas, about strolling down the lane between the house and the barn lot and watching the sparrows dive and flutter in and out of the loft. It was a powerful image for a boy—powerful enough to linger into adulthood, pungent enough to evoke nostalgia for a lost boyhood, a lost way of life.

Over the years, I have talked with a few people in academe—city or town kids—who recalled fondly those summer days on the farm of their grandparents or an aunt and uncle. There is something timeless about our fascination with and nostalgia for life on the farm, especially when our livelihood doesn't depend on the farm or when we're free to leave it at any time. Growing up on a little hill farm when I did, I always had the feeling that I was somewhere in between my dad's generation on the one hand and the city folk whose farm memories consisted of a two-week summer vacation on Grandpa's old place in the country on the other.

Life was not as stark, and work not as constant, as in the days of my grandpa's youth, or even of my dad's. Gone were the row crops, the work stock, the plowing and cultivating and picking and gathering. By the time I started to school, my grandparents had sold the family milk cow and all the chickens. We continued to raise large gardens, but the activities of the farm were reduced to those necessary to maintain a herd of thirty or so beef cattle—cutting and baling hay in the spring, feeding hay in the winter, working the cattle at various times throughout the year, and fixing fence. Whether from nostalgia for the agricultural diversity of earlier days or from a desire to see to it that my brother and I were exposed to more than just cows and fence posts, my grandpa and dad busied themselves, and us, with a variety of sideline activities. Grandpa brought home hogs to fatten for slaughter, calves for my brother and me to feed on bottles, guineas to rid the yard of ticks and grasshoppers, and logs to be fashioned into feed troughs, gunstocks, ax handles, or walking sticks. We even kept a contrary mare for a couple of years and dusted off my dad's old saddle to ride her once or twice. Dad made sure that my brother and I learned to plow and disc and other things that one does with a tractor and equipment, if for no other reason than to smell the earth in freshly turned furrows. And we hauled rocks—lots and lots of big rocks—to clog up washed-out ditches and to stay busy when idleness was uncalled for.

There were moments when—sitting on a tractor on a Saturday evening or stacking bales of hay beneath a tin loft roof on a summer afternoon or getting out of bed thirty minutes before daylight to feed the cows before going to school—I wondered what my non-farm friends were doing, wallowing in the certainty that they were sipping Mountain Dew in a movie theater or floating the river with pole in hand or simply sleeping blissfully and snugly. But I was never too far from the edge of the farm, and thus the edge of the wider world. We traveled the state to play basketball and baseball games. We visited relatives in other states, at least the relatives who lived within reach of a major league baseball team, and, though it took an hour to get to the nearest McDonald's or stoplight, Walmart was closer by, and what else do you really need?

WHEN MY WIFE AND I moved back to the farm in 1996, the county was still free of stoplights and fast-food franchises. (It would have one of each within a few years.) The farm was still there, too, and for the most part looked like it had looked for many years, at least to the casual glance. A closer inspection revealed a loft barn leaning to the west, so severely in fact that the entrances on the east side had the tilted look of cellar doors. The old chicken house, which had housed nothing more than hay bales, mice, and burlap bags full of Mason jars for more than twenty years, had a sagging roof and holes in the walls big enough for a half-grown calf to walk through. The garden spot was grown over, the little apple tree in the center of it—just like the Garden of Eden, I thought as a child— withered and stooped. My grandparents had been gone not even a year and a half, but already the place seemed in danger of being licked back into the fecund wildness of the untilled hillsides. Had I not realized beforehand that the rural idyll exists only in fairy tales or in the nostalgia-tinged haze of the past, I probably would have ended up as disenchanted as the urban homesteaders of the twentieth century, those backcountry Thoreaus of the Teddy Roosevelt era or the communitarians of the 1970s who took to the land to live but instead were forced to survive. In our first year back on the place, during which I wrote nairy a word of the dissertation, I battled a family of skunks who had taken up residence under the house, fixed leaky water lines and worried as drought and a general drop in the water table took away what water there was in the lines, hunted missing cows and pulled calves, and watched one newborn calf die of pneumonia on my back porch because I waited too late to give it a shot.

Eventually I settled into a routine, finished the dissertation, taught a few community-college classes on the side, and handled many more hay bales than just about anyone that I knew of in the academic world. By the time I began applying for jobs, I had come to the realization that my time on the farm was limited. Two schools offered me a faculty position, one on the edge of the Ozarks some four hours away and the other in the Deep South, 350 miles from home. We packed up and moved south. I made my peace with that acute sense of place, satisfied that the scraggly cedar would reemerge somewhere down the road, that I would nestle into the life of the academic, the life of the mind. Sure enough, the visions of the cedar returned, the pull of the farm as powerful as ever. That cedar had something to do with it the following year when I left a perfectly good job to take a paycut and one-year position that would allow us to move back to that rocky, hilly farm.

Funny thing, that sense of place, the feel for not just any old creek bottom and barn lot. And powerful pull, that agrarian ideal, the longing to strike the balance between the life of the mind and the life on the land. In many ways the academic lifestyle and the agrarian life are perfect bedfellows, at least when the academic side provides enough money to support the agrarian side. The time clock of modern, industrial society has only a minimal bearing on either, and both require a willingness to forego material comfort. Both lifestyles are fueled in large part by idealism, by the quest for the perfect, most complete existence—the intellectual on the one hand and the romantic/agrarian on the other. The two also complement each other, combining the elements of vigorous intellectual activity with sometimes equally vigorous physical activity. And for many people this is what the agrarian ideal boils down to. Deep within the recesses of our consciences, there is a voice that reminds us that the best labor, the most fulfilling and God-ordained work, requires the hands and the back and takes place in the open air, on the dirt or grass, and among the trees and streams and birds and beasts.

For those whose consciences speak too softly, there has been no shortage of philosophers and public figures willing to tell us this is so, even if their actions sometimes undermined the ideal. The Roman statesman and writer Cato championed the agrarian life and recorded instructions for a variety of farming activities, but his servants did most of the actual physical work. Thomas Jefferson, perhaps more than any other American, praised the natural superiority of the agrarian life, though he spent much of his life chasing his conflicting desires to live the life of a country gentleman and to achieve political prominence. He, too, left the physical labor to others: the enslaved. The Roman general and statesman Cincinnatus left no doubt about the moral superiority of the agrarian life when he relinquished the power he earned in battle to return to his farm on the banks of the Tiber. George Washington, the American Cincinnatus, went back to the banks of the Potomac, but like Jefferson he only partially suppressed a longing for public life. Despite the fact that most of the people who have exalted the agrarian ideal—from Cato to the iconoclastic Southern Agrarians of the 1920s and 1930s—took part in little of the strenuous activity that farming requires, we continue to champion the ideal and to try and heed its mandates.

It is this physical element that helps account for the concept of the agrarian *ideal*. It's what balances the intellectual simply by preventing one from overindulgence in the purely cerebral experience of life. And it's why the academics and the part-time farmers found in the countryside— not the drivers and mechanics of agribusiness—are the true, modern-day bearers of the agrarian ideal. But, like most Americans who live the "farm" life today, I am constantly reminded that my rural life is a luxury afforded only by a steady off-farm income and dependent on the vagaries (in my case) of the academic world.

REVISITING THIS ESSAY after nearly twenty years, I conclude this book while sitting at a computer in a shed on the farm. The rhythmic churning of a baler echoes in the distance as my grown son finishes a little "jag" of hay that my dad cut and raked. My son is a good hand at hill farming, much more skilled and confident on a tractor than I ever was and much less distracted. In fact, his increasing expertise and heightened role has rendered my input less crucial in the last few years, freeing me to spend more time conducting research and writing books.

That's a valuable thing, because my professional life still lies within the academic world. Shortly before this essay was first published—at the very moment when it looked like leaving the land was my only option if I were intent on pursuing a career in academia—I was fortunate enough to secure a tenure-track job at Lyon College, my little alma mater on the White River near the spot where the Delta meets the Ozarks. I fully expected to be there until retirement. But our biggest opportunities seem to find us when we least expect them. Just two years into that tenure-track job, I received a call from the chair of a search committee at Missouri State University.

The institution's newly created endowed professorship in Ozarks studies seemed tailor-made for me—which is why the chair was shocked when I told her I wasn't interested. And I wasn't feigning disinterest as a bargaining tool. Well, if you've looked at the book jacket you already know how this comes out. The persuasive chair eventually convinced me to apply for the job—"just to see what happens"—and I accepted the offer, but only with the understanding that I wouldn't have to leave the farm more than a couple of days a week.

I've now spent almost two-thirds of my career at Missouri State. My dual life—shuttling between the university world in the largest city in the Ozarks and the rural backcountry of a perpetually depressed section of the region—has been a valuable vantage for understanding the place I study and call home. It has provided for balance of various kinds—between the intellectual and the physical, the ideal and the practical. It has also been a good place to raise a family, including the daughter who arrived not long after I wrote the first iteration of this essay. I'm not sure what lies ahead for her, but my son remains on the farm, the fourth generation to call this rocky, hilly piece of the earth home.

A large vegetable garden sprawls just steps from my writing shed. A barn full of hay stands fifty yards away on the spot that was my grandparents' garden. Cows take their mid-morning rest along the yard fence in the shade of two catalpas my grandpa planted before I was born. A line of trees along a wet-weather creek impedes my view of the cedar on the hillside from those dreams in younger days. That cedar no longer enters my mind. In fact, I've never once looked to see if it is there. And that is why I came back, to be able to look or put off looking anytime I want. The acute sense of place is a fixed thing. The old homeplace can't be moved, but the ivory tower can.

NOTES

Chapter One

1. This essay is derived from a paper first presented at the annual conference of the Arkansas Historical Association held in Batesville, Arkansas, in April 1998. Any similarity in content and spirit to Paul K. Conkin's presidential address at the sixty-third annual meeting of the Southern Historical Association in Atlanta in November 1997 (later published in the February 1998 issue of the *Journal of Southern History*) is purely coincidental and simply underscores the demographic and social similarities between the Ozarks and Appalachia. I was not present at the Atlanta conference and did not read the published version of the speech until well after my April 1998 presentation.

2. John Shelton Reed, "The South: What Is It? *Where* Is It?" in *The South for New Southerners*, eds. Paul D. Escott and David R. Goldfield (Chapel Hill: University of North Carolina Press, 1991), 19.

3. Ulrich B. Phillips, "The Central Theme in Southern History," *American Historical Review* 34 (October 1928): 31.

4. See chapter 1 of Brooks Blevins, *A History of the Ozarks, Volume 2: The Conflicted Ozarks* (Urbana: University of Illinois Press, 2019).

5. US Census, population, 1900, 1930, 2010. Studies in the twenty-first century continue to reflect a direct correlation between race and regional identity, as places with higher densities of African Americans are more likely to identify as southern. Christopher A. Cooper and H. Gibbs Knotts, "Declining Dixie: Regional Identification in the Modern American South," *Social Forces* 88 (March 2010): 1095.

6. See Kimberly Harper, *White Man's Heaven: The Lynching and Expulsion of Blacks in the Southern Ozarks, 1894–1909* (Fayetteville: University of Arkansas Press, 2010); James W. Loewen, *Sundown Towns: A Hidden Dimension of American Racism* (New York: W. W. Norton, 2005); Guy Lancaster, *Racial Cleansing in Arkansas, 1883–1924: Politics, Land, Labor, and Criminality* (Lanham, MD: Lexington Press, 2014). For an example of one Ozark town that became all white due to racial strife, see Jacqueline Froelich and David Zimmermann, "Total Eclipse: The Destruction of the African American Community of Harrison, Arkansas, in 1905 and 1909," *Arkansas Historical Quarterly* 58 (Summer 1999): 131–59.

7. US Department of the Interior, Office of the Census, *Eleventh Census of the United States, 1890: Agriculture*, Washington, DC: Government Printing Office (GPO), 1895.

8. US Department of Commerce, Bureau of the Census, *Census of Agriculture, 1935: Reports for States, With Statistics by Counties*, vol. 1, part 2, Washington, DC: GPO, 1936.

9. US Dept. of Commerce, *Census of Agriculture, 1935*, vol. 1, pt. 2.

10. Reed, "South: What Is It?," 21.

11. Oliver E. Baker, "Agricultural Regions of North America, Part II—The South," *Economic Geography* 3 (January 1927): 65; Oliver E. Baker, "Agricultural Regions of North America, Part III—The Middle Country Where South and North Meet," *Economic Geography* 3 (July 1927): 309.

12. Clarence Cason, *90 Degrees in the Shade* (Chapel Hill: University of North Carolina Press, 1935). See also Ulrich B. Phillips, *Life and Labor in the Old South* (Boston: Little, Brown, 1929).

13. Wayne L. Decker, "Climate of Missouri," http://climate.missouri.edu/climate .php, accessed May 29, 2022; "Climate of Arkansas," https://static.ark.org /eeuploads/anrc/Climate_of_Arkansas_maybe_from_2014.pdf, accessed May 29, 2022.

14. For a scholarly examination of the place of the mule in southern culture and history, see Charles F. Lane, "Southern and Quasi-Southern Cultural Landscapes," in *The South in Perspective*, ed. Francis B. Simkins (Farmville, VA: Longwood College, 1959); and George B. Ellenberg, *Mule South to Tractor South: Mules, Machines, and the Transformation of the Cotton South* (Tuscaloosa: University of Alabama Press, 2008).

15. US Department of Commerce, Bureau of the Census, *Fifteenth Census of the United States: 1930, Agriculture*, vol. 2, part 1 (Washington, DC: Government Printing Office, 1932), 1004–1013, 1162–1167, 1310–1315.

16. Reed, "South: What Is It?," 23.

17. John Gould Fletcher, *Arkansas* (Chapel Hill: University of North Carolina Press, 1947), 269, 368.

18. See Brooks Blevins, "Fireworking Down South," in this volume.

19. See chapter 4 of Blevins, *History of the Ozarks, Volume 2*.

20. W. J. McCuen, *Historical Report of the Secretary of State, 1986*, ed. Steve Faris (Little Rock: Arkansas Secretary of State, 1986), 385–420.

21. US Department of Commerce, Bureau of the Census, *Religious Bodies: 1926, Summary and Detailed Tables*, Vol. 1 (Washington, DC: GPO, 1930), 580–83, 635–38, 661–63; "Largest Participating Religious Group" map, *2010 U.S. Religion Census: Religious Congregations and Membership Study*, http:// www.usreligioncensus.org/images/002.jpg, accessed July 16, 2020; Reed, "South: What Is It?," 16.

22. Bureau of the Census, *Religious Bodies: 1926*, 580–83, 635–38, 661–63. At the time of the 1926 census, the Presbyterians were also divided into

northern and southern denominations, along with the Cumberland Presbyterians. In only a handful of Ozarks counties, however, did all Presbyterians
constitute as much as 10 percent of the total religious population. Thus, the
more substantial presence of the Methodists (who accounted for more than a
quarter of the population in a dozen counties in the region) provided a larger
pool for the southern test.

23. C. Vann Woodward, "The Search for Southern Identity," in Woodward, *The
Burden of Southern History* (Baton Rouge: Louisiana State University Press,
1968), 3–25. (Originally published in the *Virginia Quarterly Review* 34
(1958): 321–38.)

24. Reed, "South: What Is It?," 40.

25. Christopher A. Cooper and H. Gibbs Knotts, "Declining Dixie: Regional
Identification in the Modern American South," *Social Forces* 88 (March
2010): 1092; John Shelton Reed, "The Heart of Dixie: An Essay in Folk
Geography," *Social Forces* 54 (June 1976): 934.

26. David L. Smiley, "The Quest for the Central Theme in Southern History,"
South Atlantic Quarterly 71 (Summer 1972): 325.

Chapter Two

1. This and all subsequent epigrams are taken from Helen Norris, "The Cracker
Man," in Norris, *The Burning Glass: Stories* (Baton Rouge: Louisiana State
University Press, 1992). Norris's "The Cracker Man" inspired a motion pic-
ture: *The Cracker Man*, produced by Bruce Kuerten, John DiJulio, and Tom
Luse and directed by Rudy Gaines, 57 min., Alerion Films, Auburn, AL,
1999. For more information, visit the film's website at www.crackerman.com.

2. See Alan St. H. Brock, *A History of Fireworks* (George G. Harrap & Co.,
1949).

3. John Gould Fletcher, *Arkansas* (Chapel Hill: University of North Carolina
Press, 1947), 269; Ron Taylor, "True South; Illegal Fireworks," *Atlanta
Journal and Constitution*, June 30, 1991, M2; Diana Karter Appelbaum,
The Glorious Fourth: An American Holiday, An American History (New
York: Facts on File, 1989), 98; C. Vann Woodward, ed., *Mary Chesnut's Civil
War* (New Haven, CT: Yale University Press, 1981), 832. See also Leonard I.
Sweet, "The Fourth of July and Black Americans in the Nineteenth Century:
Northern Leadership Opinion within the Context of the Black Experience,"
Journal of Negro History 61 (July 1976): 256–75.

4. George Plimpton, *Fireworks: A History and Celebration* (New York:
Doubleday, 1984), 55. The reference here is to the tradition called "firing
the anvil," whereby blacksmiths would turn one anvil upside down, fill the
hollow with powder, place another anvil right-side-up on top of it, and then
light a fuse, sending the anvil on top flying into the air. In Europe this custom was most often associated with the November 23 feast of St. Clement,

patron saint of the blacksmith. Americans enjoyed firing the anvil so much that the celebration came to mark marriages, Christmas, New Year's, and the Fourth of July. Nancy McDonough, *Garden Sass: A Catalog of Arkansas Folkways* (New York: Coward, McCann & Geoghegan, 1975), 108.

5. Matthew Dennis, *Red, White, and Blue Letter Days: An American Calendar* (Ithaca, NY: Cornell University Press, 2002), 70–71; Appelbaum, *Glorious Fourth*, 135; "Lingering Glory of the Old Fourth," *Life*, July 4, 1955, 53.

6. Information on fireworks fatalities for December 2001 gathered from the Chemical Incident Reports Center of the U.S. Chemical Safety and Hazard Investigation Board, http://www.chemsafety.gov/circ; Appelbaum, *Glorious Fourth*, 156, 158; Michael A. Greene and Patrick M. Race, "2001 Fireworks Annual Report: Fireworks Related Deaths, Emergency Department Treated Injuries, and Enforcement Activities During 2001," U.S. Consumer Product Safety Division, June 2002, http://www.cpsc.gov/library/2001fwreport.PDF. In the years since the original publication of this essay, state laws have continued to liberalize the sale of consumer fireworks. Georgia allows the sale of some fireworks, as does almost every other state in the union. As of 2021, only Massachusetts completely banned the sale of fireworks, and three other states (Illinois, Ohio, and Vermont) limited sales to sparklers and novelty items. American Pyrotechnics Association, "Directory of State Laws," https://www.americanpyro.com/state-law-directory, accessed August 26, 2021.

7. American Pyrotechnics Association, "Industry Facts and Figures," https://pyro.memberclicks.net/industry-facts-figures, accessed August 28, 2021.

8. Taylor, "True South; Illegal Fireworks," M2; Shelley Emling, "Fireworks Are Fun But Can Land User in Jail," *Atlanta Journal and Constitution*, July 3, 1994, C12.

9. Lane DeGregory, "The Ruse before the Fuse," *St. Petersburg Times Online Floridian*, 1 July 2002.

10. Paul Thorn and Billy Maddox, "Mission Temple Fireworks Stand," *Mission Temple Fireworks Stand*, Perpetual Obscurity Records/Back Porch Records, 2002.

11. Dennis, *Red, White, and Blue Letter Days*, 69. Marjorie Kinnan Rawlings, "Fish Fry and Fireworks," in *Short Stories by Marjorie Kinnan Rawlings*, ed. Rodger L. Tarr (Gainesville: University Press of Florida, 1994), 287.

12. Norris, "Cracker Man," 105.

Chapter Three

1. *The Andy Griffith Show* (hereafter *Andy*), "Dogs, Dogs, Dogs," episode 93, CBS Television, April 22, 1963.

2. *Andy*, "The Arrest of the Fun Girls," episode 155, CBS Television, April 5, 1965; "Barney and the Choir," episode 52, February 19, 1962; "Mountain

Wedding," episode 94, April 29, 1963; "The Songfesters," episode 115, February 24, 1964; "Floyd, the Gay Deceiver," episode 72, November 26, 1962; "Barney and the Governor," episode 78, January 7, 1963.

3. Alon Harish, "Jerry Seinfeld's Secret Andy Griffith Tributes," *ABC News*, July 4, 2012, http://abcnews.go.com/blogs/entertainment/2012/07/jerry -seinfelds-secret-andy-griffith-tributes/. The tribute involved having the *Seinfeld* characters greet each other "Hey, Jerry," "Hey, George," and so on in homage to the common greeting "Hey, Andy" used by many Mayberrians, especially Gomer and Goober.

4. Daniel de Visé, *Andy and Don: The Making of a Friendship and a Classic American TV Show* (New York: Simon & Schuster, 2015), 80–88.

5. De Visé, *Andy and Don*, 80–88. One notable exception to the typical stable of coastal writers was North Carolina native Harvey Bullock, who penned a number of classic episodes during the show's golden era.

6. Fred Pfister, *Insiders' Guide to Branson and the Ozark Mountains*, 7th ed. (Guilford, CT: Insiders' Guide, 2009), 119; *Today*, NBC Television, March 4, 1996.

7. Allison Graham, *Framing the South: Hollywood, Television, and Race During the Civil Rights Struggle* (Baltimore: Johns Hopkins University Press, 2001), 158.

8. *Andy*, "Barney's Replacement," episode 34, CBS Television, October 9, 1961. Regarding the show's campaign against the "Organization Man," see John O'Leary and Rick Worland, "Against the Organization Man: *The Andy Griffith Show* and the Small-Town Family Ideal," in *The Sitcom Reader: America Viewed and Skewed*, ed. Mary M. Dalton and Laura R. Linder (Albany: State University of New York Press, 2005): 73–84.

9. O'Leary and Worland, "Against the Organization Man," 76.

10. *Andy*, "Man in a Hurry," episode 79, CBS Television, January 14, 1963.

11. *Andy*, "The Sermon for Today," episode 99, CBS Television, October 21, 1963.

12. Derek H. Alderman, Terri Moreau, and Stefanie Benjamin, "*The Andy Griffith Show*: Mayberry as Working-Class Utopia," in *Blue-Collar Pop Culture: From NASCAR to Jersey Shore, Vol. 2: Television and the Culture of Everyday Life* (Santa Barbara, Cal.: Praeger, 2012), 60; Graham, *Framing the South*, 159–160; Michael B. Kassel, "African Americans and Entertainment TV," *The Guide to United States Popular Culture*, ed. Ray B. Browne and Pat Browne (Madison: University of Wisconsin Press, 2001), 18.

13. Tim Funk, "This Andy, Plain-Spoken," *Charlotte Observer*, February 7, 1993, 1E; de Visé, *Andy and Don*, 178.

14. Rochelle Riley, "Another Member of Our Family Passes," *Detroit Free Press*, July 4, 2012, 2A. See also Shani O. Hilton, "Black & White in Mayberry," *The Awl*, July 5, 2012, https://www.theawl.com/2012/07/black-white-in -mayberry/; Mary C. Curtis, "Andy Griffith Was a Democrat, and N.C.

Disapproved," *Washington Post*, July 4, 2012, http://www.washingtonpost
.com/blogs/she-the-people/post/andy-griffith-was-a-democrat-and-nc
-disapproved/2012/07/04/gJQAb27FNW_blog.html; Richard Prince, "Was
'The Andy Griffith Show' Postracial," *The Root*, July 5, 2012, https://www
.theroot.com/was-the-andy-griffith-show-postracial-1790884245.

15. "Why Come There Ain't No Black People in Mayberry?" *Northwest History*,
July 28, 2008, http://northwesthistory.blogspot.com/2008/07/why-come
-there-aint-no-black-people-in.html; Elijah Gosier, "Race Was Never an
Issue in Mayberry," *St. Petersburg Times*, March 15, 1993, 1 (City Times
Section).

16. Alderman et al., *"Andy Griffith Show,"* 60.

17. Lee Pfeiffer, *The Official* Andy Griffith Show *Scrapbook* (New York: Citadel
Press, 1994), 19; US Bureau of the Census, *Census of the Population:
1960, Vol. I: Characteristics of the Population, Part 35: North Carolina*
(Washington, DC: Government Printing Office, 1963), 237; Graham,
Framing the South, 159.

18. James Flanagan, "Deconstructing Mayberry: Utopia and Racial Diversity in
the *Andy Griffith Show*," *Continuum: Journal of Media & Cultural Studies*
23 (June 2009): 314.

19. Pfeiffer, *Official* Andy Griffith Show *Scrapbook*, 168–69, 172, 176–77, 182,
186, 189, 193, 205.

20. Jeremy B. Jones, "Notes on a Mountain Man," in *Appalachian Reckoning:
A Region Responds to Hillbilly Elegy*, ed. Anthony Harkins and Meredith
McCarroll (Morgantown: West Virginia University Press, 2019), 272, 278.

21. See David C. Hsiung, *Two Worlds in the Tennessee Mountains: Exploring
the Origins of Appalachian Stereotypes* (Lexington: University Press of
Kentucky, 1997.)

22. Pfeiffer, *Official* Andy Griffith Show *Scrapbook*, 19; de Visé, *Andy and
Don*, 30.

23. Pfeiffer, *Official* Andy Griffith Show *Scrapbook*, 130, 165, 135, 153.

24. *Andy*, "Briscoe Declares for Aunt Bee," episode 100, CBS Television,
October 28, 1963.

Chapter Four

1. Nathan R. Lane, "A Godly Man," in *Climbing Higher: New Gospel Songs*
(Knoxville, TN: Cumberland Valley Music Company, 2011), 30–31. This essay
focuses on the gospel singing school tradition. There are specific denominations that also sponsor singing schools, especially those that maintain a
tradition of a cappella music, such as Primitive Baptists and the Churches of
Christ. Such schools, though similar to gospel schools in many respects, are
outside the purview of this essay.

2. James R. Goff Jr., *Close Harmony: A History of Southern Gospel* (Chapel Hill: University of North Carolina, 2002), 15, 21, 23, 22; Douglas Harrison, *Then Sings My Soul: The Culture of Southern Gospel Music* (Urbana: University of Illinois Press, 2012), 52; Gavin James Campbell, "'Old Can Be Used Instead of New': Shape-Note Singing and the Crisis of Modernity in the New South, 1880–1920," *Journal of American Folklore* 110 (1997): 172. At its most basic usage, the term *diatonic scale* refers to the seven major notes or tones that correspond with the white keys on the piano: C-D-E-F-G-A-B. In the seven-note shape-note system, these are identified as do-re-mi-fa-sol-la-ti.

3. Goff, *Close Harmony*, 35 (quotation), 37; William Lynwood Montell, *Singing the Glory Down: Amateur Gospel Music in South Central Kentucky, 1900–1990* (Lexington: University Press of Kentucky, 1991), 18.

4. Goff, *Close Harmony*, xii. The label *southern gospel* can be problematic, as the phrase is most often associated with commercialized quartet music. Though singing schools have only a tenuous connection with this commercial arm of the southern gospel world, I use the term *southern gospel* to differentiate the particular brand of gospel music at singing schools and singing conventions from other strains of gospel music, such as Black gospel. I also use the term *southern gospel* because it accurately reflects the geographic nexus of the world of white gospel singing schools. The "primitivist" resurgence refers here to the human impulse to connect with something original and authentic.

5. Interview with Orgel Mason, July 14, 1993, Ozark Oral History Program, transcript and video available at Arkansas History Commission, Little Rock; Anna Floyd, "History of Brockwell Gospel Music School of Brockwell, Arkansas," *Izard County Historian* 37 (July 2012): 3. See also David Stricklin, "Brockwell Gospel Music School," *Encyclopedia of Arkansas*, updated March 9, 2016, https://encyclopediaofarkansas.net/entries /brockwell-gospel-music-school-5/. Unless otherwise noted, all historical information regarding Mason and the Brockwell Gospel Music School from this point forward is derived from the interview with Mason. Orgel Mason died in 2002; subsequent directors of the Brockwell Gospel Music School have been Anna Floyd and Beverly Meinzer.

6. Drew Beisswenger, "Singing Schools in Southcentral Kentucky," MA thesis, Western Kentucky University, 1985, 48; Harrison, *Then Sings My Soul*, 65; Goff, *Close Harmony*, 113; Charles Wolfe, "'Gospel Boogie': White Southern Gospel Music in Transition, 1945–55," *Popular Music* 1 (1981): 74; James R. Goff Jr., "The Rise of Southern Gospel Music," *Church History* 67 (December 1998): 729; Goff, *Close Harmony*, 38 (first quotation); Mason interview (second quotation).

7. Harrison, *Then Sings My Soul*, 15. The term *Sacred Harp* is sometimes

used erroneously to refer to all singers and singings utilizing the four-shape system. The term actually defines only those singers and singings using *The Sacred Harp*, a tune book first published in 1844 and reissued in various editions since that time.

8. Kiri Miller, *Traveling Home: Sacred Harp Singing and American Pluralism* (Urbana: University of Illinois Press, 2008), 143 (first quotation); John Bealle, *Public Worship, Private Faith: Sacred Harp and American Folksong* (Athens: University of Georgia Press, 1997), 243 (second quotation); Beisswenger, "Singing Schools in Southcentral Kentucky," 89 (third quotation); Stephen A. Marini, *Sacred Song in America: Religion, Music, and Public Culture* (Urbana: University of Illinois Press, 2003), 92 (fourth quotation) and 93 (fifth quotation).

9. Campbell, "'Old Can Be Used Instead of New,'" 183.

10. Minutes of Camp Fasola 2011 Adult Session, June 12–15, 2011, accessed December 12, 2013, http://fasola.org/minutes/search/?n=3623.

11. Beisswenger, "Singing Schools in Southcentral Kentucky," 87.

12. Mason interview (first quotation); Alabama School of Gospel Music Website, accessed May 30, 2022, https://www.alabamagospel.com/ (second quotation); Ben Speer's Stamps-Baxter School of Music Website, accessed May 30, 2022, https://www.stampsbaxterschool.com/ (third quotation); Texas Southern Gospel School of Music Website, accessed May 30, 2022, https://tsgsm.com/ (fourth quotation).

13. "Preserving the Heritage of Shape Note Gospel Music," Do Re Mi Gospel Music Academy Website, accessed December 11, 2013, http://www.doremigospelmusicacademy.com/ (first quotation); "Our Mission Statement," Leoma Music Company Website, accessed December 11, 2013, http://www.leomamusic.net/ (second quotation). The website of the Leoma Music Company was not available as of 2022.

14. Montell, *Singing the Glory Down*, 26.

15. Harrison, *Then Sings My Soul*, 114. Because there is no association of singing schools or anything resembling a clearing house for such institutions, there is no hard-and-fast data on the number and location of singing schools. A couple of websites maintained by individual singing schools provide lists of gospel singing schools, such as this example from the website of the Alabama School of Gospel Music, http://www.alabamagospel.com/othersingschools.html. I have identified at least eighteen different institutions operating at least twenty singing schools. (The National School of Music operates singing schools in three different states: Tennessee, Texas, and California.) I have included only those singing schools that meet annually at permanent locations and are thus most easily documented. I have excluded one-time schools and the few singing schools still taught by itinerant teachers. Limited evidence suggests that these itinerants are generally affiliated with one of the permanent schools.

16. Harrison, *Then Sings My Soul*, 104 (first and third quotations); interview with Marty Phillips, by telephone, January 10, 2014 (second quotation).
17. Harrison, *Then Sings My Soul*, 106. As of 2016 there were at least five music publishers that cater to the paperback, singing convention/singing school market. The oldest, Jeffress/Phillips Music Co. of Crossett, Arkansas, has been in business since 1945. The others, all established since the 1970s, include: Leoma Music Company of Leoma, Tennessee; Cumberland Valley Music Company of Knoxville, Tennessee; Gospel Heritage Music of Cleveland, Tennessee; and Southern Legacy Music of Pensacola, Florida. There are additional clothbound shape-note hymnals available to congregations today. The most popular is *Heavenly Highway Hymns*, first compiled by Luther G. Presley and released by Stamps-Baxter in 1956 and now available through Brentwood-Benson Publishing.

Chapter Five

1. Interview with Sarah Stone, by telephone, September 26, 2013; J. Blake Perkins, *Hillbilly Hellraisers: Federal Power and Populist Defiance in the Ozarks* (Urbana: University of Illinois Press, 2017), 137.
2. Will Sarvis, "A Difficult Legacy: Creation of the Ozark National Scenic Riverways," *Public Historian* 24 (Winter 2002), 35–36; Missouri Division of Resources and Development, *Plan for Preservation and Development of Recreation Resources Current and Eleven Point River Country Missouri* (Jefferson City, MO, 1956), 24, Folder 136, Box 5, Series 7, Leo Drey Papers, SL 531, State Historical Society of Missouri, St. Louis.
3. Sarvis, "Difficult Legacy," 38.
4. Sarvis, "Difficult Legacy," 36; Donald L. Stevens Jr., *A Homeland and a Hinterland: The Current and Jacks Fork Riverways* (Omaha, NE.: National Park Service Midwest Region, 1991), 200.
5. Stevens, *Homeland and a Hinterland*, 201–2; Sarvis, "Difficult Legacy," 38–44; James M. Guldin, Greg F. Iffrig, and Susan L. Flader, eds., *Pioneer Forest: A Half Century of Sustainable Uneven-Aged Forest Management in the Missouri Ozarks*, USDA Forest Service General Technical Report SRS-108 (Asheville, NC: Southern Research Station, 2008), 9–16; Leonard Hall, *Stars Upstream: Life along an Ozark River* (Chicago: University of Chicago Press, 1958.)
6. Stevens, *Homeland and a Hinterland*, 202; Sarvis, "Difficult Legacy," 45, 47; Local Hearing on S. 1381: Ozark Rivers National Monument, bulleting of Current-Eleven Point Rivers Assn., June 23, 1962, Folder 210, Box 7, Drey Papers.
7. Stevens, *Homeland and a Hinterland*, 202–3; Will Sarvis, "Old Eminent Domain and New Scenic Easements: Land Acquisition for the Ozark National Scenic Riverways," *Western Legal History* 13 (Winter/Spring

2000): 4, 18, 20, 24–34; Steve Kohler, *Two Ozark Rivers: The Current and the Jacks Fork*, with photos by Oliver Schuchard (1984; Columbia: University of Missouri Press, 1996), 110; Sarvis, "Difficult Legacy," 18.

8. Neil Compton, *The Battle for the Buffalo River: A Twentieth-Century Conservation Crisis in the Ozarks* (Fayetteville: University of Arkansas Press, 1992), 77, 222.

9. Compton, *Battle for the Buffalo River*, 23.

10. Compton, *Battle for the Buffalo River*, 52–57, 66–68, 80, 122.

11. Compton, *Battle for the Buffalo River*, 88–97, 106–9, 119, 128.

12. Compton, *Battle for the Buffalo River*, 150–51, 187, 197, 203, 211–12, 225–36, 242, 281, 291, 464.

13. Compton, *Battle for the Buffalo River*, 294, 106, 212–14.

14. Compton, *Battle for the Buffalo River*, 79, 182.

15. Compton, *Battle for the Buffalo River*, 106, 399, 108; Orphea Duty, interviewed by Kris Morrow and Nancy Sneed, Boxley, AR, June 7, 1983, Folder 35, Upper Big Buffalo Area Boxley Valley Oral History Project, Box 11, RG 8, Center for Ozarks Studies Records, Missouri State University Special Collections, Springfield (unless otherwise noted, all oral histories cited are from this collection); Suzie Rogers, "Buffalo National River," *Encyclopedia of Arkansas*, https://encyclopediaofarkansas.net/entries/buffalo-national-river-7/, accessed July 30, 2022.

16. Theodore Catton, "Life, Leisure, and Hardship Along the Buffalo," Historic Resources Study, Buffalo National River (Omaha, Neb.: Midwest Region, National Park Service, 2008), 266; Rogers, "Buffalo National River." On ONSR accounts of friction between residents and the NPS, see the above-cited articles by Will Sarvis; Kelly Fish-Greenlee, "We Are the Horses: Identity Work in the Southeastern Missouri Ozarks," PhD diss., University of Kansas, 2009; and Stephen N. Limbaugh, "The Origin and Development of the Ozark National Scenic Riverways Project," in *The Ozarks in Missouri History: Discoveries in an American Region*, ed. Lynn Morrow (Columbia: University of Missouri Press, 2013), 272–85.

17. Jim Liles, *Old Folks Talking: A Place of Special Value in the Ozarks of Arkansas*, rev. ed. (Fort Washington, PA: Eastern National, 2009), 288–89; Suzanne Rogers, "Foreword," in Liles, *Old Folks Talking*, vii; Jim Liles, "The Boxley Valley of Buffalo National River: A U.S. National Park Service Historic District in Private Hands," *George Wright Forum* 7, no.3 (1991): 2–5.

18. A few follow-up interviews were conducted in 1984.

19. Jared M. Phillips, *Hipbillies: Deep Revolution in the Arkansas Ozarks* (Fayetteville: University of Arkansas Press, 2019); Hurchal Fowler, Norma Fowler, and Eddie Fowler, interviewed by Lynn Morrow and Kay Murnan, Boxley, AR, June 6, 1983, Folder 38; Lynn Emmett, by Robert Flanders and Lynn Morrow, Jasper, AR, January 10, 1984, Folder 36.

20. Emmett interview, January 10, 1984; Judge Alton Campbell, interviewed by
    Kris Morrow and Nancy Sneed, Jasper, AR, June 8, 1983, Folder 30; Bertha
    Sparks, interviewed by Kay Murnan and Nancy Sneed, Pruitt, AR, June 10,
    1983, Folder 43.

21. Lynn Fowler Emmett, interviewed by Robert Flanders, Kris Morrow, and
    Lynn Morrow, Boxley, AR, June 7, 1984, Folder 36; Wayman and Norma
    Lee Villines, interviewed by Kris Morrow, Lynn Morrow, and Kay Murnan,
    Boxley, AR, June 5, 1983, Folder 45.

22. Hubert and Mary Virginia Ferguson, interviewed by Robert Flanders and
    Lynn Morrow, Boxley Valley, AR, June 9, 1983, Folder 37.

23. Roy and Katy Keaton, interviewed by Kris Morrow, Kay Murnan, and Nancy
    Sneed, Marble Falls, AR, June 9, 1983.

24. Sanford J. Rikoon and Theresa L. Goedeke, *Anti-Environmentalism and
    Citizen Opposition to the Ozark Man and the Biosphere Reserve* (Lewiston,
    NY: Edwin Mellen Press, 2000), i; Sanford J. Rikoon, "Wild Horses and the
    Political Ecology of Nature Restoration in the Missouri Ozarks," *Geoforum*
    37 (March 2006): 200–211; Fish-Greenlee, "We Are the Horses," 122, 126.
    See also Erika Brady, "Mankind's Thumb on Nature's Scale: Trapping and
    Regional Identity in the Missouri Ozarks," in *Sense of Place: American
    Regional Cultures* ed., Barbara Allen and Thomas J. Schlereth (Lexington:
    University Press of Kentucky, 1990): 58–73.

25. Compton, *Battle for the Buffalo*, 366–68.

26. "Wild Rivers Bill Assailed at Hearing," *St. Louis Post-Dispatch*, May 3, 1967,
    no page number, clipping; "Compromise for Scenic Rivers," *Kansas City
    Times* editorial reprinted in *St. Louis Post-Dispatch*, no date, no page num-
    ber, clipping; SLPD clipping, 4-21-70, 1 & 8, Patrick Strickler, "Scenic Rivers
    Bill Is Result of Impatience with Legislature," *St. Louis Post-Dispatch*,
    April 21, 1970, 1, 8, clipping; SLPD clipping, 3-6-71, 7A, "Sportsmen
    Banned," *St. Louis Post-Dispatch*, March 6, 1971, 7A, clipping, Folder 151,
    Box 6, Leo Drey Papers, State Historical Society of Missouri, St. Louis.

27. Jacob H. Wolf, "1000 Oppose Scenic Rivers," *St. Louis Post-Dispatch*,
    March 11, 1971, 1, 5, clipping; Jerry W. Venters, "Scenic Rivers Dissent is
    Split," *St. Louis Post-Dispatch*, March 1, 1971, no page number, clipping,
    Folder 151, Box 6, Leo Drey Papers; "Two Scenic Rivers," November 18, 1975,
    unidentified clipping, Folder 150, Box 6, Drey Papers.

28. Rikoon and Goedeke, *Anti-Environmentalism*, 16–17.

29. Liles, *Old Folks Talking*, 290–98.

Chapter Six

1. Thomas D. Clark, *Pills, Petticoats, and Plows: The Southern Country Store*
   (1944; repr., Norman: University of Oklahoma Press, 1964), viii. Written
   by a late treasure of southern history, this book offers our best peek into

the historical significance of the country store, as well as an example of the historian's folly of era-izing too neatly a past that is equal parts finality and perseverance. Clark's book is much more than just a history of the country store. It is really Clark's ruminations on southern history, letters, and folklore set against the backdrop of the whittler's bench and potbellied stove. The nostalgia embedded in the topic obviously played on Clark's narrative and analysis. See also Lewis E. Atherton, *The Southern Country Store, 1800–1860* (1949; repr., New York: Greenwood Press, 1968).

2. Unless otherwise noted, information on stores and storekeepers presented in the following pages was gathered in firsthand visits to stores and/or discussions with storekeepers.

3. *Douglas County Herald* (Ava, MO), June 23, 1988, 6, 7. As of the date of this book's publication, Spurlock's was closed and appeared to be down for the count.

4. Dorothy Spurlock died in 2018 at age ninety-three.

5. Interview with Randy Spurlock, Squires, Missouri, May 12, 2009.

6. Sandy Deckard died in 2019 at age seventy-two.

7. Interview with Charlotte Fountain, Tilly, Arkansas, May 21, 2009.

8. http://www.rayscountrystore.com/?About_Us, accessed September 22, 2010. As of the date of this book's publication, the website for Ray's Country Store was no longer available. However, the store remained in operation and had an internet presence through this Facebook page: https://www.facebook.com/profile.php?id=100047092167088&ref=py_c.

9. http://www.rayscountrystore.com/?About_Us, accessed September 22, 2010. (As of 2022, website no longer available.)

10. Heather Berry, "Henson's General Store: A Relic of the Past," *Rural Missouri*, Septembe 2002, http://www.ruralmissouri.org/02pages /02septstore.html, accessed September 21, 2010.

11. Garrison Keillor, *Lake Wobegon Days* (New York: Viking, 1985), 95.

12. National Geographic Society, *America's Hidden Corners: Places Off the Beaten Path* (Washington, DC: National Geographic Society, 1983), 151.

13. Interview with Betty Henson, Champion, Missouri, October 7, 2010.

Chapter Seven

1. Lawrence Dalton, *History of Randolph County, Arkansas* (Little Rock, AR: Democrat Printing and Lithographing Company, 1946), 182.

2. Warren R. Hofstra, "From the North of Ireland to North America: The Scots-Irish and the Migration Experience" in *Ulster to America: The Scots-Irish Migration Experience, 1680–1830*, ed. Warren R. Hofstra (Knoxville: University of Tennessee Press, 2012), xiii.

3. See the "Borderlands to the Backcountry" chapter in David Hackett Fischer,

Albion's Seed: Four British Folkways in America (New York: Oxford University Press, 1989).

4. Colleen Morse Elliott and Lois Mashburn Ott, eds., *A Reminiscent History of the Ozark Region* (1894; Easley, SC: Southern Historical Press, 1978), 41–78.

5. Theodore Roosevelt, *The Winning of the West, Volume One: From the Alleghanies to the Mississippi, 1769-1776* (New York: G. P. Putnam's Sons, 1889), 124–30.

6. Michael Forster, "Johann Gottfried von Herder," *Stanford Encyclopedia of Philosophy*, plato.stanford.edu/entries/herder/, accessed January 5, 2016; Vernon Louis Parrington, *Liberalism, Puritanism and the Colonial Mind*, Main Currents in American Thought Series (New York: Routledge, 2011), 134 (quotation). See Horace Kephart, *Our Southern Highlanders* (New York: Outing Publishing Company, 1913).

7. Hofstra, "From the North of Ireland," xiii.

8. See James Leyburn, *The Scotch-Irish: A Social History* (Chapel Hill: University of North Carolina, 1962); Robert B. Cochran, *Vance Randolph: An Ozark Life* (Champaign: University of Illinois Press, 1985); Ethel C. Simpson, "Otto Ernest Rayburn, an Early Promoter of the Ozarks," *Arkansas Historical Quarterly* 58 (Summer 1999): 160–79; Forrest McDonald and Grady McWhiney, "The Antebellum Southern Herdsman: A Reinterpretation," *Journal of Southern History* 41 (May 1975): 147–66; McDonald and McWhiney, "The Celtic South," *History Today* 30 (July 1980); McDonald and McWhiney, "The South from Self-Sufficiency to Peonage: An Interpretation," *American Historical Review* 85 (December 1980): 1095–1118; McWhiney and McDonald, "Celtic Origins of Southern Herding Practices," *Journal of Southern History* 51 (May 1985): 165–82; McWhiney, *Cracker Culture: Celtic Ways in the Old South* (Tuscaloosa: University of Alabama Press, 1988). See also Fischer, *Albion's Seed*.

9. Mary Lee Douthit, Robert Flanders, Barbara Fischer, and Lynn Morrow, *Overview of Cultural Resources in the Mark Twain National Forest, Missouri*, Vol. I., Center for Archaeological Research Report No. 94 (Springfield, MO: Center for Archaeological Research, Southwest Missouri State University, 1979), 154 (first quotation), 176 (second quotation). There is no evidence that the few scholars focusing on the Ozarks in the period between publication of Leyburn's book in 1962 and McDonald and McWhiney's earliest Celtic articles in the mid-1970s incorporated the Scots-Irish thesis into their work. Cultural geographer E. Joan Wilson Miller, relying heavily on Randolph's publications, found in the Ozarks "no melting pot . . . but massive homogeneity of mainly Anglo-Saxon origins." Anthropologist Elizabeth Hagens Herlinger likewise omitted any discussion of the Scots-Irish. E. Joan Wilson Miller, "The Ozark Culture Region as Revealed by

Traditional Materials," *Annals of the Association of American Geographers* 58 (March 1968): 66; Elizabeth Hagens Herlinger, "A Historical, Cultural, and Organizational Analysis of Ozark Ethnic Identity," PhD diss., University of Chicago, 1972.

10. Milton D. Rafferty, *The Ozarks, Land and Life*, 2nd ed. (Fayetteville: University of Arkansas Press, 2001), 60 (first quotation); Russel L. Gerlach, "The Ozark Scots-Irish," in *Cultural Geography of Missouri*, ed. Michael O. Roark (Cape Girardeau: Southeast Missouri State University Department of Earth Science, 1983), 12 (second quotation), 19, 20; Gerlach, *Settlement Patterns in Missouri: A Study of Population Origins, with a Wall Map* (Columbia: University of Missouri Press, 1986) 16; Gerlach, "A Contrast of Old World Ideology: Germans and Scots-Irish in the Ozarks," in *Ideology and Landscape in Historical Perspective: Essays on the Meanings of Some Places in the Past*, ed. Alan R.H. Baker and Gideon Biger (New York: Cambridge University Press, 1992), 291, 292, 296, 298; Donald L. Stevens Jr., *A Homeland and a Hinterland: The Current and Jacks Fork Riverways* (Omaha, NE: National Park Service Midwest Region, 1991), 37–38 (third quotation). See Steven D. Smith, *Made in the Timber: A Settlement History of the Fort Leonard Wood Region*, ERDC/CERL Special Report 03-5 (Fort Leonard Wood, MO: Maneuver Support Center, 2003); and *Thematic Context for Rural Farmsteading, Mark Twain National Forest*, Contract No. AG-447U-C-09-0080 (Austin, TX: Hardy-Heck-Moore Inc., 2010).

11. Gerlach, "Contrast of Old World Ideology," 289–302; Carl O. Sauer, *The Geography of the Ozark Highland of Missouri* (1920; New York: Greenwood Press, 1968), 148 (first quotation), 152 (second quotation). On the "retarded frontier" thesis, see George E. Vincent, "A Retarded Frontier," *American Journal of Sociology* 4 (July 1898): 1–21.

12. On the Palatine immigration to America, see A. G. Roeber, *Palatines, Liberty, and Property: German Lutherans in Colonial British America* (Baltimore, MD: Johns Hopkins University Press, 1993).

13. Brooks Blevins, *A History of the Ozarks, Volume 1: The Old Ozarks* (Urbana: University of Illinois Press, 2018), 77–79. On the Shaver family, see Mark B. Arslan, *Biography of Jacob Blackwelder Shaver* (n.p., 2005), available at http://arslanmb.org/shaver/shaver.html, accessed November 1, 2015.

14. Terry G. Jordan-Bychkov, *The Upland South: The Making of an American Folk Region and Landscape* (Santa Fe, NM: Center for American Places, in association with the University of Virginia Press, 2003), 9 (first quotation), 10 (second quotation); Leyburn, *Scotch-Irish*, 319.

15. Patrick Griffin, "Searching for Independence: Revolutionary Kentucky, Irish American Experience, and Scots-Irish Myth, 1770s-1790s," in Hofstra, *Ulster to America*, 223.

16. Robert Flanders, "Ozarks Legacy of the High Scots-Irish," *Gateway Heritage*

6 (Spring 1986): 49 (first quotation), 50 (second quotation); Robert Flanders, "Caledonia: An Ozarks Village: History, Geography, Architecture," unpublished report prepared to accompany nomination to National Register of Historic Places (Springfield: Center for Ozarks Studies, Southwest Missouri State University, ca. 1984), Missouri State University Special Collections, Springfield, 1 (third quotation), 2, 6, 12, 13; Robert Flanders, "Kith and Kin," *OzarksWatch* 5 (Spring 1992): 2, 3.

17. Jordan-Bychkov, *Upland South*, 10 (first quotation); Gerlach, *Settlement Patterns in Missouri*, 1 (second quotation); J. A. Banks and G. Gay in "Ethnicity in Contemporary American Society: Toward the Development of a Typology," *Ethnicity* 5 (1978): 248 (third quotation); Conrad M. Arensberg, "American Communities," *American Anthropologist*, New Series 57 (December 1955): 1155 (fourth quotation).

18. James Webb, *Born Fighting: How the Scots-Irish Shaped America* (New York: Random House, 2004); J. D. Vance, *Hillbilly Elegy: A Memoir of a Family and Culture in Crisis* (New York: Harper, 2016).

19. Gerlach, "Ozark Scots-Irish," 24 (quotation); Flanders, "Ozarks Legacy of the High Scots-Irish," 49.

20. Hofstra, "From the North of Ireland," xx (first quotation), xxiv (second quotation).

Chapter Eight

1. Originally published in Indiana University Press's Minorities in Modern America Series in 1979, *Dixie's Forgotten People: The South's Poor Whites* was published in a new edition in the same series in 2004.

2. Frederick Law Olmsted, *A Journey in the Back Country* (New York: Mason Brothers, 1860), 226–27.

3. Kenneth W. Noe, "'A Source of Great Economy'? The Railroad and Slavery's Expansion in Southwest Virginia, 1850–1860," in *Appalachians and Race: The Mountain South from Slavery to Segregation*, ed. John C. Inscoe (Lexington: University Press of Kentucky, 2001), 102; James C. Klotter, "The Black South and White Appalachia," *Journal of American History* 66 (March 1980): 840–42; Nina Silber, "'What Does America Need So Much as Americans?' Race and Northern Reconciliation with Southern Appalachia, 1870–1900," in Inscoe, *Appalachians and Race*, 248, 253; John C. Campbell, *The Southern Highlander and His Homeland* (1929; reprint, Lexington: University Press of Kentucky, 1969), 95.

4. Carter G. Woodson, "Freedom and Slavery in Appalachian America," *Journal of Negro History* 1 (April 1916): 150; Loyal Jones, "Appalachian Values," in *Voices from the Hills: Selected Readings of Southern Appalachia*, ed. Robert J. Higgs and Ambrose Manning (New York: Ungar, 1975), 512;

Willard B. Gatewood Jr., "Arkansas Negroes in the 1890s: Documents," *Arkansas Historical Quarterly* 33 (Winter 1974): 297; Gordon B. McKinney, "Southern Mountain Republicans and the Negro, 1865–1900," in Inscoe, *Appalachians and Race*, 199, 205.

5. W. J. Cash, *The Mind of the South* (New York: Alfred A. Knopf, 1941), 219. The mention of Arnold Toynbee here is in reference to his oft-cited criticism that "the Appalachian 'Mountain People' at this day are no better than barbarians. They are the American counterparts of the latter-day White barbarians of the Old World: the Rifis and Kabyles and Tuareg, the Albanians and Caucasians, the Kurds and the Pathans and the Hairy Ainu." Arnold J. Toynbee, *A Study of History*, vol. 2 (London: Oxford University Press, 1939), 311.

6. V. O. Key Jr., *Southern Politics in State and Nation* (New York: Alfred A. Knopf, 1950), 666.

7. Helen C. Lindley, "The Watkins Brothers and Wild Haws," *Izard County Historian* 5 (October 1974): 8; Dale Hanks, "Silent Strangers: West Africans in Izard County," *Izard County Historian* 26 (October 2001): 16.

8. Interview with Estelle Canada Rucker, August 26, 2003, Batesville, AR; interview with Norman Byrd, May and August 1994, in *Down Memory Lane*, vol. 1, ed. Betty Guthrie McCollum and Sue Shell Chrisco (n.p., 1999), 173; interview with Alta Estelle Canada Rucker, June 13, 2013, in *Down Memory Lane*, vol. 11, ed. Betty Guthrie McCollum and Diane McCollum Honey (n.p., 2014), 265–66.

9. Hanks, "Silent Strangers," 18, 20; US Department of State, Agricultural Manuscript Census Schedules, Izard County, Arkansas, 1880; US Department of Commerce, Bureau of the Census, *Fifteenth Census of the United States, 1930: Population*, vol. 3, part 1 (Washington, DC: Government Printing Office [GPO], 1932), 218–219; US Department of Commerce, Bureau of the Census, *Fifteenth Census of the United States, 1930: Agriculture*, vol. 2, part 3 (Washington, DC: GPO, 1932), 1144. Although a fire in 1889 destroyed all of Izard County's records, one early twentieth-century document suggests that the county's African American citizens were able to avoid the political disfranchisement that swept much of the South in the 1890s and early 1900s. A 1909 roll of poll-tax payers listed eighteen Black people from LaCrosse township, or 90 percent of the township's Black men listed in the same year's personal tax assessment book. (List of Poll Tax Payers, Izard County, 1909, Izard County Courthouse, Melbourne, AR; Personal Assessment, 1909, Izard County, Izard County Courthouse, Melbourne, AR.)

10. Interview with Estelle Canada Rucker, May 8, 1991, Batesville, AR; interview with Lillie Mae Darty Watkins, May 8, 1991, Batesville, AR; interview with Ray Kennard, May 8, 1991, Batesville, AR.

11. William Lynwood Montell, *The Saga of Coe Ridge: A Study in Oral History*

(Knoxville: University of Tennessee Press, 1970), 3, 166 (quote); Rucker interview, May 8, 1991; interview with Lillie Mae Darty Watkins, July 12, 1993, Batesville, AR, Ozark Oral History Project, Ozark Cultural Resource Center, Ozark Folk Center, Mountain View, Arkansas.

12. Gordon D. Morgan, *Black Hillbillies of the Arkansas Ozarks* (Fayetteville: University of Arkansas Department of Sociology, 1973), 63; William Pickens, "Arkansas—a Study in Suppression," *The Messenger* 5 (January 1923), reprinted in *These 'Colored' United States: African American Essays from the 1920s*, ed. Tom Lutz and Susanna Ashton (New Brunswick, NJ: Rutgers University Press, 1996), 34; Flynt, *Dixie's Forgotten People*, 116.

13. Interview with P. O. Wren Jr., May 10, 1991, LaCrosse, AR; Rucker interview, May 8, 1991; Izard County Real Estate Tax Book, 1909, p. 78, Izard County Courthouse, Melbourne, Arkansas.

14. Morgan, *Black Hillbillies*, 75; Edward Cabbell, "Black Invisibility and Racism in Appalachia," *Appalachian Journal* 8 (Autumn 1980), 48; Edward J. Cabbell, "Black Invisibility and Racism in Appalachia: An Informed Survey," in *Blacks in Appalachia*, eds. William H. Turner and Edward J. Cabbell (Lexington: University Press of Kentucky, 1985), 3; Gatewood, "Arkansas Negroes in the 1890s," 297.

15. W. Fitzhugh Brundage, *Lynching in the New South: Georgia and Virginia, 1880–1930* (Urbana: University of Illinois Press, 1993), 128, 143. See also George C. Wright, *Racial Violence in Kentucky, 1865–1940: Lynchings, Mob Rule, and 'Legal Lynchings'* (Baton Rouge: Louisiana State University Press, 1990).

16. Jacqueline Froelich and David Zimmermann, "Total Eclipse: The Destruction of the African American Community of Harrison, Arkansas, in 1905 and 1909," *Arkansas Historical Quarterly* 58 (Summer 1999): 141; Kimberly Harper, *White Man's Heaven: The Lynching and Expulsion of Blacks in the Southern Ozarks, 1894–1909* (Fayetteville: University of Arkansas Press, 2010); James W. Loewen, *Sundown Towns: A Hidden Dimension of American Racism* (New York: W. W. Norton, 2005); Guy Lancaster, *Racial Cleansing in Arkansas, 1883–1924: Politics, Land, Labor, and Criminality* (Lanham, MD: Lexington Press, 2014). See also Katherine Lederer, *Many Thousand Gone: Springfield's Lost Black History* (Springfield, MO: Missouri Committee for the Humanities and the Gannett Foundation, 1986); and Elliott Jaspin, *Buried in the Bitter Waters: The Hidden History of Racial Cleansing in America* (New York: Basic Books, 2007).

17. Steven Teske, "Clinton," *Arkansas Encyclopedia of History and Culture*, https://encyclopediaofarkansas.net/entries/clinton-1001/, accessed April 19, 2022; Brooks Blevins, *A History of the Ozarks, Volume 3: The Ozarkers* (Urbana: University of Illinois Press, 2021).

18. Watkins interview, July 12, 1993; interview with Lillie Mae Darty Watkins, September 3, 1997, in *Down Memory Lane*, vol. 2, ed. Betty Guthrie

McCollum and Sue Shell Chrisco (n.p., 2000), 163 (first quote), 158 (second quote).

19. Rucker interview, August 26, 2003.
20. Interview with Knoxie Canada Brown, May 8, 1991, Batesville, AR; Wren interview, May 10, 1991.
21. Edward L. Ayers, *The Promise of the New South: Life after Reconstruction* (New York: Oxford University Press, 1992), 158; Joel Williamson, *The Crucible of Race: Black-White Relations in the American South Since Emancipation* (New York: Oxford University Press, 1984), 308, 309. See also Lillian Smith, *Killers of the Dream* (1949; New York: W. W. Norton, 1961.)
22. Ayers, *Promise of the New South*, 156, 157 (quotes).
23. Froelich and Zimmermann, "Total Eclipse," 137; Patrick Huber, "Race Riots and Black Exodus," unpublished paper in possession of author, 5.
24. John C. Inscoe, "Slavery and African Americans in the Nineteenth Century," in *High Mountains Rising: Appalachia in Time and Place*, ed. Richard A. Straw and H. Tyler Blethen (Urbana: University of Illinois Press, 2004), 40–41, 42. See also John C. Inscoe, "Olmsted in Appalachia: A Connecticut Yankee Encounters Slavery and Racism in the Southern Highlands, 1854," in Inscoe, *Appalachians and Race*, 154–164, as well as Inscoe's "Introduction" in the same volume.
25. US Department of Commerce, Bureau of the Census, *Fifteenth Census of the United States, 1930: Population*, vol. 3, part 1 (Washington, DC: GPO, 1932), 218–219; US Department of Commerce, Bureau of the Census, *Census of Population, 1950: Characteristics of the Population—Arkansas*, vol. 2, part 4 (Washington, DC: GPO, 1952), 79; US Department of Commerce, Bureau of the Census, *Fifteenth Census of the United States, 1930: Agriculture*, vol. 2, part 3 (Washington, DC: GPO, 1932), 1138, 1144; US Department of Commerce, Bureau of the Census, *Census of Agriculture, 1950: Counties and State Economic Areas—Arkansas*, vol. 1, part 23 (Washington, DC: GPO, 1952), 69, 72.

Chapter Nine

1. Wayman Hogue, *Back Yonder: An Ozark Chronicle*, ed. Brooks Blevins (Fayetteville: University of Arkansas Press, 2016), 155–56; Walter F. Lackey, *History of Newton County, Arkansas* (Independence, MO, n.d.), 214; Anderson McFall Journal, R 365, State Historical Society of Missouri, Rolla; Omer E. Brown, *Son of Pioneers: Recollections of an Ozarks Lawyer* (Point Lookout, MO: School of the Ozarks Press, 1973), 91.
2. Brooks Blevins, *Hill Folks: A History of Arkansas Ozarkers and Their Image* (Chapel Hill: University of North Carolina Press, 2002), 181–87.
3. Marvin Lawson, *By Gum, I Made It! An Ozark Arkie's Hillbilly Boyhood*

(Branson, MO: Ozarks Mountaineer, 1977), 81; Ellen Gray Massey, *A Candle within Her Soul: Mary Elizabeth Mahnkey and Her Ozarks* (Lebanon, MO: Bittersweet, 1996), 172; John K. Hulston, *An Ozarks Boy's Story, 1915–1945* (Point Lookout, MO: School of the Ozarks Press, 1971), 61.

4. Leland Fox, *Tall Tales from the Sage of Cane Hill* (Greenfield, MO: Vedette Publishing, 1971), 121; James West, *Plainville, U.S.A.* (New York: Columbia University Press, 1945), 24–28; Don West, *Broadside to the Sun* (New York: W. W. Norton, 1946), 192; Z. Evalena Pemberton, *Precious Memories of My Arkansas Mother, Edna Pugh Lee* (n.p., 1980), 188–89.

5. Blevins, *Hill Folks*, 106–9.

6. Erma Humphreys, *Down on the Farm* (Fort Dodge, KS: s.p., 1976), 109–25; Pat Lendennie, "Buffalo Island," *Encyclopedia of Arkansas*, https://encyclopediaofarkansas.net/entries/buffalo-island-3071/, accessed June 9, 2020.

7. Interview with Zela Rhoads, Agnos, AR, October 2, 1998.

8. V. R. "Jack" Thomas, *Life in the Heart of the Ozarks* (Kearney, NE: Morris Publishing, 2007), 55–60.

9. Narrative Report of County Extension Agents, Stone County, 1947, Box 289, Federal Extension Service Records—Arkansas, RG 33, National Archives and Records Administration, Southwest Region, Fort Worth, TX.

10. Interview with Geneva and Steve Emerson, Calamine, AR, September 30, 2011.

11. Emerson interview; Stonewall Treat, interviewed by Vaughn Brewer, Big Flat, AR, ca. 1979, Ozark Heritage Institute and Ozark Oral History Office, University of Central Arkansas, Conway, AR; interview with Walter Severs, Ralph, AR, October 18, 2012.

12. Interview with Ray Joe Hastings, Doniphan, MO, October 13, 2011.

13. Interview with L. V. Waddell, Imboden, AR, August 19, 1993, Ozark Oral History Project, Ozark Folk Center, Mountain View (now housed at Arkansas State Archives, Little Rock); interview with R. W. Lyerly, by telephone, March 22, 2004.

14. Severs interview; Ernest J. Webber, *Growing Up in the Ozarks* (Naples, FL: Adams Press, 1988), 165; Hastings interview; Emerson interview; Lyerly interview.

15. Lyerly interview.

16. Julie M. Wiese, *Corazón de Dixie: Mexicanos in the U.S. South since 1910* (Chapel Hill: University of North Carolina Press, 2015), 87; *Migratory Labor in American Agriculture: Report of the President's Commission on Migratory Labor* (Washington, DC: GPO, 1951), 20.

17. Wiese, *Corazón de Dixie*, 83–85, 89–90, 99–100, 116; interview with Carolyn Blevins, Violet Hill, AR, June 12, 2020.

18. Donald Holley, *The Second Great Emancipation: The Mechanical Cotton*

Picker, Black Migration, and How They Shaped the Modern South
(Fayetteville: University of Arkansas Press, 2000), 131; Lyerly interview.
19. Interview with Totsie Wood, Melbourne, AR, date unknown.

Chapter Ten

1. Van Allen Tyson, "Folklore in the Life and Work of John Gould Fletcher,"
PhD diss., University of Arkansas, 1981, 182.
2. Rachel Reynolds Luster, "Mary Celestia Parler," *Encyclopedia of Arkansas*,
https://encyclopediaofarkansas.net/entries/mary-celestia-parler-3616/,
updated May 10, 2018.
3. The first Ozarks collection to be digitized was the Max Hunter Collection,
housed at the Springfield-Greene County Library in Springfield, Missouri. It
is available at https://maxhunter.missouristate.edu. Inspired by the Hunter
Collection, staff members at Lyon College's Mabee-Simpson Library soon
thereafter digitized the Ozarks recordings of John Quincy Wolf Jr. They are
available at https://home.lyon.edu/wolfcollection/ozarks.htm.
4. John Burgess, "Francis James Child: Brief Life of a Victorian Enthusiast:
1825–1896," *Harvard Magazine*, May-June 2006, harvardmagazine.
com/2006/05/francis-james-child.html. See also Sigrid Rieuwerts, "'The
Genuine Ballads of the People': F. J. Child and the Ballad Cause," *Journal
of Folklore Research* 31 (Dec. 1994): 1–34.
5. Cecil James Sharp, *English Folk-Songs from the Southern Appalachians,
Collected by Cecil J. Sharp; Comprising Two Hundred and Seventy-four
Songs and Ballads with Nine Hundred and Sixty-eight Tunes, Including
Thirty-nine Tunes Contributed by Olive Dame Campbell*, ed. Maud Karpeles
(London: Oxford University Press, 1932); H. M. Belden, "Balladry in
America," *Journal of American Folklore* 25 (Jan.-March 1912): 2; Scott B.
Spencer, ed., *The Ballad Collectors of North America: How Gathering
Folksongs Transformed Academic Thought and American Identity*
(Lanham, MD: Scarecrow Press, 2011), 10; Henry D. Shapiro, *Appalachia
on Our Mind: The Southern Mountains and Mountaineers in the American
Consciousness, 1870–1920* (Chapel Hill: University of North Carolina Press,
1978), 252–59; David E. Whisnant, *All that Is Native & Fine: The Politics of
Culture in an American Region* (Chapel Hill: University of North Carolina
Press, 1983), 110–27.
6. Carl Sandburg, *The American Songbag* (New York: Harcourt, Brace and
Company, 1927.)
7. Susan L. Pentlin and Rebecca B. Schroeder, "H. M. Belden, the English Club,
and the Missouri Folk-lore Society," *Missouri Folklore Society Journal* 8–9
(1986–87), https://missourifolkloresociety.truman.edu/home/missouri
-folklore-studies/belden/, accessed May 31, 2022; H. M. Belden, "Balladry in
America," *Journal of American Folklore* 25 (January–March 1912): 1, 3.

8. Robert B. Cochran, "Vance Randolph," *Encyclopedia of Arkansas*, https://encyclopediaofarkansas.net/entries/vance-randolph-2265/. See also Cochran, *Vance Randolph: An Ozark Life* (Champaign: University of Illinois Press, 1985).

9. Vance Randolph and Frances Emberson, "The Collection of Folk Music in the Ozarks," *Journal of American Folklore* 60 (April-June 1947): 119–123; Vance Randolph, "Ballad Hunters in North Arkansas," *Arkansas Historical Quarterly* 7 (Spring 1948): 4–9. See also Samantha C. Horn, "Wayfaring Stranger: Sidney Robertson, American Folk Music, and the Resettlement Administration, 1936–37," MA thesis, University of North Carolina, Chapel Hill, 2016.

10. Luster, "Mary Celestia Parler"; Ethel C. Simpson, "Ozark Folklore Society," *Encyclopedia of Arkansas*, https://encyclopediaofarkansas.net/entries /ozark-folklore-society-6239/. See also Rachel Reynolds, "Mary Celestia Parler (1904–1981): Folklorist and Teacher," in *Arkansas Women: Their Lives and Times*, eds. Cherisse Jones-Branch and Gary T. Edwards (Athens: University of Georgia Press, 2018), 287–304.

11. Spencer, *Ballad Collectors of North America*, 10; Luster, "Mary Celestia Parler."

12. Brooks Blevins, "John Quincy Wolf Jr.," *Encyclopedia of Arkansas*, https://encyclopediaofarkansas.net/entries/john-quincy-wolf-jr-3033/.

13. Finding aid to the Loman D. and Laura M. Cansler Collection, 1820–2005, C 4018, State Historical Society of Missouri, Columbia, https://files.shsmo .org/manuscripts/columbia/C4018.pdf, accessed May 31, 2022; https://maxhunter.missouristate.edu, accessed August 22, 2015; David Stout, "Max Hunter, Ozark Folklorist of Tunes and Tales, Dies at 78," *New York Times*, November 15, 1999, www.nytimes.com/1999/11/15/arts/max-hunter-ozark -folklorist-of-tunes-and-tales-dies-at-78.html.

14. Finding aid to the Robert P. Christeson Collection, 1808–1995, C 3971, State Historical Society of Missouri, Columbia, https://files.shsmo.org /manuscripts/columbia/C3971.pdf, accessed May 31, 2022; Jeff Joiner, "Doorway to the Past," *Rural Missouri*, November 2002, 14; Drew Beisswenger, "Gordon McCann: The Improbable Ascent of the Ozarks Fiddle Man," *Old-Time Herald* 10 (2003): 32–36. See also Drew Beisswenger and Gordon McCann, *Ozarks Fiddle Music* (St. Louis, MO: Mel Bay Publications, 2008.)

15. https://www.arkansasstateparks.com/parks/ozark-folk-center-state-park, accessed August 22, 2015. See Norm Cohen's chapter on the Ozarks in Spencer, *Ballad Collectors of North America*.

Chapter Eleven

1. Manuscript Census Returns, Twelfth Census of the United States, 1900, Population Schedules, Wayne County, Illinois; Manuscript Census Returns,

Fourteenth Census of the United States, 1920, Population Schedules, Woodford County, Illinois; *Minnie E. Gardner v. John E. Gardner*, Divorce File, Book 29, Wayne County (IL) Chancery, Wayne County Courthouse, Fairfield, Illinois; *J.S. Atteberry v. Minnie E. Atteberry*, Divorce File, Book 32, Wayne County (IL) Chancery Court.

2. File 7, Box 1, Minnie E. Atteberry Papers (hereafter MEAP), University of Arkansas Special Collections, Fayetteville. The frequent ellipses in the diary quotations reflect the author's editing in an attempt to streamline Minnie's dense and wordy entries.

3. *J.S. Atteberry v. Minnie E. Atteberry.*

4. Doris Thompson, "History of an Ozark Utopia," *Arkansas Historical Quarterly* 14 (Winter 1955): 359, 360, 361, 364. See also Leslie Wayne Boldt, "John Adam Battenfield and the Incoming Kingdom Missionary Unit," MA thesis, Lincoln Christian Seminary (IL), 1986.

5. Francis Albert Mathes, World War I Registration Card, Ancestry.com, accessed January 14, 2014; 1921 Personal Property Assessment Tax Book, Searcy County (AR) Clerk Office, Searcy County Courthouse, Marshall, AR; Minnie Atteberry to Lawrence Gardner, February 9, 1943, letter in possession of Mary Lou Helton of Odessa, TX, copy in possession of author.

6. Thompson, "History of an Ozark Utopia," 372–73.

7. Minnie's Diary, February 14, 1967, File 7, Box 2, MEAP.

8. Deed Book 40, page 433, Searcy County (AR) Clerk Office.

9. Minnie E. Atteberry to Lavinna Mayes, May 10, 1942, File 12, Box 2, MEAP.

10. Alan Kraut, "Dr. Joseph Goldberger & the War on Pellagra," National Institutes of Health website, http://history.nih.gov/exhibits/goldberger/index.html, accessed January 28, 2014. See also Elizabeth W. Etheridge, *The Butterfly Caste: A Social History of Pellagra in the South* (Westport, CT: Greenwood Press, 1972.)

11. Atteberry to Mayes, May 10, 1942, File 12, Box 2, MEAP.

12. List of "all the money I have rec'd since Lawrence left for the Army", File 3, Box 1, MEAP; Floyd W. Hicks and C. Roger Lambert, "Food for the Hungry: Federal Food Programs in Arkansas, 1933–1942," *Arkansas Historical Quarterly* 37 (Spring 1978): 34, 40.

13. Minnie's Diary, December 26, 1942, File 3, Box 1, MEAP.

14. Minnie's Diary, March 5, 1946, File 4, Box 1, MEAP.

15. Minnie E. Atteberry to Brother Ben and Sister Chloe Mathes, July 8, 1951, File 12, Box 2, MEAP (quotation); Ben F. Johnson III, *Arkansas in Modern America, 1930–1999* (Fayetteville: University of Arkansas Press, 2000), 76.

16. George Daniel, interview by author, Marshall, AR, October 3, 2013; Robert "Ace" Hensley, interview by author, Marshall, AR, October 3, 2013; Leon Cooley, interview by telephone, January 10, 2014.

17. File 1, Box 1, MEAP. See Ethan Kross, Emma Bruehlman-Senecal, Jiyoung Park, Aleah Burson, Adrienne Dougherty, Holly Shablack, Ryan Bremner,

Jason Moser, and Ozlem Ayduk, "Self-Talk as a Regulatory Mechanism: How You Do It Matters," *Journal of Personality and Social Psychology* 106, no. 2 (2014): 304–324; Ethan Kross and Ozlem Ayduk, "Making Meaning out of Negative Experiences by Self-Distancing," *Current Directions in Psychological Science* 20 (June 2011): 187–191.

18. US Department of Commerce, Bureau of the Census, *Census of Housing: 1950: Volume I: General Characteristics: Part 2: Alabama-Georgia* (Washington, DC: Government Printing Office, 1953), 4–17, 4–48.

19. File 6, Box 1, MEAP.

20. File 6, Box 1, MEAP.

21. File 6, Box 1, MEAP.

22. File 6, Box 1, MEAP.

23. Cooley interview.

24. Minnie's Diary, April 18, 1959, File 8, Box 1, MEAP.

25. Minnie's Diary, June 26, 1957, File 7, Box 1, MEAP.

26. According to Searcy County historian James J. Johnston, during Minnie's lifetime she and other rural Searcy Countians could not get television reception. In the early 1950s, a businessman in Marshall erected a tower on Backbone Mountain and installed an early cable system for residents of the county seat and those living nearby. Johnston to author, email, March 31, 2015.

27. See Patti McCord and Kristene Sutliff, eds., *Queen of the Hillbillies: Writings of May Kennedy McCord*, Chronicles of the Ozarks Series (Fayetteville: University of Arkansas Press, 2022.)

28. See Floyd Hitchcock, *The March of Empires—Daniel* (1944), http://baptistbiblebelievers.com/OTStudies/MarchofEmpiresTheBookofDaniel.aspx, accessed June 1, 2022.

29. Minnie's diary, April 4, 1959, File 8, Box 1, MEAP.

30. Minnie's diary, May 18, 1957, File 7, Box 1, MEAP.

31. Mary Lou Helton, interview by telephone, ca. 2014.

32. Minnie's diary, August 5, 1959, File 11, Box 1, MEAP.

33. Lawrence's Diary, April 10, 1959, File 9, Box 1, MEAP; Lawrence's Diary, July 16, 1959, File 8, Box 1, MEAP; Lawrence's Diary, February 10, 1959, File 8, Box 1, MEAP (quotation).

34. US Department of Commerce, Bureau of the Census, *Census of Population: Supplementary Report: Poverty Status in 1969 and 1959 of Persons and Families, for States, SMSA's, Central Cities, and Counties: 1970 and 1960* (Washington, DC: U.S. Government Printing Office, 1975), 3, 46; Minnie's Diary, February 21, 1967, File 7, Box 2, MEAP.

35. American Psychiatric Association, *Diagnostic and Statistical Manual of Mental Disorders: DSM-5* (Washington, DC: American Psychiatric Publishing, 2013), 678–679.

36. Cooley interview.

37. Minnie's Diary, June 4, 1954, File 6, Box 1; for examples of the dumping of whey, see especially entries from April and May 1954, File 7, Box 1, MEAP.

38. Minnie's diary, June 6, 1961, File 3, Box 2, MEAP.

39. Minnie's diary, June 12, 1957 (first quotation), July 3, 1957 (second quotation), File 7, Box 1, MEAP.

40. Minnie's Diary, April 27, 1959 (first quotation), May 31, 1959 (second quotation), File 8, Box 1, MEAP. Five years after their departure, some of the Bradberrys stopped by for a visit. Learning that they were living in Indiana and doing well for themselves, Minnie noted, "I am glad for them." Minnie's Diary, July 5, 1964, Folder 5, Box 2, MEAP.

41. Minnie's Diary, May 18, 1957, File 7, Box 1, MEAP.

42. Minnie's diary, July 23, 1965, File 6, Box 2, MEAP.

43. *Mountain Wave* (Marshall, AR), February 14, 1974 (quotation), June 2, 1974; Certificate of Death: Lawrence Harry Gardner, 1992, Searcy County (AR) Clerk Office.

Chapter Twelve

1. John Alexander Williams, *Appalachia: A History* (Chapel Hill: University of North Carolina Press, 2002), 198.

2. See the chapter "The Local-Color Movement and Appalachia" in Henry D. Shapiro, *Appalachia On Our Mind: The Southern Mountains and Mountaineers in the American Consciousness, 1870–1920* (Chapel Hill: University of North Carolina Press, 1978.)

3. Minna Caroline Smith, "A Camp in the Mountains of Arkansas," *Outing*, August 5, 1887, 436–45.

4. Mary Stewart, *Unspotted from the World* (New York: Robert Lewis Weed, 1897), 20–21.

5. "About Big Stone Gap," https://bigstonegap.com/history/, accessed August 29, 2021.

6. Williams, *Appalachia*, 200.

7. Brooks Blevins, "Mountain Mission Schools in Arkansas," *Arkansas Historical Quarterly* 70 (Winter 2011): 398. Technically, the first mission schools in the Ozarks were founded by Congregationalists: Rogers Academy in northwestern Arkansas in 1883 and Iberia Academy in the Osage River country of central Missouri in 1890. For the first two decades or so of their existence, however, these academies operated primarily as rigorous preparatory schools and evinced none of the rhetoric and programming associated with mission schools designed for "mountain whites." Only in the early twentieth century would the necessity of fundraising among New Englanders motivate the academies to adopt the conscious trappings of the mountain mission-school movement. See also Brooks Blevins, "Region, Religion, and

Competing Visions of Mountain Mission Education in the Ozarks," *Journal of Southern History* 82 (February 2016): 59–96.

8. David E. Whisnant, *All That Is Native and Fine: The Politics of Culture in an American Region* (Chapel Hill: University of North Carolina Press, 1983), xiii.

9. *Southern Mountain Schools Maintained by Denominational and Independent Agencies*, rev. ed. (New York, 1929), 1–10.

10. Williams, *Appalachia*, 207.

11. James Watt Raine, *The Land of Saddle-bags: A Study of the Mountain People of Appalachia*, foreword by Dwight B. Billings (Lexington: University Press of Kentucky, 1997.)

12. Horace Kephart, *Our Southern Highlanders* (New York: Macmillan, 1922), 6.

13. Vance Randolph, *The Ozarks: An American Survival of Primitive Society* (New York: Vanguard Press, 1931), v.

14. Kephart, *Our Southern Highlanders*, 7; Randolph, *The Ozarks*, v.

15. Otto Ernest Rayburn, *Ozark Country* (New York: Duell, Sloan and Pearce, 1941); Charles Morrow Wilson, *Backwoods America* (Chapel Hill: University of North Carolina Press, 1935.)

16. Catherine Barker, *Yesterday Today: Life in the Ozarks* (Caldwell, ID: Caxton Printers, 1941.)

17. Michael Harrington, *The Other America: Poverty in the United States* (New York: Macmillan, 1962.)

18. Williams, *Appalachia*, 10, 340–42.

19. J. Blake Perkins, "Growing the Hills: The Ozarks Regional Commission and the Politics of Economic Development in the Mid-American Highlands, 1960s-1970s," *Missouri Historical Review* 107 (April 2013): 144, 145 (quotation).

20. J. Blake Perkins, *Hillbilly Hellraisers: Federal Power and Populist Defiance in the Ozarks* (Urbana: University of Illinois Press, 2017), 179.

21. Ozarka College Self-Study, ca. 2000, available on https://www.ozarka.edu, 2–3; Kim Whitten, "Ozarka College," *Encyclopedia of Arkansas*, https://encyclopediaofarkansas.net/entries/ozarka-college-3220/; Perkins, *Hillbilly Hellraisers*, 184.

22. Perkins, *Hillbilly Hellraisers*, 163.

23. See, for instance, Robert H. Wiebe, *The Search for Order, 1877–1920* (New York: Hill and Wang, 1977); Steven Hahn and Jonathan Prude, eds., *The Countryside in the Age of Capitalist Transformation: Essays in the Social History of Rural America* (Chapel Hill: University of North Carolina Press, 1985); Ronald D. Eller, *Miners, Millhands, and Mountaineers: Industrialization of the Appalachian South, 1880–1930* (Knoxville: University of Tennessee Press, 1982).

24. See Richard H. Brodhead, *Cultures of Letters: Scenes of Reading and Writing in Nineteenth-Century America* (Chicago: University of Chicago Press, 1993); Durwood Dunn, *Cades Cove: The Life and Death of a Southern Appalachian Community, 1818–1937* (Knoxville: University of Tennessee Press, 1988); Mary Beth Pudup, Dwight B. Billings, and Altina L. Waller, eds., *Appalachia in the Making: The Mountain South in the Nineteenth Century* (Chapel Hill: University of North Carolina Press, 1995); Brooks Blevins, *Hill Folks: A History of Arkansas Ozarkers and Their Image* (Chapel Hill: University of North Carolina Press, 2002).

25. *Southern Mountain Schools*, 1–10; Elmer T. Clark, *Healing Ourselves: The First Task of the Church in America* (Nashville: Cokesbury, 1924), 151 (quotation).

26. See Blevins, *Hill Folks*; Brooks Blevins, "Wretched and Innocent: Two Mountain Regions in the National Consciousness," *Journal of Appalachian Studies* 7 (Fall 2001): 257–71; Blevins, *Arkansas/Arkansaw: How Bear Hunters, Hillbillies, and Good Ol' Boys Defined a State* (Fayetteville: University of Arkansas Press, 2009); Anthony Harkins, *Hillbilly: A Cultural History of an American Icon* (New York: Oxford University Press, 2005).